Routledge Revivals

A Critical, Old-Spelling Edition of William Rowley's a New Wonder, a Woman Never Vexed

A Critical, Old-Spelling Edition of William Rowley's a New Wonder, a Woman Never Vexed

Trudi Laura Darby

First published in 1988 by Garland Publishing, Inc.

This edition first published in 2018 by Routledge
2 Park Square, Milton Park, Abingdon, Oxon, OX14 4RN
and by Routledge
52 Vanderbilt Avenue, New York, NY 10017, USA

Routledge is an imprint of the Taylor & Francis Group, an informa business

Publisher's Note
The publisher has gone to great lengths to ensure the quality of this reprint but points out that some imperfections in the original copies may be apparent.

Disclaimer
The publisher has made every effort to trace copyright holders and welcomes correspondence from those they have been unable to contact.
A Library of Congress record exists under ISBN:

ISBN 13: 978-0-367-11002-4 (hbk)
ISBN 13: 978-0-367-11003-1 (pbk)
ISBN 13: 978-0-429-02426-9 (ebk)

GARLAND PUBLICATIONS IN AMERICAN AND ENGLISH LITERATURE

Editor
Stephen Orgel
Stanford University

GARLAND PUBLISHING, INC.

A Critical, Old-Spelling Edition of William Rowley's *A New Wonder, A Woman Never Vexed*

Trudi Laura Darby

GARLAND PUBLISHING, INC.
NEW YORK & LONDON 1988

Library of Congress Cataloging-in-Publication Data

Rowley, William, 1585?-1642?
[New wonder, a woman never vexed]
A critical, old-spelling edition of William Rowley's A new wonder, a woman never vexed / Trudi Laura Darby.
p. cm. — (Garland publications in American and English literature)
Originally presented as the author's thesis (Ph. D.)—King's College, London.
Bibliography: p.
ISBN 0-8240-6385-6
1. Rowley, William, 1585?-1642? New wonder, a woman never vexed I. Darby, Trudi Laura. II. Title. III. Series.
PR2742.N49 1988
822' .3—dc 19 88-16474

Printed on acid-free, 250-year-life paper
Manufactured in the United States of America

CONTENTS

Preface

This book originated in a thesis submitted to the University of London which was supervised by Professor Richard Proudfoot and examined by Professor Nigel Alexander and Dr Elizabeth Brennan. I am most grateful for their advice and continued support, and particularly for Professor Proudfoot's help over several years. My fellow graduate students at King's College London have been generous with ideas, especially Mrs Akiko Kusunoki, Mr Stephen Miller, Mrs Fleur Rothschild and Dr Jo Udall. My thanks also to Professor Albert Braunmuller of UCLA.

I owe a debt of gratitude for support and encouragement to many members of London University in various departments in both the Arts and Sciences. I owe a special debt to five members of the Board of Studies in Classics: Professor John Barron, the late Professor Frank Goodyear, Dr Barrie Hall, Mr Peter Howell and Dr Sue Sherwin-White, who all took an enthusiastic and informed interest in this project. It would not have been completed without them.

Photographic work was done by Mike Peirce from microfilms of the copies of the 1632 quarto in the Bodleian Library, Oxford.

This edition has been proof-read, corrected and re-corrected by Constance Darby. The tribute to her impeccable work is the number of errors which do not appear in the published text; those that remain are entirely my fault.

This book is dedicated to the memory of my grandfather, Charles Foley.

Trudi Darby
October 1987

Copies Collated

The following abbreviations are used for the copies which have been collated.

BL[1]	British Library, 644.c.12
BL[2]	British Library C.12.f.1
Ashley	Ashley 1453 (Thomas J. Wise's copy, now in the British Library)
Dyce	Victoria and Albert Museum, D.26. Box 39.1
Bodl.[1]	Bodleian, Mal. 167
Bodl.[2]	Bodleian, Mal.B.164
Bodl.[3]	Bodleian, Douce R.123
Worc.[1]	Worcester College, 3.35
Worc.[2]	Worcester College, 3.48
Keynes	King's College Cambridge, Keynes C.7.63
Bute	National Library of Scotland, Bute 452
Hunt.	Henry E. Huntingdon Library, Bridgewater copy C21423/69158

Abbreviations

Annals	Annals of English Drama 600-1700, Alfred Harbage rev. Samuel Schoenbaum.
Bentley	The Jacobean and Caroline Stage, G.E. Bentley, 7 vols.
Bibliography	A Bibliography of the English Printed Drama to the Restoration, Sir W.W. Greg, 4 vols.
BL	British Library.
Canon	The Canon of Thomas Middleton's Plays, David Lake.
Court Records	Records of the Court of the Stationers' Company 1602-1640, ed. W.A. Jackson.
Dilke	Old English Plays being a selection from the early dramatic writers, ed. C.W. Dilke.
Dodsley	A Collection of Old Plays, ed. R. Dodsley, rev. C.W. Hazlitt.
Dramatic Records	The Dramatic Records of Sir Henry Herbert, ed. J.Q. Adams.
Inquiry	An Inquiry into the Authorship of the Middleton-Rowley Plays, Pauline G. Wiggin.
Internal Evidence	Internal Evidence and Elizabethan Dramatic Authorship, Samuel Schoenbaum.
Lamb	Specimens of the English Dramatic Poets, Charles Lamb.
MLR	Modern Language Review.
Mynshul	Certain Characters and Essays of Prison and Prisoners, Geoffrey Mynshul.
ODEP	Oxford Dictionary of English Proverbs.
OED	Oxford English Dictionary.
RES	Review of English Studies.
SB	Studies in Bibliography
Southern	'On Reconstructing a Practicable Elizabethan Playhouse', Richard Southern, Shakespeare Survey, 12.
SQ	Shakespeare Quarterly.
Tilley	A Dictionary of Proverbs in England in the Sixteenth and Seventeenth Centuries, Morris P. Tilley.

Authorship

A New Wonder, A Woman Never Vext was entered on the Stationers' Register as the work of Rowley and published as by William Rowley. Until the end of the nineteenth century, it was accepted as being solely by him by critics including Langbaine, Baker, Lamb, Dilke, Swinburne and, on two occasions, Fleay. It was, however, Fleay himself who suggested in the Biographical Chronicle[1] that the play was a revision by Thomas Heywood of an earlier play by Rowley:

> A New Wonder, or A Woman never vexed, C., was published as by "William Rowley, one of His Majesty's servants," in 1632, by Constable, who issued only L. Elizabeth plays (with one exception, The Fatal Dowry, a King's play). It is clearly altered from an old rhyming play, the part from iii.2 onward being slightly changed. The insertion in v.1, "Good husband. Gentle brother. Dear uncle," and a passage in iv.1 which originally stood thus -
>
> "But for his father, hang him!
> Brew. Fie [fie] fie.
> Steph. By heaven!
> Brew. Come, come, live in more charity!
> He is your brother: if that name offend[s]
> I'll sing that tune no more. Jane, bid your friends
> Welcome.
> Jane They must be, sir, that come with you," &c
>
> evidently prove a revision...I think the original author was Heywood, whose Fortune by Land and Sea may also have been put on the stage, but certainly in no part written, by Rowley.

Whatever investigation or intuition lay behind Fleay's theory, it is presented here almost as an inspired guess and does not promote confidence; but it was enough to arouse Pauline Wiggin's scepticism about the play's authorship[2] and she accepts that the last two acts may be taken from another play. Since then, Heywood's claim as collaborator has not met favour and Dewar M. Robb,[3] while recognising some similarities with Heywood's work, remarks that once the play is seen as being written under Heywood's influence, it fits the pattern of Rowley's writing in about 1610. Writers on Heywood have also rejected A Woman Never Vext from his canon. A.M. Clark says that,[4]

> The crabbed style, even allowing for revision, is quite foreign to Heywood, with whose mannerisms Fleay does not elsewhere display such an acquaintance that we can trust to his recognizing them when buried under the peculiarities of Rowley.

For Michel Grivelet,[5]

> Il n'y a aucune raison d'attribuer à Heywood cette pièce de Rowley mais il est intéressant de noter l'influence du premier sur le second dans cet ouvrage.

The majority of critical opinion, then, and such external evidence as there is - Stationers' Register and title-page - unite in ascribing the play to Rowley. The first of Samuel Schoenbaum's principles for canonical investigators[6] is that,

> External evidence cannot be ignored, no matter how inconvenient such evidence may be for the theories of the investigator.

(David Lake, however, takes a slightly more flexible approach.[7]) It is, therefore, with some reluctance that one considers the possibility that Heywood did indeed collaborate with Rowley on this play.

In examining the text of the 1632 quarto, one notices certain idiosyncracies, notably in the spelling 'I'l' for the contraction normally found as 'Ile', 'I'le' or 'ile'. This spelling is unlikely to be compositorial; it does not occur in any other text from Purslowe's shop, and in particular it is not found in *Changes* printed in the same year. It is found in two plays in MS Egerton 1994: *The Captives* and *Calisto or The Escapes of Jupiter*, both generally acknowledged to be by Thomas Heywood and in the author's handwriting. Although not a spelling unique to Heywood (it also occurs in, for example, Brome's *The Queen's Exchange*, printed by Henry Brome in 1657), it is sufficiently unusual to warrant an investigation into Heywood's possible involvement with the quarto text. Fredson Bowers has suggested[8] that Massinger copied out both his own and Fletcher's share in *Beggars' Bush*. One may speculate that Heywood transcribed a play written by himself and Rowley, without necessarily crediting him with a large share of the composition. Other small indications in *The Captives* point to a Heywood manuscript behind the quarto of *A Woman Never Vext*. Heywood tends to write 'de-' for 'di-' in, for example, 'desasters'; press variants show that in the quarto (F4) 'devide' and 'devision' were corrected to the more usual 'divide' and 'division'. He has a habit of placing the comma one word too early: 'what gurles weare, these thou spakest off,' (line 1212, *The Captives*). This may explain the rather odd punctuation, 'When charity tunes the, pipe the poore man sings,' (5.1.235, emended in this edition). Finally, on two occasions the compositor confused 'a' and 'o', setting 'apposite' for 'opposite' and 'sok'd' for a word ending in '-ak'd' (2.1.312 and 3.3.190), mistakes easy to make in Heywood's hand. Admittedly this is a common enough feature of secretary hand; but a letter which Greg thought to be in Rowley's hand[9] shows 'a' and 'o' very carefully distinguished, even in a letter which appears to have been dashed off in a hurry. It is virtually impossible to confuse the two characters, suggesting that the compositor was not working from copy in this handwriting (unless he made two foul case errors); but the text is consistent with a MS in Heywood's handwriting, or a very close scribal transcript.

It thus seems possible that Heywood had some part in writing _A Woman Never Vext_. The authorship problem is here inverted; usually an anonymous play is searching for an author, here we are looking for evidence to support an author already postulated. The situation of course gives scope for self-deception, and it is perhaps as well to remember the laws laid down by investigators such as Samuel Schoenbaum and David Lake. '_Textual analysis logically precedes stylistic analysis_', is Schoenbaum's fourth principle, having already stated that, '_If stylistic criteria are to have any meaning, the play must be written in a style_'.[10] He also demands a reasonable amount of unchallenged writing by the author in question and the recognition that, '_Intuitions, convictions, and subjective judgments_' are not evidence.[11] David Lake, for his part, requires evidence which cannot be due to compositorial intervention and which is objective and quantifiable.[12]

In what follows I have therefore followed the tests advocated by MacDonald P. Jackson in _Studies in Attribution: Middleton and Shakespeare_ and by David Lake in _The Canon of Thomas Middleton's Plays_, as well as following some suggestions in Cyrus Hoy's 'The Shares of Fletcher and his Collaborators in the Beaumont and Fletcher Canon (V)'. Unfortunately, the only attempt to define Heywood's characteristics was made by H.D. Gray, in his article suggesting him as a collaborator on _A Cure for a Cuckold_,[13] and he relied almost exclusively on parallels and metrical tests. I have thus used the tables supplied by MacDonald Jackson and David Lake in their works, while recognizing that their tests, aimed at distinguishing Middleton from other writers, are not always ideally suited to Heywood and Rowley's works.

The simplest test is Cyrus Hoy's; he notes that Rowley uses ''em' or ''um', an abbreviation for 'them', in a relatively high proportion.[14] The quarto's contraction, ''m', disappears after G4, 4.1 (which has no significance as far as compositors are concerned; see below, 'Printing'), and appears only once in this scene and in 3.2. David Lake gives a wide range of linguistic evidence to be tested but in many cases Heywood and Rowley's usages are similar and cannot plausibly be distinguished. This category includes all connective synonyms, such as 'among/amongst' and contractions such as 'it's', 'y'are', 'i'th', and 'o'th'. However, certain features are distinctive. Heywood is not recorded as using 'swounds' (quarto 'zoundes') and last used 'tut' in 1605, in <u>II If You Know Not Me</u> (apparently the only play in which he used it). He scarcely uses ''em', prefers 'hath' to 'has', 'doth' to 'does', 'I am' to 'I'm'[15] and never uses ''has' for 'he has', while Rowley never uses 'y'ave'. The 'has/hath', 'does/doth' test does not show a significant distribution through the play and will not be considered as evidence. 'Y'ave' occurs once, in 3.3, 'I'm' occurs in 1.1, 2.1, 3.1, 3.3 and 5.1. 'I'faith' and 'in troth' present special problems since usage in the quarto breaks down into two forms each: 'faith' in 3.1 and 5.1, 'i'faith' in 1.1, 1.2, 2.1, 3.1, 3.2, 4.1; 'troth' in 3.1, 4.3, 5.1, 'in troth' in 1.1, 4.1. From MacDonald Jackson's table, Rowley's use of 'i'faith' far outweighs Heywood's, while Heywood uses 'faith' slightly more often than Rowley (six times to Rowley's five). It therefore seems that 'i'faith' - which Heywood last used in <u>The Royal King and the Loyal Subject</u> - is more likely to indicate Rowley than Heywood, although 'faith' does not necessarily indicate Heywood rather than Rowley. 'Zoundes' occurs in 4.1 and 4.3 and 'e'en', also used by Rowley but not by Heywood, in 4.3. 'Tut' is in 1.1 only.

Some of MacDonald Jackson's tests overlap David Lake's. Of his others, one of the most useful is for exclamations and oaths. Rowley never uses 'pox on' and only once, in <u>A Shoemaker, A Gentleman</u>, uses 'forsooth'. He used 'cry you mercy' once, in All's Lost by Lust.[16] 'Cry you mercy' occurs twice in 4.2, 'pox on' four times in the gambling scene at the beginning of 2.1, 'forsooth' once each in 3.2 and 3.3. One must bear in mind the influences of characterization in the gambling and prison scenes; oaths are no doubt used to create an atmosphere of roguery and dishonesty, while the Keeper is being established as a courteous, kindly man. On the other hand, scope for such vocabulary occurs elsewhere in Rowley's work and it is perhaps significant that he does not use it. Heywood and Rowley both use 'how now', 'prithee', 'I warrant' and their usages are indistinguishable. 'Alas' presents the same problem as 'i'faith' and 'in troth'; it occurs once each in 1.1, 1.2, 4.2, but ''las' occurs once in 4.1, three times in 4.2 and once in 5.1. The dual form also occurs in 'foot/sfoot' but Heywood and Rowley both used 'sfoot' elsewhere, so this feature cannot be used to distinguish between them. Heywood used 'foot' in II If You Know Not Me. MacDonald Jackson records 'faith' and 'i'faith' separately, but neither he nor David Lake treats the forms of 'in troth' and 'alas' as distinct.

MacDonald Jackson also introduces a new test, of function words. This takes the first 1,000 occurences in total of the thirteen function words ('a', 'and', 'but', 'by', 'for', 'from', 'in', 'it', 'of', 'that', 'the', 'to', and 'with') and analyses the way in which that total is made up, say, 148 'and', 152 'to' and so on. Obviously, this test can only be applied as confirmation of a hypothesis already formulated, since contamination from a substantial number of lines from a second writer will give a faulty result. The figures can also vary more from one play to another by the same author than from one author to another. Certain characteristics, on the other hand, remain relatively constant for all writers, since 'by', for example, is less common than 'to'. However, a useful pattern can emerge. From MacDonald Jackson's table, it is apparent that Rowley uses 'a' more than 'and' - a feature he shares only with Webster, and with Marston and Wilkins who show this ratio in half of their plays. I have carried out this test on The English Traveller, A Maidenhead Well Lost, A Challenge for Beauty and The Captives; Heywood consistently uses 'and' more than 'a' by a substantial margin.

These tests thus give several types of evidence, all quantifiable, objective and unlikely to be influenced by external factors such as compositorial habits or printing-house style, or by imitation of another writer. Most represent the sort of habits which may be unthinking, since few writers are likely to be aware how often they use the small, basic words which create their language. In evaluating the results, a clear division becomes visible after 4.1, chiefly in the use of 'troth' and ''las' for 'in troth' and 'alas'. 'Cry you mercy' in 4.2 suggests Heywood's authorship, as does 'y'ave' in 3.3, while 'e'en' and 'zoundes' are firm indicators of Rowley in 4.1 and 4.3, at least in Lambskin's speeches, of which 'zoundes' is a feature. The distribution of 'I'm' makes me think that Rowley wrote much of the first three acts and possibly part of 5.1. ''Has' confirms his writing in 4.1, 'forsooth' indicates that Heywood wrote some of the Clown's speeches in 3.1 and 3.3. I would suggest that ''las' (which is only used by the Widow/Wife) is a Heywood form since it appears in 4.2, a scene in which there is no convincing evidence for Rowley, and 'cry you mercy' appears twice. It seems to me that, with the exception of some of Stephen's speeches to which I shall return, 1.1 was written almost entirely by Rowley (''m' four times, 'them' only once), 4.2 is Heywood's work, and the remaining scenes show traces of both writers. The tables which follow at the end of this section summarise the evidence presented above and relate it to each scene of the play. In general terms, from 4.2 onwards Heywood's share of the writing becomes greater and he replaces Rowley as the dominant author. The function word test confirms this. The Heywood pattern, 'and' more than 'a', is found in this second segment of the play, 4.2-5.2, while the Rowley pattern, 'a' more than 'and', is found in a sample section taken from the first segment of the play, scenes 1.1, 2.1-3.1. In order to be absolutely certain that this section did not contain a significant number of Heywood lines, 1.2, which bears a superficial resemblance to 4.2 in the verse, was excluded.

The 'I'l' problem is not quite resolved. Throughout 1.1, 'Ile' or 'I'le' is the usual form with the exception of a cluster of five occurrences of 'I'l' in Stephen's speeches on B1. I suggest that copy for this scene was Rowley's foul papers, or at least written out by him, with one passage revised by Heywood; or that in this early scene the scribe had not decided whether or not to copy Rowley's forms exactly or substitute his own. In view of the way 'Ile' gives way to 'I'l' at the end of Act 1, and the way 'I'l' appears in a group of five on B1, I would prefer the first explanation. However, 'Ile' appears twice in 2.1, and 'I'le' occurs sporadically until $G2^v$ in 4.1; Heywood - or an anonymous copyist - may have copied these examples from Rowley's foul papers, failing totally to replace them with his own forms, or they may indicate that Heywood revised Rowley's work. This spelling is found in every scene up to and including 4.1, with the exception of 3.1. Again, this confirms the picture which emerges of Rowley writing the largest share of the first three acts and part of Act 4, with Heywood taking over at the beginning of the prison scene, 4.2.

One further point should be made. Heywood habitually used 'ey' for 'ay'. Quarto prints 'I', although 'ey' is used in, for example, A Maidenhead Well Lost.[17] David Lake's tables show Heywood's preference for 'yes' rather than 'ay' although he uses both; however, 'yes' is the only form in 4.2, the scene containing the greatest indications of Heywood's work. Possibly, then, 'I' is more likely to represent Rowley, although not in all cases; it occurs in every scene except 4.1, 4.2 and 5.2.

Finally, one should consider the verse. David Lake remarks that metrical tests have acquired a bad reputation[18] and I do not intend to use them. The quarto contains many speeches which are mislined and much relineation has been necessary, more so in the first three acts than in the last two. Of course I hope that my lining is as near the author's intention as possible, but even so some passages can be arranged in two or more ways. There is, then, a possibility that it is the editor's metrical sense which is being tested rather than the playwright's. That said, however, two distinct styles of verse can be seen in the play, one irregular and close to prose, the other more regular and containing a high proportion of rhyming couplets. The difference can be illustrated by the two passages following:

There let him howle, tis the best stay he hath; a)

For nothing but a prison can containe him
So boundlesse is his ryot; twice have I raysde
His decayed fortunes to a faire estate
But with as fruitlesse charity, as if I had throwne
My safe landed substance backe into the Sea,
Or dressd in pitty some corrupted Iade,
And he should kick me for my courtesie.
I am sure you cannot but heare, what quicke-sands
He findes out, as Dice, Cards, Pigeon-holes,
And which is more, should I not restraine it,
Hee'd make my state his prodigality. 1.1.45-56

I see mine error now: oh can there grow b)
A Rose upon a Bramble? did there e'r flow
Poyson and health together in one tide?
I'm borne a man; reason may step aside
And leade a father's love out of the way:
Forgive me, my good Boy, I went astray;
Looke, on my knees I beg it; not for joy
Thou bringst this golden rubbish, which I spurne
But glad in this, the heavens mine eye balls turne,
And fixe them right to looke upon that face
Where love remaines with pitty, duty, grace.
Oh my deare wronged boy! 5.1.76-87

Passage a) clearly tends to vary the number of syllables in a line, and lines 54-55 are so irregular as to be almost prose. This verse type is typical of 1.1, the verse passages of 2.1, and of 3.1 and 3.3. Passage b), which adheres more closely to the ten-syllable line, resembles the verse of the Wife's conversations with the Doctor in 1.2, with Stephen and Robert in 3.2, and of 4.2, 5.1 and 5.2 after the second entry. The verse thus shows a somewhat 'rough and ready' distinction of the scenes most closely related to the 'woman never vext' plot. There is, I think, little doubt that Rowley, notorious for his irregular verse,[19] wrote passage a), and that the passage b) verse is in a notably different style. I would suggest that the scenes showing the more regular verse are those most likely either to be written in part or wholly by Heywood, or at least written under his influence. It may be significant that the passage b) verse is found mainly in speeches by the Widow, Stephen, Robert, the King and the Keeper, while Mrs. Foster and Bruine speak in the verse of passage a). Mrs. Foster (like the Wife in *A Shoemaker, A Gentleman*) is distinguished by the phrase 'I, I', while the anomalous 'I'l' passage on B1, it will be remembered, occurs in Stephen's speeches.

In conclusion, the linguistic features preserved in the quarto text are not incompatible with the suggestion of divided authorship. The exact nature of any collaboration is impossible to prove - whether Heywood and Rowley worked together or Heywood revised a play almost completed by Rowley, adding most to the scenes following 4.1. In view of the sporadic nature of much of the evidence I think this latter is perhaps the most likely hypothesis; but as Samuel Schoenbaum has reminded us, opinions are not evidence. Where it is necessary to refer to the author of the play in this Introduction, I shall assume it is substantially the work of William Rowley, possibly revised by Thomas Heywood.

FEATURES USED TO DISCRIMINATE BETWEEN ROWLEY & HEYWOOD

a) Features used exclusively by Rowley or Heywood.

Rowley only	Heywood only
zoundes	pox on
'has (= he has)	y'ave
e'en	
foot	

b) Features favouring Rowley or Heywood but not offering conclusive proof.

Rowley	Heywood
tut	cry you mercy
I'm	forsooth
i'faith	I'l
I'le/Ile	yes
I (= ay)	'las
'm	them

DISTRIBUTION OF DISTINCTIVE FEATURES

a) by scene.

1.1 tut; I'm; i'faith; I; I'le; Ile; 'm.
I'l; them.

1.2 i'faith; I'le; Ile; I; 'm.
yes; them.

2.1 I'm; i'faith; I'le; Ile; I; 'm.
pox on; I'l; yes; them.

3.1 I'm; i'faith; I; 'm.
I'l; yes; them.

3.2 i'faith; I'le; I; 'm.
forsooth; I'l; yes; them.

3.3 I'm; I'le; I; 'm.
y'ave; forsooth; I'l; yes; them.

4.1 zoundes; 'has; i'faith; I'le; 'm.
I'l; yes; 'las; them.

4.2 ----------------------
cry you mercy; I'l; yes; 'las; them.

4.3 zoundes; I'le; I; e'en.
I'l; them.

5.1 I'm; I.
I'l; yes; 'las; them.

5.2 I.
I'l; yes; them.

b) by feature.

tut: 1.1(3)
zoundes: 4.1(3), 4.3(1)
'has: 4.1(2)
e'en: 4.3(1)
pox on: 2.1(4)
y'ave: 3.3(1)
I'm: 1.1(2), 2.1(1), 3.1(2), 3.3(1), 5.1(5)
i'faith: 1.1(1), 1.2(1), 2.1(3), 3.1(1), 3.2(1), 4.1(2)

Ile: 1.1(6), 1.2(5), 2.1(2)

I'le: 1.1(1), 1.2(2), 2.1(2), 3.2(1), 3.3(1), 4.1(1), 4.3(3)

I: 1.1(8), 1.2(4), 2.1(6), 3.1(7), 3.2(1), 3.3(4), 4.3(1), 5.1(1), 5.2(1)

'm: 1.1(4), 1.2(7), 2.1(9), 3.1(5), 3.2(1), 3.3(2), 4.1(1)

cry you mercy: 4.2(2)

forsooth: 3.2(1), 3.3(1)

I'l: 1.1(5), 2.1(41), 3.1(12), 3.2(2), 3.3(5), 4.1(11), 4.2(9), 4.3(10), 5.1(10), 5.2(3)

yes: 1.2(3), 2.1(2), 3.1(3), 3.2(1), 3.3(1), 4.1(5), 4.2(3), 5.1(4), 5.2(1)

'las: 4.1(1), 4.2(3), 5.1(1)

them: 1.1(1), 1.2(2), 2.1(5), 3.1(6), 3.2(4), 3.3(3), 4.1(6), 4.2(3), 4.3(4), 5.1(6), 5.2(1)

FEATURES WHICH DO NOT DISCRIMINATE BETWEEN ROWLEY & HEYWOOD

prithee	among/amongst	's (= his)	i'th
how now	beside(s)	I'd	o'th
I warrant thee	between/betwixt	th'art	has/hath
why	toward(s)	'tas	does/doth
heavens	while(s)/whilest	it's	sfoot
marry	ye	y'are	
speech prefixes			

Not found in other Rowley or Heywood works:

foot; hold my life; th'are; by...copy; third part of.

Analysis of function words in <u>All's Lost by Lust</u>, <u>A Shoemaker, A Gentleman</u>, late Heywood plays and two sections of <u>A New Wonder, A Woman Never Vext</u>.

	a	and	but	by	for	from	in	it	of	that	the	to	with
Eng. T	99	182	56	14	34	23	103	33	78	76	133	135	34
MWL	112	146	54	21	58	9	69	43	72	79	138	154	45
Chall.	98	162	48	23	50	14	99	31	105	75	140	121	34
LM	95	178	56	20	42	18	88	18	104	65	129	127	60
Cap.	98	187	32	19	47	17	84	34	104	72	144	132	30
ALL*	144	127	34	19	39	23	77	75	86	54	158	111	53
Shoe*	137	115	41	14	54	15	64	100	87	56	140	138	39
WNV 1	141	128	52	21	72	8	89	42	69	68	137	122	51
WNV 2	95	153	32	12	73	29	74	50	69	74	139	154	46

* MacDonald Jackson's figures.

Eng. T	<u>The English Traveller</u>
MWL	<u>A Maidenhead Well Lost</u>
Chall.	<u>A Challenge for Beauty</u>
LM	<u>Love's Mistress</u>
Cap.	<u>The Captives</u>
ALL	<u>All's Lost by Lust</u>
Shoe.	<u>A Shoemaker, A Gentleman</u>
WNV 1	<u>A New Wonder, A Woman Never Vext</u> 1.1, 2.1-3.1
WNV 2	<u>A New Wonder, A Woman Never Vext</u> 4.2-5.2

The Author

William Rowley's name first appears in 1607, as collaborator with Day and Wilkins on <u>The Travels of the Three English Brothers</u>. The play was written for Queen Anne's Men, a company for which Rowley wrote two other plays: <u>A Shoemaker, A Gentleman</u> in 1608 and, with Heywood, <u>Fortune by Land and Sea</u> in 1609.[1] In the same year, his pamphlet <u>A Search for Money</u> was printed - the only prose work which he is known to have written.

By March 1610 Rowley was associated with the Duke of York's Men[2] (later known as Prince Charles' Men) with whom he worked until 1623. He acted as their payee at Court[3] and became one of the leading members of the company.[4] As an actor, he seems to have specialised in playing clowns.[5]

Rowley's collaboration with Middleton, who had been writing for Lady Elizabeth's Men, began in 1615-16, when their companies merged;[6] Wit at Several Weapons was their first work,[7] then came A Fair Quarrel (1617), The Old Law (with Massinger, 1618) and following All's Lost By Lust (Rowley, 1619-20) The World Tossed at Tennis (1620), The Changeling (1622) and The Spanish Gipsy (1623). Rowley was also collaborating with other playwrights; in 1621 he worked with Dekker and Ford on The Witch of Edmonton and, following his move to the King's Men in 1623, he and Fletcher wrote The Maid in the Mill. A Cure for a Cuckold, with Webster, and A New Wonder, A Woman Never Vexed both belong to the period 1624-25.

In 1624, the Prince's Men attempted to repeat the success of The Witch of Edmonton by hiring Rowley, Dekker, Ford and Webster to write a play about two recent scandals. The Late Murder of the Son Upon the Mother, or, Keep the Widow Waking provoked a Star Chamber case; Rowley was named with the other writers in the indictment, but died before he could give evidence, in the early weeks of 1626.[8] 'William Rowley, householder' was buried at St. James Clerkenwell, on February 11th 1626, leaving a widow, Grace.[9]

Of Rowley's works, only The Travels of the Three English Brothers, A Fair Quarrel, A Search for Money and The World Tossed at Tennis were published in his life-time. Apart from Keep the Widow Waking, five plays are known to be lost;[10] three others present difficulties. The Thracian Wonder (1623) by 'Rowley and Webster' is of doubtful authorship, as is A Match at Midnight (1621) by 'W.R.' The Birth of Merlin (published 1662) by 'Shakespeare and Rowley' is of uncertain date and authorship. The Parliament of Love, entered on the Stationers' Register in 1660 as by Rowley, is almost certainly the unaided work of Massinger.[11]

Date

A New Wonder, A Woman Never Vext was not entered on the Stationers' Register until 1631. If the Master of the Revels issued a licence for stage production, it has not survived; nor has any record of a performance. Revisions could have been made to the play until 1631, but most of the writing must have been finished before Rowley's death early in 1626. I have found no evidence of major interpolation in the text; on the contrary, one of the striking aspects of the play is its unity.[1]

Two dates have previously been suggested for composition. Dewar M. Robb favours 1610[2] because of similarities to Heywood's works. Rowley and Heywood collaborated on Fortune by Land and Sea, published in 1655 as acted by the Queen's Men. This is usually taken to refer to Queen Anne's Men, in whom Heywood was a sharer and for whom Rowley is thought to have acted, rather than Queen Henrietta's Men (for whom Heywood wrote and who inherited Rowley's plays for Lady Elizabeth's Men). Fortune by Land and Sea is thus dated about 1609, and A Woman Never Vext, according to Dewar Robb's theory, is of roughly the same period.

I.A. Shapiro has pointed out[3] that the Clown's 'Tittere Tu Tattere' at 2.1.323 is a reference to a Catholic association formed in the regiment of Lord Vaux while it was serving in the Low Countries. This regiment was created after April 1622; on December 6th, 1623, Chamberlain wrote to Dudley Carleton of the Tityre-tus and said that they had come to London, 'the number of eight score already knowne'.[4] Chamberlain seems to be passing on recent gossip; so if the news of the association was to be sufficiently well known for Rowley's audience to recognise the allusion,[5] the passage cannot pre-date Chamberlain's letter by any significant period. This suggests that Rowley was working on the play in the last weeks of 1623 or later and gives composition dates of December 1623-January 1626.[6]

The Text

I. The Publisher and the Printer

A New Wonder, A Woman Never Vext was entered on the Stationers'

Register on 24th November 1631:

> Master Constable Entred for his Copy vnder the handes of Sir HENRY HERBERT and Master Islip warden a booke called A new wonder or a woman neuer vext (a Comedy) by WILLIAM ROWLEY vj[d].

It was printed by George Purslowe in 1632; the quarto title-page replaces the 'or' of the Register's entry with a comma.

This was the sixth play which Francis Constable had published since he started business in 1615; seven more were to follow before 1640. He had published the King's Men's The Maid's Tragedy in 1619 and 1622, but after 1630 he dealt almost exclusively in the Lady Elizabeth's/ Queen Henrietta's/Beeston's Boys stock of plays.[1] However, The Fatal Dowry, another King's Men play, was also printed for him in 1632 and registered on March 30th.

George Purslowe had previously printed one play for Francis Constable, The Maid's Tragedy edition of 1622. In 19 years as a master printer, he printed ten dramatic works, including two pageants and a masque;[2] apart from A New Wonder, he also printed Changes in 1632, for W. Cooke. He had one press,[3] but as a member of the Eliot's Court printing house he probably shared his type stock with his partners, John Haviland and Ann Griffin.[4] His staff at this time included two apprentices: William White, bound on January 14th 1629, and Thomas Wilson, bound December 25th 1629. William Gay was freed on January 12th 1631 and agreed to work for Purslowe one further year. He was probably a pressman, since he contracted to work 'XXX[c]' per day for eight shillings per week.[5]

The Stationers' Register records that on February 17th, 1647 (i.e., 1648) 'M[rs] Alice Constable widd' sold to Richard Thrale 'these copies following wch lately apperteyned to M[r] Francis Constable dec[d],' item ten being 'A new wonder, a woman never vext by W[m] Rowley.' The title, it will be noticed, is now that on the title-page of the quarto. The Fatal Dowry was item eleven in Richard Thrale's list, and the two plays were again entered together when, on April 11th 1681, Richard's widow Dorothy assigned 'all her estate, right, title, and interest, of, in, and to the severall bookes or coppies or parts of bookes or coppies hereafter menco̅ned' to Benjamin Thrale. A New Wonder, A Woman Never

Vext does not appear in the Stationers' Register again; there were no reprints.

II. Printing

There is no reason to doubt that formes A-H were set by a single compositor working by formes. With gathering I, however, two changes enter the text. Most noticeably, the use of the italic type is altered; for the first time, on I1, I2 and I2^v the names of places - here London and Ludgate - are italicised. 'Ludgate' appears in Roman again on I3 and 'London' on I4^v, but on K1, K2 and K2^v place-names are again italicised[6] with one exception on K2,[7] and finally on L1. I would suggest that the printer's copy did not italicise place-names and the first compositor followed his copy faithfully, but a new compositor became involved at the beginning of I who followed Purslowe's more normal practice.[8]

This supposition is supported by the punctuation-spacing test advocated by T.H. Howard-Hill.[9] Certain features remain constant throughout the text, notably the preference for a space before colons and semi-colons, and until gathering I there is a strong preference for commas to be set without a space, either before or after the punctuation. From I1-2^v the pattern alters, and the tendency is to set a comma followed, but not preceded by, a space, and this preference is again marked at K1-2^v and L1-1^v. K3-4^v do not show a strong preference either way; and L2, consisting of seven lines of text, has four commas, all set as on I1-2^v. Against this evidence, we might argue that the punctuation of this section of the play is bound to show changes because it includes the greatest number of rhymed couplets. These tend to be end-stopped and thus syntactically different from the prose of Acts 1-3, resulting in a somewhat lighter punctuation; but this should not affect the compositor's spacing of commas, and we are still left with I3-4^v which follow the pattern of the rest of the text. It will also be noticed that I1-2^v, K1-2^v and L are the areas showing a change in italic usage.

From B1-I4^v, the running-titles show two distinct skeleton formes used in regular sequence. However, a new set of running-titles was introduced at inner K, and L, a half-sheet, used another new combination.

Inner K was imposed before the second I forme[10] was stripped and before outer K. L was imposed before outer K was stripped. So we can say that one man worked on most of the book; but when he reached I, a second compositor was brought in, and they worked together, dividing the gathering into two four-page sections rather than taking a forme each. The second compositor set the first half of the gathering. This arrangement continued through K, and the second compositor set the final half-sheet L.

The play is printed in five acts, with no scene divisions, and running-titles _A new wonder,_ on the verso, _A woman never vext._ on the recto.[11] It is lined as verse throughout, although much of the play is in prose, affecting particularly 1.2, 3.2, 4.1, 4.3. Rhyming couplets are sometimes mislined even when, as on K1, the lines do not reach the full measure. The pages contain between 27 and 37 lines of type, depending on the occurrence of act-headings and stage-directions. Most of the extant copies have an end ornament[12] in the centre of L2, but it is lacking in some copies. It has not proved possible to discover whether it was added or removed during the print-run; it is damaged, but was used again by Elizabeth Purslowe (who took over George's business) in _Certain Learned and Elegant Works of the Right Honourable Fulke Lord Brooke_, 1633.[13] Other variants caused by press-corrections occur at A (inner and outer), B (inner and outer), D (inner), E (outer), F (inner), G (inner and outer), K (inner) and L (outer). E outer and F inner both show a relatively high proportion of corrections.

Twelve copies have been collated for this edition: two at the British Library (644.c.12 and C.12.f.1) and the Wise copy also housed there (Ashley 1453), the Dyce collection copy at the Victoria and Albert Museum, three copies at the Bodleian, two at Worcester College, King's College Cambridge's copy, the Bute collection copy at the National Library of Scotland, and one of the Huntington Library's copies (C 21423/69158). The copies at Cambridge, Huntington and Worcester College copy 3.48 lack the end ornament. The title-page and L2 (with ornament) are illustrated on the following pages.

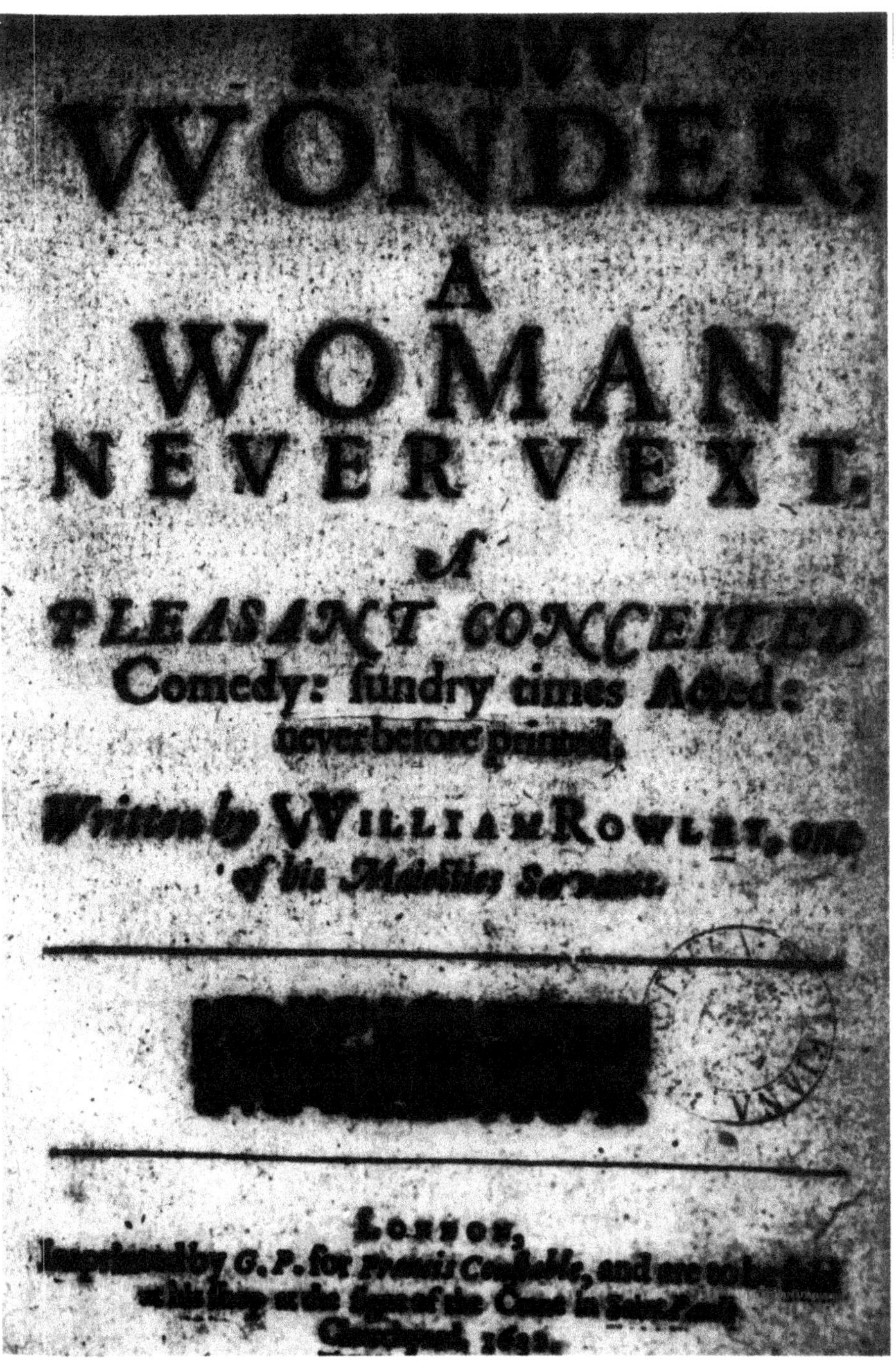

WONDER,
A
WOMAN
NEVER VEXT,
A
PLEASANT CONCEITED
Comedy: sundry times Acted:
never before printed.

Written by WILLIAM ROWLEY, one
of his Majesties Servants.

LONDON,
Imprinted by G. P. for Francis Constable, and are to be sold
at his shop at the signe of the Crane in Saint Pauls
Churchyard, 1632.

Title page from the 1632 quarto.
Copy Mal. 167, reproduced by permission of
The Bodleian Library, Oxford.

(Enlarged)

A woman wonder, brothers reconcil'd ;
You worthy Sir, did invite us to a feast,
Wee'l not forget it, but will bee your guest,
Because wee'l veiw these wonders o're agen,
Whose records doe deserve a brazen Pen,
But this above the rest, in golden text,
Shall be insculpt ; *A Woman never Vext.*

Exeunt.

FINIS.

End ornament from the 1632 quarto.
Copy Douce R.123, reproduced by permission of
The Bodleian Library, Oxford.

(Enlarged)

III. The Printer's Copy

At first glance, the printer's copy seems to have been the author's foul papers, or a copy of them. The text shows none of the convenient signs of prompt-book copy; no references to the actors by name, no warnings to be ready, no annotations about properties. In an article on the Lambarde manuscript of _Beggars' Bush_,[14] however, Fredson Bowers has suggested that a text printed from prompt-book may very easily be mistaken for one from the author's foul papers. The permissive nature of some of the stage directions, in Act 2 especially, seems to imply that this text was never prepared for staging. Surely any theatre company seeing the direction, _Enter the Bowlers_, would want to know how many Bowlers? (This is their one and only appearance.) One would also expect exits to be tidied up, but at least two are missing. Yet Bowers points out that Edward Knight's prompt-book of _Beggars' Bush_ must have been surprisingly vague:[15]

> But the prompt-book seems to have omitted on several occasions to specify necessary action beyond Massinger's incomplete or ambiguous directions as found in F...This appears to be a clear case of Knight's failing to make good the inadequacies of the author's copy for staging.

The possibility that we are dealing with prompt-book copy, then, must at least be borne in mind.

The placing and form of the stage directions may give us some help. On G4^{v} there is the direction, _Ent. Stepen's_ [sic] _Wife_ placed in the right-hand margin. Up to this point, entrances have taken the form _Enter..._ and have been centred, but _Ent. Robert_ appears on I1 and _Ent. Stephen_ on I1^{v}, both on the right of the text. The change in form and placing does not agree with the change of compositors, for the second compositor did not take over until I1, after the G4^{v} direction, and the usual form of directions appears on I2^{v}, also set by the second compositor, and throughout the rest of his work. Further, the G4^{v} direction is a repetition of _Enter Stephens Wife_ at the bottom of G4. (Since G4 is in the inner forme, and G4^{v} in the outer, the compositor cannot be blamed for not noticing the repetition; as he was not setting the pages in numerical sequence, he need not have realised that only two lines of text separate the directions.) The most likely explanation is that someone went through the manuscript and in a desultory fashion began to prepare it for the stage. The G4 direction is too early; the Wife uses Bruine's speech 'Here comes...vext' to walk across the stage, arriving by Bruine as he says, 'Y'are welcome Mistris Foster', and she does not need to enter on the first line of his speech. As it stands in the quarto, the direction is also in an awkward place and would certainly need to be written in again by Bruine's speech; but the quarto layout of course probably has nothing to do with the manuscript arrangement in division of pages. The entrances on I1 and I1^v may have been omitted in the author's papers; the prompter realised they were necessary and added them. Surviving manuscript plays such as _Demetrius and Enanthe_, _Bonduca_, _The Witch_, _The Soddered Citizen_, _Hengist King of Kent_, indicate a tendency to put stage directions in the right-hand margin.

Of the other stage directions, it is impossible to tell which are authorial, which, if any, supplied later. The printer habitually sets all stage directions to the right, unless they require a full line or more of print, and remembering Rowley's long experience in writing for the theatre, it is not unlikely that he himself wrote the directions where the prompter would look for them - in the margin on the right. It is, I think, futile to guess whether Rowley was more likely to have written _Robin puts in money_ or the prompter _Kisse him_. As W.W. Greg remarked,[16]

> The fact is that there is hardly a stage-direction that has been cited as characteristic of the prompter that cannot be paralleled from texts for which the author was probably alone responsible.

IV. The Title-page

The printing of the title, as we have remarked, shows a slight alteration from the one registered: the Stationers' Register shows 'A new wonder or a woman neuer vext', implying a double title of the formula of Shirley's _Changes, or Love in a Maze_ (although of Rowley's other works only the collaborative _The Birth of Merlin, or the Child hath Found its Father_ and _Keep the Widow Waking_ take this form). The running-titles, however, agree with the title-page and, indeed, with subsequent entries in the Stationers' Register, so whatever the author's intention, this is the title by which the play is known.

The phrase 'sundry times Acted' is a common-place and need not necessarily be taken to indicate a stage success. In other respects the title-page is uninformative; in particular, it is unusual that no acting company is mentioned. A Shoemaker, A Gentleman was 'Acted/ at the Red Bull and other Theaters, with a/general/ and good Applause'; All's Lost by Lust was 'Divers times Acted by the Lady Elizabeths/ SERVANTS./And now lately by her Maiesties Servants, with/great applause, at the Phoenix in Drury Lane'; and A Match at Midnight was printed 'As it hath beene Acted by the Children/of the Revells'. There are two areas which might repay investigation in this respect: the publisher, and the author.

The Publisher Francis Constable usually published plays which belonged to companies connected with Christopher Beeston: Lady Elizabeth's Men, Queen Henrietta's Men, Beeston's Boys. The exceptions are the King's Men's The Maid's Tragedy, of which he was joint owner, and Field and Massinger's The Fatal Dowry, also belonging to the King's Men, and published in the same year as A Woman Never Vext. But these two plays were entered on the Stationers' Register on different days, March 30th 1632 (The Fatal Dowry) and November 24th 1631 (A Woman Never Vext), and there is thus no evidence that they were bought at the same time. Indeed, since a publisher might be expected to register a new book quickly in order to establish his copy, the plays were probably bought on separate occasions. Of course, having once dealt with the King's Men in 1619, Constable might have briefly renewed the association in 1631-32; but the chances are that Field and Massinger's play was the first he had bought from the company since The Maid's Tragedy and that he obtained A Woman Never Vext from his usual source, Christopher Beeston.

The Author Between 1623-25, when the play was completed, Rowley was a member of the King's Men and was collaborating with John Fletcher on The Maid in the Mill for his own company. One might suppose, then, that A Woman Never Vext was also written for the King's Men. However, during the same period Rowley and Webster wrote A Cure for a Cuckold for an unidentified company and they also worked with Dekker and Ford on Keep the Widow Waking for the Prince's Men, the company which had produced The Witch of Edmonton in 1621. His recent plays - All's Lost by Lust, The Changeling, The Spanish Gipsy - had all been written for the Lady Elizabeth's Men.

A play written for the King's Men about 1625 would probably still be owned by them in 1631 when Francis Constable bought it. One written for the Lady Elizabeth's Men would have had a more complex history, since the company was disbanded about 1625, some of the members joining Beeston in forming Queen Henrietta's Men. A Woman Never Vext was probably completed at about the time of the change-over; the theatres were closed for eight months during 1625 because of plague,[17] and a play becoming available at this time would stand little chance of immediate production. Beeston apparently took the play-stock with him[18] and so Francis Constable would have bought A Woman Never Vext from Queen Henrietta's Men, with whom Rowley himself was never associated. This may account for the unusual wording of the title-page.

Sources

1. John Stow's 'A Survey of London'

Stow's Survey may be quite readily identified as a source for A Woman Never Vext since Stow is the only writer to mention Walter Bruine and the foundation of St. Mary's Spittle. He includes both Bruine and Foster in his Abridgement of the English Chronicle but it is the Survey which ties in most closely with the play.

The Survey went through three editions in Rowley's lifetime, in 1598, 1603 and 1618, the last enlarged by a reviser. I have quoted throughout from the 1618 edition as the most 'up-to-date' one to which Rowley could have had access, but none of the editions varies in the sections which concern us.

Because Stow arranges his material topographically rather than chronologically, Foster and Bruine appear several times. Foster, for example, is mentioned in the list of temporal government as well as in the sections on gates and on charitable citizens. Since Stow thus tends to duplicate information, I quote below the passages which deal most fully with Bruine and the Fosters.

I reade in a Charter, dated the yeare 1235, that Walter Brune, Citizen of London, and Rosia his wife, hauing founded the Priory or new Hospital of our blessed Lady, since called S. Marie Spittle without Bishopsgate, confirmed the same to the honour of GOD and our blessed Lady, for Chanons regular. E6

Also in the yeere 1463. the third of Edward the fourth,...in a common Councell, at the request of the well disposed, blessed, and deuout Woman, Dame Agnes Forster, widow, late wife to Stephen Forster, Fishmonger, sometime Maior, for the comfort and reliefe of all the poore prisoners, certaine Articles were established. Inprimis, That the new works, then late edified by the same Dame Agnes, for the enlarging of the prison of Ludgate, from thence-forth should be had and taken, as a part and parcell of the said prison of Ludgate, so that both the old & new work of Ludgate aforesaid, to be one prison, Gaile, keeping, and charge for euermore.

The said Quadrant, strongly builded of stone, by the before-named Stephen Forster, and Agnes his wife, containing a large walking place by ground, of 38. foot and a halfe in length, besides the thicknesse of the walles, which are at the least six foot, makes all together 44. foot and a halfe, the breadth within the walles is 29. foote and a halfe, so that the thicknesse of the walles maketh it 35. foote and a halfe in breadth. The like roome it hath ouer it for lodgings, and ouer it againe faire Leades to walke vpon, well imbattailed, all for fresh ayre, and ease of prisoners, to the end they should haue lodging, and water free without charge, as by certaine verses grauen in...Copper, and fixed on the said Quadrant, I haue read, in forme following.

> Deuout soules that passe this way,
>   for Stephen Forster, late Maior, heartily pray,
> And Dame Agnes his spouse, to God consecrate,
>   that of pitie, this house made for Londoners in Ludgate.
> So that for lodgings and water, prisoners here nought pay,
>   as their keepers shall all answere at dreadfull doomes day.

This place, and one other of his Armes, being three broad Arrow-heads, taken downe with the old Gate, I caused to be fixed ouer the entrie of ye said Quadrant: but the verses being vnhappily turned inward to the wall, procured ye like in effect to be ingrauen outward in prose, declaring him to be a Fishmonger, because some, vpon a light occasion (as a Maydens head in a glasse window) had fabled him to be a Mercer, and to haue begged there at Ludgate. F2-3

In the yeere 1197. Walter Brune, a Citizen of London, and Rosia his wife, founded the Hospital of our Lady, called Domus Dei or S. Mary Spittle, without Bishopsgate of London, a house of such reliefe to the needy, that there was found standing at the surrender thereof, nine score beds, well furnished for receit of poore people. M2v

Wherefore I wish men to make their owne hands their Executors, and their eyes their Ouerseers, not forgetting the old Prouerbe:

Women be forgetfull, Children be vnkind,

> Executors be couetous, and take what they find.
> If any body aske where the deads goods became,
> They answere:
> So God me helpe and holydome, he dyed a poore man. 07

> 1454, Maior, Sir Stephen Foster, Fishmonger, sonne of Robert Foster of London, Stock-fishmonger. This man enlarged Ludgate, for ease of the prisoners there. 306

A further passage ($X8^v$-Y1) deals with the history of the *Domus Dei* until the Dissolution of the Monasteries and has no relevance to the play.

Rowley has, therefore, taken the following aspects of the play from Stow:

1. The character of Walter Bruine; his foundation of St. Mary's Spittle; the historical setting (the reign of Henry III).
2. The characters of Stephen Foster and his wife; their building at Ludgate; the legend that Stephen began his career as a Ludgate beggar (which Stow rejects); the name 'Robert Foster'.
3. The proverb 'women be forgetful'.

Equally striking, however, are the changes which he has made to his source material. The most important are these:

1. Bruine and Foster have been made contemporaneous, bridging an historical gap of some 200 years. The juxtaposition of the two characters is important to the play's thematic structure, allowing Rowley to show 'charity' in its various aspects.
2. 'Robert Foster' has been displaced by two generations, from Stephen's father to his nephew; Old Foster, his son and wife are Rowley's inventions and are, of course, central to the plot.
3. Rosia Bruine has disappeared and has been replaced by Jane, who brings with her the two foolish suitors, Lambskin and Speedwell. Jane provides the romantic sub-plot; Lambskin and Speedwell act as foils to Robert but also contribute to the structural unity by their link with Stephen and the Widow.

It will be noticed that there is no source for the Widow's marriage to Stephen. This story does not appear in the *Survey* until Strype's revision and expansion[1] but it is clear from Stow's comments that it was current at the turn of the seventeenth century. According to

Strype, the Widow heard Stephen Foster begging for bread at Ludgate. She gave him the £20 which he needed to obtain release, and hired him; he proved a good business man and sometime later she married him. Rowley does not show Stephen in Ludgate; he makes Robert buy his release; and he makes the Widow marry him immediately on meeting him. The legend which Rowley knew may have differed from that which Strype records or he may have altered the story as he did the material from the Survey.

One should also notice that Stow's Survey appears to have been a source for Heywood's II If You Know Not Me You Know Nobody, first printed in 1606 and reprinted in 1610 and 1623. This play also deals with the City's benefactors, and at one point brings in the Fosters:

> They are two that haue deseru'd a memorie,
> Worthy the note of our Posteritie;
> This Agnes Foster, wife to sir A. Foster,
> That fre'd a Beggar at the grate of Ludgate,
> Was after Maior of this most famous Citie,
> And builded the South-side of Ludgate vp,
> Vpon which wall these Verses I haue read... (1606, D1)

Stow's verses are then quoted and, a little later, the first two lines of the 'women are forgetful' proverb (D1^{v}). These lines would tend to suggest that the Foster story which was available to Heywood was substantially the same as Strype's. The play provides an interesting parallel to A Woman Never Vext, for both plays are concerned to show how citizens have helped the City. A discussion of the similarities and differences between the plays belongs more properly to a critical consideration of A Woman Never Vext but it is, I think, probable that Rowley knew II If You Know Not Me, if not from the stage then from one of the reprints.

Cooke's play Greene's Tu Quoque has an incident in which a widow releases an apprentice from debt, hires him and eventually marries him. A couplet in the preliminaries of the 1614 edition, signed W.R., is almost certainly by Rowley; since he probably knew the play, it should be included among the sources.

2. The Legend of Polycrates

Herodotus tells the story of the fish and the ring in Book 3 of *The Histories*. Polycrates, the tyrant of Samos, was so lucky that Amasis king of Egypt advised him to throw away his most precious possession to avert the displeasure of the gods. Polycrates threw a ring into the sea; some days later a fisherman took a large fish to the tyrant's cook, who found the ring inside. Amasis broke off his alliance, to avoid the disaster which he knew must follow, and Polycrates, having been captured by the Persian Orontes, was crucified.[2] The Augustan historian Strabo summarised the story in book 14 of *De Situ Orbis*;[3] he gives only the following outline: Polycrates threw a ring into the sea which was later found in a fish, a king of Egypt foretold that Polycrates' life would not end fortunately, and the tyrant was hanged by Orontes. These two works had not been translated into English but were available in Latin translations and in parallel texts. Summaries could be found in, for example, *Dictionarium Historicum ac Poeticum* (1579) and Bishop Cooper's *Dictionarium*; these are closer to the shorter account in Strabo than to Herodotus, and omit Amasis.

Rowley uses the Polycrates legend in three ways.

1. The Widow and Polycrates are both unnaturally lucky - although one might argue that in the Widow's case this is partly the result of her generous outlook and a refusal to be ill-tempered, rather than just luck. In this respect her character owes something to Candido, the merchant in *I The Honest Whore*.
2. In 1.2, the Widow's maid buys a fish and finds inside the wedding ring which the Widow had lost in the Thames.
3. Like Polycrates, the Widow deliberately gives away her most precious possession - her wealth, which she invites Stephen to waste. Also like Polycrates in the Herodotus version, she has a religious conscience about her luck and, by using the passage from *Hebrews*[4] and introducing the character of the Doctor, Rowley achieves a synthesis with Christian theology. In view of this religious element, it seems likely, although not conclusive, that an edition of Herodotus was Rowley's source.

There is also, however, evidence of a further possible source. Vox Piscis[5] was entered on the Stationers' Register on 13th September 1626, and contains three treatises, 'found in the belly of a Cod-fish in Cambridge Market, on Midsummer Eue last, Anno Domini 1626.' It cannot, therefore, have been written before Rowley's death in February 1626. However, after giving the Polycrates legend, the author gives this story:

> A citizen of Newcastle (whose name I take to be M. Anderson) talking with a friend of his vpon Newcastle bridge, and fingring his Ring, before he was aware let it fall into the Riuer; and was much troubled at the losse of it, till by a fish caught in the Riuer that losse was repaired, and his Ring restored him. ($A8^v$-9)

This story is very close to the incident in A Woman Never Vext; the Widow, one recalls, was crossing the Thames when she lost her ring. It is unlikely, I think, that the Vox Piscis author had seen an unrecorded performance of A Woman Never Vext and been inspired by it to fabricate the Newcastle story; but it is possible that the pamphlet and the play share an undiscovered source. However, I have been unable to find any reference to this incident before Vox Piscis, or anything that could be an analogue.

The Foster Family[1]

Stephen Foster was baptised, at an unrecorded date, (probably close to the year 1400) at Staunton Drew, Somerset; his brother, nephew and great nephew were still living there in 1458, and throughout his life Foster retained links with the West Country.[2] One of his successful trading ventures was with William Cannynges, a wealthy Bristol merchant; together they owned the profitable 'Katherine' which traded to Iceland under a special dispensation from the King. Cannynges remained a life-long friend.[3]

Precisely when Foster based his business in London is unknown, but his family had held land in the city since 1385.[4] The date and circumstances of his marriage to Agnes are also unknown, but in view of his prosperous family background and subsequent career it seems unlikely that his wife rescued him from penury at Ludgate. One may conjecture that the legend which Rowley uses and Stow dimisses[5] grew up to explain the family's unusual interest in prison reform. Foster's career in the administration of London began on August 29th, 1435, when he was elected M.P. Between 1439 and 1443 he was an auditor, and again 1446-7;[6] in 1441 he stood, unsuccessfully, for Castle Baynard Ward,[7] and was elected alderman for Bread Street Ward in 1444.[8] His work to enlarge Ludgate was also begun in this year.[9] He was sheriff 1444-5, Mayor 1454-5;[10] 1453-4 found him engaged in legal action over the manor of Ashton[11] and on February 3rd 1458 he was exonerated from his duties as alderman because of ill-health.[12] He died between December 4th, 1458, when he made his will, and December 27th, when it was proved.[13]

Rowley's picture of him as a merchant trading in a variety of wares is probably accurate in substance. By the fifteenth century, merchants were not confined to the trade of the guild to which they nominally belonged. Foster was a fishmonger, but also traded in grocers' wares - he purchased 22 bales of pepper, worth £529, in one deal - and left money to both the grocers and fishmongers. He traded to Iceland for stockfish, and bartered Cornish tin for Venetian silk and spices.[14]

Rowley is, however, wrong to suggest that Agnes pre-deceased her husband; she survived until at least 1477. The work at Ludgate was not completed when Foster died and, while it was being finished, she appears to have visited Newgate, Ludgate and the Counters to study prison conditions. In December 1463, when the Ludgate Addition was officially given to the Mayor and aldermen, she made suggestions for reform which would curb cruelty and extortion by the keepers and ensure that no man was imprisoned without cause.[15]

In 1465, Agnes was given custody of a prisoner-of-war, the Sieur de Graville, who remained with her twelve years awaiting ransom. The money was owed to 'John Forster', probably Agnes' son.[16] The evidence for the structure of Stephen Foster's family is given by Sylvia Thrupp in her appendix on aldermanic families.[17] Robert Foster was the name both of Stephen's father and of one of his three sons (the father a stockfishmonger, the son a grocer); Rowley's choice of the name for Stephen's nephew and adopted son perhaps reflects a garbled history of the family. Of his brothers, one was called Thomas, another Richard; the Fords, William and John, are also described as 'brother'. There is no evidence that any of his kinsmen quarrelled with him. Agnes, his daughter, took for her second husband Robert Morton gentleman of Lincoln's Inn, a relative of Cardinal Morton, confirming the family's position as gentry.

The Play

Structure and Technique

A New Wonder, A Woman Never Vext is an impressively homogeneous play, uniform in tone and clear in exposition. Its structure is its greatest asset: not only is it satisfyingly tidy in plotting but its framework is also made to work positively within the play, supporting the action and pointing up themes. It must, therefore, be a highly artificial structure (in the sense that it is carefully contrived); but the fact that the artifice does not obtrude into the play is not the least of its triumphs. One is never aware that the natural impetus of the drama has been impeded or distorted.

But the first task is to determine the structure which shapes the action. In its printed form the play uses the five-act division inherited from the Terentian school but this need not necessarily be authorial. If, as has been suggested as a possibility in the remarks on text and authorship, a scribal copy intervened between author's papers and printed text, then the act divisions could have been introduced there. Rowley's other plays - A Shoemaker, A Gentleman, All's Lost by Lust and the doubtful A Match at Midnight - all use the formula Actus primus; A Match at Midnight adds scaena Prima in the first act before adopting the formula Actus 2. scaena 1 etc. (In each case, only the first scene of each act is marked.) R.V. Holdsworth suggests that this was Rowley's usage for A Fair Quarrel;[1] however, it is not sufficiently unusual to prove Rowley's responsibility for A Woman Never Vext's act headings. In collaboration, at least, Rowley appears to have thought in terms of an act-structure; The Changeling preserves the stage direction, 'In the act-time De Flores hides a naked rapier.'[2] The staging of A Woman Never Vext provides one hint that the present act-division is at times at odds with the action. Stephen leaves the stage at the end of 5.1 and immediately re-appears in Henry III's train at the beginning of 5.2. A pause in the action is inevitable here and is arguably more appropriate than at the end of 4.3, allowing the momentum of the prison scenes to continue through 5.1. But the arrangement of the printed text is by no means impossible, although I have noticed no other occasion on which Rowley demands a halt between scenes rather than acts. The question is in some ways an artificial one, since in production the position of act-divisions would not always be obvious.[3]

To regard this play in terms of five-act structure is, in any case, misleading, since the act-divisions do not arise organically from the text. Act 2 starts a new phase of action in the gaming-house, but it is so well correlated with Act 1 that it is virtually a continuation of it. It can be more helpful to see the plot as comprising three movements. Acts 1 and 2 establish the family relationship which is a cohesive factor in plotting. Characters are delineated, the history of the family before the action starts is made clear, and the Widow's marriage to Stephen completes the division of the major characters into two groupings: Old Foster and Mrs. Foster, and Stephen and his Wife, with Robert and Bruine the go-betweens caught between the two camps. Act 3 is an act of reversals. Stephen is seen in his new character, Old Foster's hopes are raised and destroyed, the brothers' financial positions are exchanged. The Bruine sub-plot is also set going. Acts 4 and 5 examine the new relationship in which the Fosters find themselves and bring them to a reconcilement; the Bruine plot is also finished. Act 5 does not truly present a dénouement but rather a resolution before the conflict can reach a climax. There is no convincing reason for Old Foster's reformation in 5.1, and the audience has always been aware that Stephen is not really opposed to his brother; the point at which the action concludes is somewhat arbitrary. I shall return to this idea later.

To talk of a three-part structure is doing no more than to say that the play has a beginning, a middle and an end; but A Shoemaker, A

Gentleman demonstrates that even such a basic structure is not always easy to achieve. In this play, Rowley possibly had too much material for one work; thus the main-plot, describing how the princes Crispin and Crispianus are forced to take disguise as shoemakers but eventually are made kings under the Roman emperors, splits into two plots. Crispin, in his role of shoemaker, wooes and marries the Emperor's daughter, in an action which has substantially the same material as the main-plot of The Shoemaker's Holiday, but at the same time Crispianus performs heroic deeds fighting the Vandals and Goths. In addition, there are two sub-plots: Hugh's love for the saintly princess Winifred, and Amphiabell's conversion of Alban. As a result, the central three acts are almost clogged with action. Motivation is left unclear; why, for example, does Crispianus suddenly become loyal to Dioclesian in 3.4 when, in 1.1, Dioclesian had caused the death of Crispianus' father? What, apart from Amphiabell's holiness, which we have to take for granted, persuades Alban to suffer martyrdom? The tone of the Winifred-Hugh plot is uncertain, since it is marked by a somewhat grisly humour in the shoemakers' treatment of 'St. Hugh's bones' and Winifred at times appears comically impatient with her unwanted lover.[4] In order to bring the twin main-plots to a satisfactory conclusion, the four saints have to be martyred in 4.2, thus bringing a premature climax, which can only be overcome by the confusion of short scenes in 5.1. The blend of the tragic and the ridiculous is a feature of the early-British history plays; one thinks of the Clown's horse-play in The Birth of Merlin while Artesia poisons Aurelius, or the Mayor of Queenborough's jokes in close company with the murderous trio of Vortiger, Roxena and Horsus in Hengist King of Kent; so the uneasy tone of A Shoemaker, A Gentleman is not necessarily a fault. What one can criticise Rowley for, however, is not knowing when to stop or what to leave out.

In contrast, the material for A Woman Never Vext is kept to a minimum and carefully distributed. Acts 1 and 2, for example, cover the action of a single day. The first set of speeches gives us the information we need to understand the plot and by the time Mrs. Foster makes her first entrance we have learned that Old Foster and Bruine are merchants and business partners, that Old Foster is antagonistic towards his wastrel brother and resents the aid his son gives him, and that he has recently married a wealthy widow who supports his business venture but has a bad temper. We anticipate Mrs. Foster's scolding as she enters, and the quarrel which breaks out as Stephen and Robert come on stage; and when Mrs. Foster leaves the stage with her husband and Bruine, she is setting off for the Widow's house, as we realise when she appears there in 1.2. Similarly, the Widow's own position is made clear in 1.2, her scene with the Clown and the Doctor; we see her as easy-going - witness her conversation with the Clown - but thoughtful and concerned, as her dialogue with the Doctor reveals. Mrs. Foster's entry establishes a sense of community or neighbourliness and brings the women together for theirvisit to the gaming-house in Act 2. The gambling-scene in 2.1 is tightly controlled; only five characters are on stage; the illusion of a noisy, crowded tavern is created by the noises off and the Host's repeated exits to quell the disturbances. The technique of the first act is utilised again when the Widow and Mrs. Foster appear in the inn, on their way to the Widow's suburb-garden. Their visit to the gaming-house is well-motivated: we know from 1.1 that Stephen intended gambling the money he borrowed from Robert and we have already seen enough of Mrs. Foster to realise that it is entirely plausible that she should catch sight of and follow him, while a gaming-house is quite likely to be in the same area as a suburb-garden.[5] The betrothal between Stephen and the Widow ends the action of the first day.

The same stage-practices will be used throughout the play. Act 3 shows the comings and goings around Bruine's house, interrupted by a brief scene at the Widow's; it must take place several days later at least if Stephen and the Widow are already married.[6] Acts 4 and 5 follow shortly after Act 3[7] and concentrate on Ludgate and Bruine's house, with characters moving between the two, until the royal procession in the last scene - to attend which, Stephen leaves Ludgate at the end of 5.1. Thus Rowley constructs his plot from three groups of incidents on which he focuses his attention: Stephen's release from Ludgate and marriage; Old Foster's reversal of fortune; Stephen's manipulation of Old Foster in prison. These incidents are matched by the three scenes of the sub-plot: Speedwell and Lambskin's first attempt to court Jane (3.1), their skirmish with, and defeat by, Robert

(4.1) and their final reformation (4.3). We can see how Rowley has utilised the constraints placed upon him by the need for actors to double roles: Jane appears relatively late (3.1) so that 'she' can double the maid Joan in 1.2, while Lambskin and Speedwell have to disappear at the end of Act 4 to return as Mountford and Arundell in 5.2. These restraints become an advantage in confining the sub-plot to its three scenes in the central acts.

One could also view the play as consisting of two parts which mirror each other and pivot around 3.2, the middle scene of the play. The major correspondences are obvious: in the first half Old Foster is rich and Stephen poor, in the second half Old Foster is destitute and Stephen wealthy. The action follows a see-saw motion. It is the pattern of Shakespeare's Richard II and is exemplified on stage by the goods which, in 3.1, Old Foster sells to Bruine and, in 3.3, Bruine sells to Stephen; the cargo of cochineal and kersey both follows and indicates the rising man. The device of pairs is used throughout the play, even in small details. Both brothers have married rich widows for their money;[8] both brothers are gamblers, although it is Old Foster who gambles away his wife's money.[9] Stephen's gambling is implicitly criticised; it is made quite clear in 1.1 that he relies on Robert to steal money for him from Old Foster, at the end of 1.1 he cheats Robert himself with a false tale about buying new clothes, and we are shown that in 2.1 he loses the money to rogues. Since Old Foster's career follows Stephen's so closely in other respects, the implication is that his gambling is to be seen in the same light as Stephen's. The women are also played against one another: Mrs. Foster's bad temper is made worse by comparison with the Widow's benevolence; the Widow's present charity[10] is contrasted with Mrs. Foster's plans for future good works;[11] and by 5.1, Mrs. Foster has taken on the Widow's role of 'ghostly comforter'.[12]

It is perhaps fitting that a notable feature of this play should be its moderation and restraint. We have already seen how an excess of material damages the structure of A Shoemaker, A Gentleman. All's Lost by Lust shows a greater control, partly in the staging of the action; the battle-scenes of the earlier play are replaced by scenes away from the field, showing Mully Mumen apostrophizing the sun (2.3),

Julianus and his commanders (2.4), Julianus and his prisoners (2.5) and, most effectively, Rodorique and Piamentelli in flight. There is no fighting on stage, until we come to the succession of deaths begun by Margaritta's murder of Lazarello (4.2). Then, indeed, one could claim that there are too many horrors, although even here the murders alternate with other scenes.[13]

In A Woman Never Vext, catastrophes are meticulously avoided. Stephen throws off 'the shadow of a face' in 5.2 before King Henry can deliver his judgement; although Old Foster enters Ludgate, both Richard and Mrs. Foster say that his debts are not beyond payment;[14] Old Foster's ships are sunk, but 'some men were sav'd' (3.3.177); Stephen's Wife insists on only what Lambskin and Speedwell can afford to pay from their debt;[15] Lambskin and Speedwell's quarrel in 3.1 stops short of a duel, just as in 4.1 they run away before Robert can do them any real harm. The effect is to isolate the tension in the play around Mrs. Foster and Old Foster; in the first three acts, we know that whenever Mrs. Foster comes on stage there will be an outburst, and in the last two acts Old Foster's anger and bitterness are at variance with the other characters.[16] The scenes between Stephen and his Wife which allow the audience to see that they are practising a deception on Old Foster and Robert are important, because they remove any fears we may have about an impending clash between the brothers; we can be confident that Stephen will stop the action before it comes to that.

A Woman Never Vext uses several structural devices which had already seen service on the Jacobean stage. A source for 1.2 and 3.2, in which the Widow talks over her problems with the Doctor, can be found in 1.3 of A Shoemaker, A Gentleman, where Winifred and Amphiabell discuss theology in rhyming couplets. In the early stages of the plot, the Physician in A Fair Quarrel performs a similar role with Jane as she reveals that she is pregnant (2.2). The technique was necessary because Rowley uses few soliloquies, preferring to give the audience the information it needs through a dialogue with a 'confessor' figure. Duelling scenes, and scenes in which duels were narrowly avoided, were not uncommon; Rowley himself had collaborated on A Fair Quarrel with its duel between Ager and the Colonel. In the same play (1.1), he has Russell take away the Colonel and Ager's swords to prevent a duel (although his ulterior motive is to ensure that they cannot rescue Fitzallen when he is arrested). The structure of the scene is similar to A Woman Never Vext 3.1: tension is created and then deflated before it can reach a climax, the true climax coming later in the scene (with Fitzallen's arrest in A Fair Quarrel, with the quarrel among the Fosters in A Woman Never Vext). A Cure for a Cuckold uses the same trick, when Lessingham confronts Bonvile on Calais sands and a fight is averted; while, outside the Rowley canon, in Brewer's The Country Girl Plush and Dwindle, two foolish suitors, are prevented from holding a duel. The gaming-house scene (2.1) has its closest analogue structurally in The Changeling 3.3 in which Lollio, on stage, shouts to the madmen off-stage, as the Host shouts to the Bowlers and Card-players; the same effect is created, of an extension of the stage-world into the tiring-house. But a brawl in an inn (with fatal consequences) had occurred in Rowley's collaboration with Heywood, Fortune by Land and Sea, and gaming-house scenes also appear in, for example, Act 2 of Michaelmas Term and in Greene's Tu Quoque.[17] A similar scene to 2.1, in which a tavern scene has noises above and below, appears in a later play, The Weeding of Covent Garden ($D2^v$) by Richard Brome. The structure of the dice-game in Act 2 may have been influenced (possibly at several removes) by Heywood's The Wise-Woman of Hogsdon (1607). As in A Woman Never Vext, a group of characters comment on their throws, enabling the audience to follow the game; both plays use the device to establish the nature of the characters before moving on to the serious business of the scene - Stephen's betrothal to the Widow, Chartley's declaration of his love for Luce. Greene's Tu Quoque also gives the details of the dice-game, but Rowley gives the device an extra dimension by adding double meanings to the calls:

> JACK In still, two theeves and choose thy fellow.
> STEPHEN Take the Miller.
> JACK Have at them i'faith.
> HUGH For a thiefe Ile warrant you. (2.1.43-6)

The point is, of course, that Jack and Hugh are thieves. It is the same device which Heywood and Middleton used with more resonance: Middleton in the 'chess' scene in Women Beware Women in which the game between Livia and the Widow reflects the Duke's seduction of Bianca; Heywood in A Woman Killed With Kindness, in the scene in which Frankford plays cards with Anne and Wendoll and watches for evidence of their adultery:[18]

> Frank. I must look to you, Master Wendoll, for you will be playing false - nay, so will my wife, too.
> (VIII.134-5)

The cloak-stealing incident may owe something to The Beggars' Bush (B4); here, Higgen and Ferret steal the Boors' cloaks while Prig distracts their attention.

Prison scenes, such as 4.2 and 5.1, are rare on the Jacobean stage; those in Eastward Ho are very different from the ones in A Woman Never Vext. Quicksilver has become pious while in prison and we are shown at length how he preaches to other prisoners. II The Honest Whore, with its Bridewell scene, also introduces the inmates of the prison as they process across the stage. The closest analogues are The Puritan, in which the cry for bread is heard at the Marshalsea (3.5) as it is heard in A Woman Never Vext at Ludgate; and Measure for Measure, in which the prison scenes of Act 4 are followed by the Duke's procession in the last scene, as A Woman Never Vext follows the Ludgate scene (5.1) with King Henry's procession (5.2). In both cases, the rulers are met by petitioners - by Isabella in Measure for Measure, by the Fosters in A Woman Never Vext - after a brief official scene: the meeting between the Duke, Escalus and Angelo, the naming of the Domus Dei. The presentation of these scenes is discussed in the section on staging.

Themes

A Woman Never Vext is an openly didactic play. This is not to deny that it is good entertainment, but to recognise that it follows in a tradition of plays which seek to send their audience home wiser and better for having seen them.[19] Precedent comes from two sources: neo-classical theory which stressed the playwright's duty;[20] and the English tradition of Morality plays - Everyman and The Castle of Perseverance, for example, or the mid-Tudor interludes with the Vice carried off to hell,[21] such as Like Will to Like.

Some plays carry their moral implicitly. Consider Middleton's

A Chaste Maid in Cheapside: here, the christening scene (3.2) and the dialogue between the Country Wench and the Promoters (2.2) are extraneous to the narrative needs of the play but are vital in creating the corruption and hypocrisy which set the tone. This technique, typical of the comedies of Chapman, Marston and, of course, Middleton, leaves the audience to form its judgements. It is not one which Rowley favours; it does not figure in any of the plays in his canon except possibly the Middleton collaboration Wit at Several Weapons and the Middleton imitation A Match at Midnight.[22] Rowley prefers to state his moral clearly and then repeat it, often in rhyming couplets:

> This is a Maxime sure, Some are made poore,
> That rich men by giving may encrease their store. (1.1.65-6)
>
> This free addition heaven hath lent my state,
> As freely backe to heaven I'l dedicate. (3.1.151-2)
>
> My charity; you can a vertue name,
> And teach the use, yet never knew the same. (3.3.145-6)
>
> For in my zealous faith I know full well,
> Where good deedes are, there heaven it selfe doth dwell.
> (4.1.236-7)
>
> ...be content;
> Blowes given from heaven are our due punishment. (4.3.2-3)
>
> Charitie's a vertue generally stands,
> And should dispersed be through all mens hands. (5.2.120-1)

Possibly the interludes are a distant influence, with their repeated catch-phrases ('"Like will to like," quoth the Devil to the Collier'); this moralising tone recalls the popular drama, especially of the late Elizabethan and early Jacobean period, plays such as A Warning for Fair Women, How a Man may choose a Good Wife from a Bad, The Miseries of Enforced Marriage, A Woman Killed with Kindness and its 1625 counterpart, The English Traveller. All these plays have a didactic theme strongly iterated.[23]

There can be no doubt about Rowley's primary concern in A Woman Never Vext: it is charity in all its forms. Civic charity is exemplified in Bruine, charity of spirit in the Widow, although each shares the virtues of the other. Charity is one of the three virtues which St. Paul recommends[24] and Rowley supports his argument with references to Biblical texts. Robert is relying on scriptural authority when he pleads, 'as well you may/Bid me love my Maker, and neglect/The Creature, which he hath bid me love' (1.1.170-2);[25] Stephen seems to echo the Good Samaritan in paying his brother's prison debts - 'Spend what he will, my purse shall pay it all'. The effect is to lend authority and dignity to the point the characters are making, while references to charity are so common that they become pervasive;[26] continual repetition of the theme is an important factor in unifying the elements of the play.[27]

Charity is, indeed, a recurring theme throughout the Elizabethan and Jacobean period. Perhaps this is not surprising, for this was an age of great civic charity[28] and the church-going citizen was exhorted from the pulpit to fulfil his duty to the poor.[29] The generosity of the wealthy Londoners was, in particular, a matter for pride. Heywood had dramatised Gresham's building of the Royal Exchange in II If You Know Not Me, and brought Dr. Nowell's gallery of notable benefactors on to the stage;[30] The Shoemaker's Holiday tells the story of Simon Eyre's charity, with much poetic licence. Beggars' Bush contains a portrait of a generous merchant:

> Is there a Virgin of good fame wants dowre?
> He is a father to her; or a Souldier
> That in his Countreyes service, from the warre
> Hath brought him only scars, and want? his house
> Receives him, and relieves him, with that care
> As if what he posses'd had been laid up
> For such good uses, and he steward of it. (1.3.45-51)

The mayoral pageants, Middleton's especially, generally contain a reference to the good deeds of earlier members of the livery company celebrated;[31] often they look back to a golden age when charity was freely and wisely given, distinguishing between Liberality and Prodigality. There is a double attack on the Jacobean citizens, for wasting money while at the same time being insufficiently generous. They are reminded that charity has lasting effects in ensuring a good reputation for the donor; here, for example, is Memory speaking of his predecessors' charity to the new Lord Mayor in The Triumphs of Integrity (1623):

I find to goodness they all bent their powers,
Which very name makes blushing times of ours;
They heap'd up virtues long before they were old,
This age sits laughing upon heaps of gold;
We by great buildings strive to raise our names,
But they more truly wise built up their fames,
Erected fair examples, large and high,
Patterns for us to build our honours by. (pp. 389-90)

It is in this light that we should see Stephen's remark,

I'l for his sake
Doe something now, that whil'st this Citty stands
Shall keepe the _Fosters_ name engraven so high,
As no blacke storme shall cloud their memory. (4.2.181-3)

Stephen and Bruine are both doing what is expected of them.

Charity in the sense 'generosity of spirit' is also an important key-note in the play. Rowley's comic characters are often marked by a spiritual _largesse_; one thinks especially of the shoemakers in _A Shoemaker, A Gentleman_, of Compass eagerly fathering Urse's bastard in _A Cure for a Cuckold_. But in _A Woman Never Vext_ he carries the trait to extremes. There are other characters in Jacobean drama who are 'never vext'; Romelio, in _The Devil's Law Case_, is unnaturally lucky in his shipping ventures (and, like Old Foster, eventually loses); Candido in I and II _The Honest Whore_ is 'the patient man'. The Widow differs in that she seeks the cause of her good fortune and even fears it; this is the only play to give a theological twist to what elsewhere is accepted as a 'humour'.[32] A minor theme in the play is the Widow's acceptance of her gift as coming from God and Mrs. Foster's acceptance of her tribulations.

...be content;
Blowes given from heaven are our due punishment. (4.3.2-3)

WIFE You must thanke heaven.
MISTRIS FOSTER I doe indeed, for all.
WIFE Sister, that hand can raise that gives the fall.
(5.1.145-6)

We have already seen, in the section on structure, how the Widow's generosity is played against Mrs. Foster's narrowness of outlook.

Tied in with the theme of civic charity is the idea of the glorification of London. II If You Know Not Me and The Shoemaker's Holiday had examined this theme in the most detail; their continuation in print suggests their enduring popularity.[33] Yet in neither play is there any sense of conviction in the merchants' charitable impulses. Sim Eyre's gift of the Leadenhall and the prentices' holiday is very much an afterthought which is not prepared for in the play; it serves, at least in part, as a practical demonstration of his wealth and power. Gresham's Royal Exchange is better integrated into the plot of II If You Know Not Me (although it is somewhat swamped by the Armada); but there is no doubt that Gresham is inspired to charity chiefly by the inconvenience of getting wet. Indeed, in the incident in which he crushes a pearl in his wine, he could be accused of the very prodigality which Middleton's mayoral pageants condemn. Bruine's Domus Dei, however, is unquestionably the result of his civic duty which he has carefully considered, and of a desire to preserve his 'name alive till Doomesday'.[34] Stephen's rebuilding at Ludgate is a compassionate act, prompted by his own sufferings as a prisoner.[35] It is this examination of the motivation behind charity which sets A Woman Never Vext apart from other plays on a similar theme.

Style

Rowley's sense of style and decorum is not necessarily always in line with theoretical ideas,[36] but it provides the frame within which he works. In its most obvious form, decorum dictates the way in which a character speaks. The Clown speaks in prose; this is in accord with contemporary stage-practice, from Shakespeare's Touchstone in Arden to Rowley's own Lollio in the madhouse. Menials also speak prose, in this case the Keeper of Ludgate. But in A Woman Never Vext it is the role, rather than the character, which is assigned its speech form: the variation between verse and prose tells the audience much about a character. Stephen, for example, moves between verse and prose. In his first argument with his brother, a potentially serious scene which marks out the division in the family, he speaks verse (1.1.190-201); but when he is left alone with Robert and tricks him out of forty shillings, he is in the role of rogue and speaks in prose for the rest of 1.1 and 2.1. The inn scene is partly 'local colour' to show Stephen at his worst, following the lines of the 'rogue' pamphlets of the 1590s and 1600s, and of Dekker's The Gull's Hornbook and The Bellman of London. The tone continues through the rather light-hearted wooing scene at the end of 2.1; but when Stephen re-appears in 3.2 his character has been transformed into that of a sober, responsible business-man:

> I finde much debts belonging to you, Sweete;
> And my care must be now to fetch them in. (3.2.26-7)

Stephen continues to speak in verse for the remainder of the play; the change in form is one way of denoting his complete reformation and of marking his more serious position as manipulator of his brother's fortunes. The same is true of Robert's two functions, in main-plot and sub-plot. As the virtuous wronged son pleading for charity he invariably speaks verse, as the gallant lover and champion of the citizens' rights against Lambskin and Speedwell, he invariably speaks prose. The change in medium again denotes a change in attitude.

There are in fact two rules governing the decorum of speech here: rank and situation. The Clown speaks prose because he is menial and comic; Speedwell and Lambskin speak prose because their role is purely comic although they are of better rank than the citizens. The Doctor and the Widow are verse-speakers because of the nature of their discussions (about theology); Jane is a prose-speaker[37] because she is the comic heroine. The system breaks down, however, in 1.1, 3.1 and 3.3, the scenes involving Old Foster and Bruine and their financial ventures. Rowley's normal usage requires that the mundane details of business are dealt with in prose; but other strands are woven so tightly into the plot that Bruine and the Factors in particular are required to move between verse and prose and sometimes, indeed, the verse structure is so loose that they seem to be speaking a mixture of both.[38]

As we have already seen,[39] the loss of Old Foster's ships is the beginning of a new phase in the play's action. Events are now moving nearer to disaster: Robert is faced with an insoluble moral dilemma and the threat of destitution; Old Foster is apparently bankrupt and is charged before the King; and the introduction of royalty in Act 5 itself moves the mood away from the comic which has run side-by-side with the serious while the Clown, Lambskin and Speedwell have been on stage. This sense of a new departure is given aural expression in the increased use of rhymed couplets, which Rowley habitually uses to give significance or dignity to a speech. In <u>All's Lost by Lust</u>, for example, Rodorigo tempts Jacinta, and she refuses, in rhymed couplets (2.1.119-25). On another level, Julianus' dying speech is in rhymed couplets (5.5.184-93). <u>A Shoemaker, A Gentleman</u> typically uses them for the martyr-plot - speeches such as the Angel's (1.3.102-19). <u>A Woman Never Vext</u> utilises them both for the long speeches of 5.2 and for shorter dialogue exchanges:[40]

> Better than your husband's hate could wish me
> That laughes to see my backe with sorrowes bow:
> But I am rid of halfe my ague now.
> WIFE Had you an ague then?
> OLD FOSTER Yes, and my heart had every houre a fit
> But now 'tas left me well, and I left it.
> WIFE O, 'tis well Cozin, what make you heare I pray?
> ROBERT To support a weake house falling to decay.
> (5.1.100-7)

The most obvious result of this technique is to give emphasis to the lines; the rhyme acts as a signal to the audience to pay extra attention. In the section on theme, we noted the occurrence of sententious couplets. Take, for example, Mrs. Foster's comment,

> You'l sing another song, and beare a part
> In my griefes descant, when y'are vext at heart:
> Your second choyse will differ from the first:
> So oft as widdowes marry they are accurst. (1.2.236-9)

This speech looks forward to the Widow's marriage in 2.1 and sets up expectations of tragedy which are pleasantly rebutted in 3.2; at the same time, it reflects on Mrs. Foster's own marriage and the Clown's rejoinder, 'I, curst widdowes are', makes us query her own estimation of herself. The speech is of some minor importance: the rhymed couplets set it apart from the surrounding dialogue and help it to stick in the memory.

The rhymed passages demonstrate that Rowley is capable of writing relatively even pentameters, although with no great flexibility; the lines are generally end-stopped and monotonous.[41] His non-rhymed verse is not always as non-metrical as it seems; again, Rowley is working within a certain discipline. Lines of twelve syllables occur,[42] but are unusual; the majority of his verse-lines have nine, ten or eleven syllables, and the second foot in particular is rarely unmetrical.[43] Rowley's skill lies in prose, especially bawdy prose. Jane, like Dionysia[44] in <u>All's Lost by Lust</u> and Leodice in <u>A Shoemaker, A Gentleman</u>, is surprisingly 'forward' in her wooing of Robert; the puns on flower-names add a touch of pastoral feeling to the verbal game without sacrificing the underlying sexuality (3.1.213ff.). Any sexual language is generally concentrated in the sub-plot, particularly in Lambskin and Speedwell's <u>double entendres</u>.[45] Jane is well aware of her superior intellectual ability and, having outwitted her foolish suitors throughout 3.1 and 4.1, finally defeats them in a verbal tourney.[46] (4.1.11ff.)

Bawdy vocabulary forms a link between Lambskin, Speedwell and the Clown. The two suitors are unaware of their obscenities; the Clown exploits his language. The extended metaphor of the holly and the ivy (1.2.11-18) is a virtuoso piece in defence of the widowed woman's state; the familiar image of barley-break (1.2.22-3) is given a new twist by the added suggestion in its phrasing of leading apes in hell.[47] Their choice of vocabulary puts Lambskin and Speedwell on the same level as the Clown, for all their pretensions to gentility; the point is made visually in their final exit, when they leave the stage escorted by him and clearly his inferiors (4.3.102). The position of the knight who offered to make Jane a lady is neatly undercut, leaving the way clear for the citizen's son.

The play's vocabulary is limited to a small range of images. Four groups predominate: storm and sea; health and poison; music and discord; wealth and markets. Sometimes the images lead into each other:

> did there e'r flow
> Poyson and health together in one tide? (5.1.77-8)

Frequently they echo each other:

> That but e'r while spread up a lofty sayle... (4.2.162)

> ...have spread
> Full and faire sayles... (5.1.141-2)

In most cases they reflect back on the main themes of the play. Old Foster's references to 'full adventurer' and 'hazard' in 3.3 point up the similarity between gambling and marketing which the play implies; 'traffique', 'merchants', 'ware', 'deale', 'faire passage', 'aloft now', 'sinkes', are all used, not by the merchants but by the Host and gamblers in 2.1. The imagery stresses a sense of duality, of paradox, of nothing being what it seems: Old Foster's phrase, 'pills with poyson to recure me' (4.2.35) is typical of this attitude; we may compare it with Mrs. Foster's reference to the viper killed by its offspring (2.1.143ff.) and Robert's to the pelican pecking its own breast (4.2.103-4). We are constantly reminded that a natural order has been upset in the play by dissension within the family, epitomised in Robert's exclamation, ''Las Sir, that Lambe/Were most unnaturall that should hate the Dam' (4.2.140-1). Many of the images suggest discord and tension; the musical image at 5.1.127ff. ends in 'frets', 'rack'd', 'crack't'. 'Rack'd' again leads back to shipwreck, the central image of the play:

> ...when all his sailes were up
> And that his proud heart danc'd on golden waves:
> ...I being sunke, and drown'd in mine owne misery,
> He would not cast out a poore line of thred
> To bring me to the shore... (4.1.59-65)

'Shipwreck' describes Old Foster's relationship with Stephen, Robert's with his father, Mrs. Foster's with her husband; marriages are seen as 'great voyages' that sometimes 'run a ground'.[48] Shipwreck is also the vital point in the plot, the cause of Old Foster's losses and, ultimately, of his reconciliation. Theme and plot are unified in this image:

> All shipwracks are no drownings. (4.3.4)

Critical History

The critical history of A Woman Never Vext is a history of short articles and entries in general surveys of English literature. Langbaine was the first to mention the play in his passage on the life of Rowley in An Account of the English Dramatic Poets (1691).[1]

His concerns were mainly biographical, however, and the first attempt to bring the work to critical notice was made by Charles Lamb, who in 1808 included three scenes[2] from A Woman Never Vext in Specimens of the English Dramatic Poets. Lamb uses the play as a spring-board for critical remarks on the drama of his own day compared to that of Rowley's:[3]

> The old play-writers are distinguished by an honest boldness of exhibition; they show everything without being ashamed...We turn away from the real essences of things to hunt after their relative shadows - moral duties.

His praise for Rowley's directness is implicit in his comments; this theme recurs through much of the criticism of the play.

Lamb's work was seminal in establishing Rowley as a writer worthy of remark, and ever since he has been included in the major surveys of literature. A Woman Never Vext is listed as Rowley's in the Biographia Dramatica of 1812 but the next important step was its inclusion in volume five of Old English Plays, edited by Dilke in 1814. Dilke provided the first full-scale essay on the play,[4] covering the life of Rowley, treatment of the sources, and commenting of the printing:

> ...a more disgraceful work never issued from the press even of the printers of that age.

Perhaps this rather sour remark was caused by the great amount of re-lining which he had to do; but he emended the quarto with caution, and warned the reader who contemplated altering the text further,

> I can only observe that he must not make too free with the pruning knife; that it is difficult to distinguish between a licentious metre and measured prose; and that very little good dramatic dialogue, of the higher walks, can be found that, with moderate torturing to the eye and ear, may not pass for such metre, -

comments which express only too well the difficulties one encounters with the play. He did, however, start a red herring which was to influence the stage image of the play in suggesting that 'Henry III' was a printer's error for 'Henry VI'. W.C. Hazlitt's edition of the play in Dodsley's Old English Plays (1875) is a reprint of Dilke's text and introduction with only minor alterations.

J.R. Planché's adaptation of the play, The Widow of Cornhill (1824), is interesting in that his changes reflect the taste of his time. Set in the mid-fifteenth century, its alterations all serve to highlight the romantic aspects of the play, while with the Lord Chamberlain in mind all trace of bawdiness has disappeared. This widow is 27, ten years younger than her original, and Robert has turned into a young gallant, his love affair with Jane being given more stress. The result is a work that lacks vigour and verges at times on the insipid; one suspects it of being a show-case for the scenic effects of Act 5.[5]

In 1820 Hazlitt had admired A Woman Never Vext for its 'pleasing simplicity and naiveté equal to the novelty of the conception.'[6] The next critic to deal with the play was F.G. Fleay. In the Shakespeare Manual of 1876, he lists it as by Rowley, written 1624-6 and played by the King's Men at Blackfriars.[7] Although he gives no source for his information his date coincides exactly with I.A. Shapiro's.[8] In 1890, he lists it as Rowley's with Middleton's name in brackets;[9] and in the Biographical Chronicle, as we have seen,[10] he asserted that the play was a Rowley revision of Heywood's original. This suggestion seems to have had little impact, except on Pauline Wiggin, who in An Inquiry into the Authorship of the Middleton-Rowley Plays (1897) considers that the last two acts 'may possibly be borrowed from an older play' and finds Jane and her lovers 'wearisome'.[11] Ward, whose A History of English Dramatic Literature to the Death of Queen Anne was the last critical history of the nineteenth century, included Rowley in his entry on Middleton. He recognized that A Woman Never Vext had its faults:

> The pathos is by no means deep, and the humour the reverse of refined; while the change in the disposition of the scapegrace uncle is too sudden to leave any moral impression.

But he approved of the 'brisk' action, 'healthy' tone and 'vigorous' action; it is a 'note-worthy play'.[12]

A Woman Never Vext's most enthusiastic critic is surely Swinburne, who likes it not least because Lamb praised it. He remarks that, 'William Rowley was the most thoroughly loyal Londoner,'[13] and says of the play, '"Agnus locutus est: causa finita est!"'[14] While deploring the 'mingle-mangle of prose and verse,' he singles out the character of Robert Foster for praise: 'so noble and attractive in its selfless and manful simplicity,'[15] and finds the woman never vexed, 'an admirable creature of broad comedy that never subsides or overflows or degenerates into farce.'[16]

J.A. Symonds was less impressed; his manuscript notes to his copy of Lamb's Specimens reveal that he thought the passages selected were 'very strained' and that Rowley 'used the weapons of his age clumsily, and though belonging to the great race was one of the least among them'.[17] In the Cambridge History of English Literature (1910), in his chapter on 'Middleton and Rowley', he expanded these comments to explain that the language was sometimes injured by emphasis. But despite the play's coarseness and clumsiness, he found no flaw in its essential truthfulness. Felix Schelling for his part found the play 'exceptionally pleasing and vigorous' as an example of the older style of London comedy.[18]

The last critic to deal in any depth with the play (with the exception of I.A. Shapiro's article on date) was Dewar M. Robb, who uses it in an attempt to determine the canon and order of Rowley's plays.[19] He thought the play to be 'entirely in Rowley's hand' and that it represented Rowley's early style. Since his article and I.A. Shapiro's, no critical study has been published, although Mrs. G. Sandeman included the play in her unpublished doctoral thesis on William Rowley.[20] She argues that Rowley's plays are the work of a professional actor writing with the stage presentation very much in mind, and that they are competent pieces of stagecraft, a view which performance of A Woman Never Vext would doubtless support.

Staging

The play should have presented no problems in performance; it is admirably adapted to the opportunities and limitations of the Elizabethan theatre, whether for the indoor or the outdoor playhouse. If we accept Harbage's division of a 'coterie' private theatre and a public theatre which produced less subtle plays,[1] then A Woman Never Vext would seem to fall into the latter category. However, the division does not always seem to have been as clear cut as might be expected; for example, Sir Henry Herbert licensed The Sea Voyage for the Globe in June 1622 and The Spanish Curate for the Blackfriars in October of the same year.[2] The determining factor seems to have been not so much a difference of tone or content as the season of the year in which the plays were produced, the Globe being used in summer and the Blackfriars in winter. Bearing this objection in mind, I would expect A Woman Never Vext to be written for the public rather than the private playhouse, but the remarks that follow would apply equally to either type of theatre.[3]

The contract for building the Fortune theatre tells us that the stage was 43 feet wide by 27 feet six inches deep.[4] The Fortune was a square theatre, and in a polygonal structure the stage may have been smaller,[5] but even so the stage would be large by modern standards and only in the procession scene in 5.2 would it be utilised to its full extent. From De Witt's drawing of the Swan - the Hope was based on the Swan's design[6] and we may suppose other theatres to have agreed in essentials - we can see that there were two doors in the tiring-house façade. The stage backed on to the tiring house, and access was thus through these doors. The contentious 'discovery space' or third door in the centre is not needed and will not concern us here. A gallery seems to have run above the stage at first storey level,[7] which we will return to in discussing the staging of 4.2. In most outdoor theatres, the canopy projecting over the stage was supported by two posts (but at the Hope it was cantilevered); and, of course, the audience surrounded the stage on three sides.

The minimum cast required is 16, including three for the female roles. This takes into account every chance to double roles, and makes no allowance for 'extras' in the procession scene, so possibly a more realistic figure would be about 20. Jane first appears in 3.1, and if necessary her part can be doubled with Joan;[8] the comic characters - the Clown, Speedwell and Lambskin - disappear after 4.3

and were probably intended to return as Henry III, Mountford and Arundel. (This would explain their absence from the general reconciliation at the end of the play, when they might be expected to be present.) The dialogue indicates clearly what properties are required and gives some hints to costume. Mrs. Foster wears a ruff and a velvet cap - old-fashioned by the 1620s but perhaps appropriate for a citizen's wife; the cheats in 2.1 must have cloaks; the Clown needs a cap and sword, Speedwell a sword and Lambskin a purse. Stephen ought to have three costumes; in Acts 1 and 2 reference is made to his tattered clothing and in Act 5 to his scarlet robes as Sheriff. Another costume comes between them, and the change between 2 and 3 is implied by Mrs. Foster's remark, 'You were kind to him in his tatter'd state;/ Let him requite it now.' The properties are all of the small, portable kind which for the most part the actors could be expected to carry on stage themselves: a purse of money, a fish and a ring, dice, a wisp of straw, bills and bonds, money bags. Only the money bags have to be carried on stage by someone else.

4.2 (at Ludgate) is the only scene which presents any ambiguity in staging, and here the difficulty is confined to the 'cry for bread'. The scene is set outside Ludgate's walls; Old Foster is about to enter and actually goes in after the quarrel with Robert. The _locale_ is established by Richard's remark, 'Your debts are not so great, that you should yeeld/Your body thus to prison unconstrain'd,' and the knowledge that the last time the audience saw Old Foster he had declared his intention of entering Ludgate. Until 5.2, the presence of the Keeper on stage also suggests a prison scene. The technique here is the same used by Shakespeare in _Measure for Measure_ (who uses the Provost from 2.3 onwards in this manner and makes the Duke comment on 'the afflicted spirits/Here in the prison'[9]) and by Dekker in _II The Honest Whore_, where the Duke begins the Bridewell scene with the line, 'Your Bridewell? that the name?' ($I3^v$). The difficulty arises with the stage direction, '_Old Foster, and above at the grate, a box hanging downe_'. Obviously, a box for money hangs down from the gallery above the stage to within the actor's reach, and indeed has probably been there since the scene began, but Old Foster's location is ambiguous. He has to be in a position from which his voice can be heard but he cannot see the stage, and this rules out either of the stage doors. It also makes the very front of the gallery awkward, but not impossible if we accept the convention that the characters on stage are not visible to those above. The gallery position would be visually desirable since it would give the impression of Old Foster in a confined space and add pathos; and it is just conceivable that Robert stood directly under the gallery, close to the tiring-house wall, and underneath Old Foster's sight-line. However, only the audience opposite the front of the stage would see this effect, as Old Foster would be hidden from those facing the stage at an angle. The exact mechanics of this piece of staging and the sight-lines depend on whether or not the gallery projected over the stage or was flush with the tiring-house wall. Obviously a gallery which projected would make Robert more easily hidden from Old Foster and Old Foster visible to more of the audience.

Unfortunately, while a close parallel for this scene occurs in *The Puritan*, the stage directions in the 1607 quarto are not complete; the direction reads:

> *The Crie at Marshalsea.*
> *Crie* Good Gentlemen ouer the way, send your reliefe,
> Good Gentlemen ouer the way.

The prisoners are apparently not on stage but in the tiring-house; possibly they appear on the gallery. There is no problem here with sight-lines on to the stage. The cry interrupts the dialogue, but the prisoners are physically separate from the stage. For *A Woman Never Vext*, I think we must accept that Old Foster's voice comes from within the tiring-house.[10] Possibly he stood back from the front of the gallery, so that the audience sitting opposite could see him,[11] but this seems a wasted gesture, and for most of the audience he would be 'within' and invisible. Basically this is the method used in 2.1 to create the illusion of a room upstairs where the direction calls for 'A noyse above at Cards,' provided from the gallery area. In turn, this is a repetition of the effect achieved of a ward on either side of the stage in the mad-house scene in *The Changeling* 3.3. It involves using the tiring-house itself as part of the acting area, so that the actors can create the impression of activity surrounding the scene on stage. A voice comes from the first storey, and the tiring-house becomes a gaming-house or Ludgate prison; from the side of the stage, and it is the interior of a mad-house. The technique reflects Rowley's ability to place a scene in the context of its surroundings with the minimum of effort, and to make the most of the physical conditions and conventions of the theatre for which he was writing.

Stage History and Adaptations

I. Early Stage History

There is no indication that the play has ever been acted as it appears in the 1632 quarto. The title-page makes no reference to a performance, successful or otherwise; Herbert's record books as they are transcribed have no entry for A New Wonder, A Woman Never Vext.

The earliest record of a production apparently dates from the reign of Mary II (1688-1694).[1] A droll called A New Wonder, A Woman never Vex'd: or The Blind Beggar of Bednal Green was advertised to appear for twelve days during Southwark Fair, at Parker's booth near the King's Bench. 'Scenes, Machines, Songs and Dances' were promised. This adaptation appears to have undergone a further mutation, for during Bartholomew Fair, August 1721, the booth owned by Pinkethman, Miller and Norris was displaying The Injured General, or, The Blind Beggar of Bethnal Green or the Woman Never Vexed. It was repeated a month later at Southwark Fair, then at Bartholomew Fair 1723, at Richmond on September 9th of the same year, at Bartholomew Fair 1724 and at Southwark Fair in 1725.[2] The 'woman never vexed' then disappears from theatrical history for almost a century.

II. Planché's Adaptation: The Widow of Cornhill

Planché's version was the only adaptation of A Woman Never Vext performed during the 19th century. It was licensed on October 25th 1824 and first acted on Lord Mayor's Day (November 9th) of the same year at Covent Garden, with Charles Kemble as Stephen and Miss Chester as Agnes Welsted, the 'woman never vexed'.[3] Planché claimed that it was the first five-act play to be produced without a prologue.[4]

The text was published in 1824; it was reprinted in Dick's Standard Plays (no. 880), in Cumberland's British Theatre (vol. 8) and in Dolby's British Theatre.

Two important external influences shaped Planché's play. First, he used Dilke's text of 1814, the only modern edition then available. Dilke, in his preface,[5] pointed out the anachronism of having Bruine and Foster in the same play. Recognising in Foster the sheriff of 1444-5, and apparently forgetting that Bruine lived in the reign of Henry III, he suggested that 'Henry III' was a printer's error for 'Henry VI' - although 'having been once noticed it becomes of little consequence.' Planché thus set his play firmly in the 15th century. Walter Bruine, the founder of the Domus Dei, becomes merely Jane's father, Brown; the Domus Dei disappears altogether; Henry III becomes Henry VI, and comes into the city, not to consecrate a charitable work but to have dinner with the new Lord Mayor. Secondly, the play was produced at a time when the 'archaeological' style of theatrical design was still very new. Planché had produced King John the year before and, against great opposition, had used historically accurate costumes representing the 13th century:[6] Samuel Meyrick, the antiquary and Planché's ally, had written to the Gentleman's Magazine as recently as 15th May 1824 in praise of the costumes Kemble was wearing and the Widow of Cornhill was to provide an excellent opportunity to demonstrate the new school of design. Consequently, in place of Rowley's modest group of royal attendants, Planché introduced the Lord Mayor's Show, as it appeared in Cheapside in 1444.[7]

The Lord Mayor's Pageant was Planché's biggest single innovation; it was described at length by the Times' reviewer:[8]

> The several companies of the city appear, not with their banners merely and devices, but each brings a pageant of its own...There is a green dragon, for instance (we don't know what company he belongs to);...Then the Fishmongers bring a salmon (on wheels) - sea and all. The Goldsmiths parade a magnificent service of plate. The Vintners exhibit a Silenus, astride upon a cask of wine; for the Armourers, a red-cross knight carries a shield of looking-glass, and treads on the neck of a prostrate Saracen; and the procession is farther graced (in addition to dignitaries innumerable who move in it) by the presence of the city waits and a company of morris-dancers, among whom the "hobby-horse" is not forgot. The scenery is some of it very curious; and the street of "practicable" houses

through which the procession passes is a new idea.

Obviously, the sheer spectacle was designed to impress and the pageant, to judge from the playbill,[9] was the play's chief selling point.

However, to accommodate the huge procession in Act 5, cuts had to be made in the rest of the play - and it already needed to be shortened to suit 19th century conditions.[10] The most serious loss is the incident of the fish and the ring; without this short scene, the Widow's character is not fully developed, there is insufficient evidence of her good luck, and she becomes frivolous, lacking in depth. Planché has not helped by taking out the Widow's vision of the comforting angels (1.2.106ff.) and replacing it with a speech which makes her seem callous and insensitive:

> My parents died
> Ere I could know their loss: and for my husband,
> Although I mourn'd him much, in grief's despight
> I joy'd withal that I had found a grief. (p. 15)

This undermines the structure of the play; in marrying Stephen, Planché's widow does not deliberately court disaster, as Rowley's does, but seems rather to be taken with a passing fancy. This was a problem the actress was unable to surmount; 'the figure of the dissipated rogue...strikes the fair widow with a sudden whim, which looks very like a sudden inclination.'[11] The loss of the _Domus Dei_ also detracts from the plot; the theme of charity lacks depth and becomes unimportant. Genest, in his _Account of the English Stage_,[12] picks out for particular condemnation a speech of Robert Foster,'in which he talks of the nymph of Elis, and Thisbe - this is injudicious, and not at all suited to the character.' He also complains that, 'when Mrs. Foster, in the 3d act, tells her husband that his brother is just married, she adds that he is also chosen sheriff - which is absurd, as there was no probability of his being chosen sheriff, till a considerable time after his marriage.'

One could produce more illustrations of Planché's alterations; the bowdlerisations one expects, although the change of a single word to remove a rhyming couplet, of which there are several instances, is perhaps more of a surprise.[13] These are matters of changing literary taste. However, the general principles of the adaptation are clear: all anachronisms have been removed and the play has been designed to lead up to the finale of Act 5. Indeed, bearing in mind that intermittently throughout 1824 the Gentleman's Magazine had carried essays on London pageants in Stuart times[14] it is hard to acquit Planché of a degree of opportunism; and, with its production on Lord Mayor's Day, The Widow of Cornhill could easily have become an occasional piece.

However, the production played to a good house[15] and was generally well received by the press. Highest praise went to Miss Lacy, who played Mrs. Foster. The Times thought her performance could not 'fail to give her considerable reputation.' Another reviewer described her role as a 'termagant wife' but thought the character 'falls off' towards the end of the play.[16] Young was 'highly impressive' as Foster and the play hinged on his performance, while Charles Kemble played Stephen with 'great manliness and spirit'; Bartley and Keeley as Speedwell and Lambskin, were 'endurable'.[17] The Times, however, did not approve of Miss Chester: 'she wore light hair (as it seemed to us), and her coiffure generally did not become her.' The anonymous reviewer also had his doubts: 'Miss Chester, by some singular mismanagement, had contrived to disfigure her head most strangely; she must wear some other head-dress.' (Stage directions tell us that the unfortunate Miss Chester was required to wear a veil, for as she woos Stephen in 2.1 she is directed to look 'archly' from under it.)[18] On the whole, The Times thought the success of the revival 'undoubted'.

The play was acted 25 times in the 1824-5 season at Covent Garden; on December 10th it opened at Bath, with Warde as Stephen Foster, and it was revived at Covent Garden on October 13th, 1825, with Warde again in Kemble's role.[19] On November 13th 1832 it was performed at the Surrey Theatre, then under the management of R.W. Elliston, as The Widow of Cornhill, or, London in 1444.[20] It was last revived at the Sadler's Wells, in 1852, for six performances.[21]

This edition

The text of this edition is based on the 1632 quarto of _A New Wonder, A Woman Never Vext_ printed by George Purslowe for Francis Constable.

Recorded alterations

Quarto spelling has been retained throughout except in cases where it is obviously in error through foul-case or misreading copy. Press-variants have been collated and the reading of the corrected state has always been preferred. A table of press-variants will be found in the textual apparatus which precedes the Commentary. Punctuation is generally the quarto's, but where it is misleading or goes against the sense of the text it has been emended. Usually this has meant moving a punctuation-mark or, in some cases, changing it to one of different emphasis; the intention has been to keep as closely as possible to quarto's punctuation, and extra marks have only rarely been added. All emendations of accidentals are recorded in the textual apparatus, including punctuation supplied at the ends of speeches, since this has not always been a case of merely adding a full-stop. However, quarto's use of roman F for italic in speech-prefixes including the name 'Foster' has not been noted.

Emendations of substantives are placed at the foot of the page of text. It has not always been easy to distinguish between substantives and accidentals; the criterion has been what the compositor intended to set. For example: at 3.2.121 'shade' was printed instead of 'shape'. Here, the 'p' was set upside-down by mistake and by coincidence produced a perfectly good word, whereas if any other letter in the word had been inverted the mistake would have been obvious. Since the compositor intended to set 'shape', 'shape' appears in the text with the alteration recorded among the emendations of accidentals. On the other hand, when at 3.1.175 'Same' was set for 'fame', the compositor misread the initial 'f' as long 's' and, since the word was at the beginning of the verse line, set 'S'. Here the compositor intended to set 'Same' instead of 'fame' and the alteration is recorded as a substantive alteration at the foot of the page. Because so many changes have been necessary to the line arrangement, alterations to the lining are recorded separately. No historical collation has been attempted. Lamb's edition in Specimens has been consulted for 1.2, 4.2 and 5.2, Dilke's and the 1875 Dodsley for the whole text, and where my line arrangement agrees with a previous editor's, this has been recorded.

Silent alterations

Movements of letters or punctuation caused by loose type have not been recorded.

Speech-prefixes, exits and entrances have been expanded throughout. The 'woman never vext' is called 'Widow' until she marries Stephen at the end of Act 2 and thereafter 'Wife'. Old Foster's son is called both 'Robert' and 'Robin' in the text; I have chosen to call him 'Robert' since this is the name used most frequently. (The variation has no significance as far as the questions of authorship and compositor analysis are concerned.) Speech headings at the beginnings of Acts have been placed on the left with all other speech-prefixes; quarto prints them in the centre of the line. Stage directions are centred, except for exits which are placed on the right. For typographical reasons, long 's' has been replaced by 's' and ligatures are not preserved.

The transition from quarto's incorrect verse lining to prose creates a specific problem: the letter which begins the line, and which the quarto prints as upper-case. In the case of words which are not nouns, these are reduced to lower-case, except where they follow a colon. (Quarto prints upper-case after a colon more often than lower-case, but lower-case more often after a semi-colon.) Nouns are printed as upper or lower-case in the quarto in a seemingly erratic manner; I have therefore chosen to retain letters moved from a position at the beginning of verse lines as upper case when they begin nouns. In this, as in all the procedures detailed above, I have tried to be consistent.

Commentary

Quotations in the Commentary are taken from the first edition of the relevant text unless otherwise specified. Shakespeare is quoted from the First Folio, edited by Charlton Hinman as the *Norton Facsimile*; Hinman's through-line numbers are given as line references, followed by the numbering of Peter Alexander's text. Dekker's works are quoted from their first editions, with a second reference to the *Dramatic Works* edited by Fredson Bowers. Full details of texts are given in the Bibliography.

Notes

Authorship

1. *Biog. Chron.* II.102; see also *Shakespeare Manual* p. 94 and *Chronicle History of The London Stage* pp. 378 and 403.
2. *Inquiry*, p. 5.
3. *Canon of William Rowley's Plays*, *MLR* XLV, 1950, p. 136.
4. *Thomas Heywood*, pp. 332-33.
5. *Thomas Heywood et le drame domestique élizabéthain*, p. 390.
6. *Internal Evidence*, p. 163.
7. *Canon*, pp. 4-6.
8. *SB* XXVII, 1974, pp. 115ff.
9. MS BL Egerton 2623 fol. 25.
10. *op. cit.* pp. 172 and 167.
11. *Ibid*, 176 and 178.
12. *Canon*, p. 6.
13. '*A Cure for a Cuckold* by Heywood, Webster and Rowley', *MLR* XXII, 1927, pp. 389-97.
14. *SB* 13, 1960, pp. 82-88.
15. Jackson records two occurrences of 'I'm' in *The Captives*, Lake none. The contradiction perhaps arises because 'I'm' is written as 'I'am', in passages where Heywood favours Jonsonian elision (ll. 2053 and 2935).
16. At 4.1.4.
17. But cf. *A Shoemaker, A Gentleman*, ed. Stork, 3.2.129, 'Ey, ey; he had better' etc. Also 3.2.165, 5.2.88.
18. *Canon*, p.14.
19. See, e.g., *Thomas Heywood*, Otelia Cromwell, p. 141: 'Heywood's lines are easily scanned; rarely is one baffled by verses, which, like Rowley's, refuse to be measured by any scheme.'

The Author

1. All dates are taken from *Annals*.
2. Bentley I.198.
3. *Ibid*.
4. *Ibid*, I.199; I.200 n.3; I.137 n.3; I.176; VI.134.
5. Plumporridge in *The Inner Temple Mask*, Jacques in *All's Lost by Lust* (cast lists).

6. Bentley I.177ff.
7. Published in the Beaumont and Fletcher Folio 1647, but assigned to Middleton and Rowley (Cyrus Hoy, 'Shares of Fletcher and his Collaborators in the Beaumont and Fletcher Canon'(V), _SB_ 13, 1960).
8. For details see C.J. Sisson's chapter on _Keep the Widow Waking_ (_Lost Plays of Shakespeare's Age_, 1936).
9. Bentley, II.556-58.
10. _The Fool without Book_; _The Four Honourable Loves_; _A Knave in Print, or One for Another_; _The Nonesuch_; _Hymen's Holiday, or Cupid's Vagaries_.
11. See Introduction, Malone Society Reprint (1925).

Date

1. See below, 'Style'.
2. _MLR_ XLV 1950, p. 136.
3. _RES_ 11. 1960, p. 55.
4. _Letters_, II.530.
5. And for Rowley to have heard the gossip himself.
6. 'Tityre-tu' also occurs in _The Beggars' Bush_ (1661, B3^v); but the context and usage are different from that in _A Woman Never Vext_. I have found no usage comparable to the Clown's prior to 1623.

The Text

1. Greg, _Bibliography_, III.1503.
2. _Ibid_, 1957. The plays were: _The Valiant Welshman_ and _Metropolis Coronata_ (1615), _Chrysanaleia_ and _The Honest Lawyer_ (1616), _The Weakest Goeth to the Wall_ (1618), _The World Tossed at Tennis_ (1620), _The Maid's Tragedy_ (1622), _Mucedorus and Amadine_ (1626) and the two 1632 plays. Purslowe was in business 1613-32.
3. _Court Records_ II.158 (July 5th 1623).
4. H.R. Plomer, 'The Eliot's Court Printing House, 1584-1676', _The Library_, 4th ser. II 1922, pp. 175-84.
5. D.F. McKenzie,'A List of Printers' Apprentices, 1605-1640', _SB_ 13, 1960, p. 131; _Court Records_ II.221. McKenzie supposes

Gay to have had a partner at the press.

6. There are no place-names on I1^{v} and K1^{v}.

7. Possibly an over-sight by the compositor, who forgot to alter his copy.

8. Purslowe usually set place-names in italic.

9. T.H. Howard-Hill, _Compositors B and E in the Shakespeare First Folio_, 1976.

10. Inner or outer, I have found no evidence to suggest which.

11. The two sets of skeleton formes are distinguished by accidentals.

12. Similar to McKerrow 379; acquired from Simon Stafford who had it from John Danter. See J.A. Lavin, 'John Danter's Ornament Stock', _SB_ XXIII 1970, pp. 37-42, where it is illustrated.

13. On i4, N4, Z4^{v}, Rr3^{v}. The width of the crack in the flourish at top right varies noticeably with each setting; it is at its narrowest on Rr3^{v}.

14. '_Beggars Bush_: A Reconstructed Prompt-book and Its Copy', _SB_ XXVII, 1974, 113-36.

15. _Ibid_, 121-22.

16. _The Shakespeare First Folio_, 1955, p. 123.

17. Bentley, I.218.

18. _Ibid_, 219.

Sources

1. 1754 ed., II.695.

2. Penguin ed., pp. 220-22.

3. Strabo, _De Situ Orbis_, Basle, 1549, 2E4.

4. _Hebrews_ 12, 6-8: 'For whom the Lord loveth he chasteneth...'

5. By Richard Tracey; Halkett and Laing, _Dictionary of Anonymous and Pseudonymous Literature_, (rev. Kennedy and Johnson), Edinburgh 1926, VI.199.

The Foster Family

1. The following section is taken largely from these works: _Studies in English Trade in the 15th Century_, 1933, Postan and Powers; _The Merchant Class of Medieval London_, 1948, Thrupp; _The Aldermen of the City of London_, 1908, Beaven; _The Yorkist Age_, 1962, Kendall.

2. Thrupp, pp. 340-1.
3. Postan and Powers, p. 168. Trade with Iceland was illegal after 1430.
4. Thrupp, pp. 340-1.
5. See above, 'Sources'.
6. Beaven, I.271, II.9.
7. *Ibid*, I.90.
8. *Ibid*, I.47.
9. *Ibid*, II.164.
10. *Ibid*, I.47.
11. Thrupp, 340-1.
12. Beaven, I.47.
13. *Ibid*, II.9.
14. Postan and Powers, pp. 271, 284-5; Kendall, pp. 288, 300.
15. Kendall, p. 429.
16. *Ibid*, p. 430.
17. *op. cit.* pp. 340-1.

The Play

1. *A Fair Quarrel*, xli and n.52.
2. *The Changeling* 3.1. The direction comes between two Middleton scenes, but the collaboration in this play appears to have been remarkably close.
3. See Emrys Jones, *Scenic Form in Shakespeare*, chap. 1.
4. E.g. 3.1.25-6, 37-40.
5. See Stubbs, *Anatomy of Abuses*, H2-2^{v}; suburb-gardens were notorious areas for assignations. The only implausibility lies in a virtuous Widow having one; but perhaps not all garden-holders were as corrupt as Stubbs suggests.
6. Unless the declaration before Robert is to be taken as constituting a valid marriage ('Here's witnesse...here's Man and Wife'). Cf. Claudio's relationship with Juliet in *Measure for Measure*; they are married *sponsalia de praesenti*, 'a mutual recognition as husband and wife in the presence of witnesses'. (New Arden, 1.2.134-44 and note.)
7. About a week later, if we take Jane's remark literally: 'I have leagu'd with'm for a weeke without any farther entercourse', 3.1.186 -7.

8. 'I'me lately married to a wealthy Widow/From whom my substance chiefely does arise,' 1.1.95-6, 'he did not marry me for loves sake nor for pitty, but love to that I had,' 1.1.122-3.

9. 'Let me once throw Dice at all, and either be/A compleate Merchant, or wracke my estate for ever', 3.3.8-9.

10. 'let bounty furnish the Table, and charity shall be the voyder.' 1.2.45-6.

11. 'Those worldly blessings, which I long enclosde,/Intending for good uses.' 1.1.126-7.

12. 'The Keeper is your friend, and powres true balme/Into your smarting wounds; therefore deare Husband/Endure the dressing with patience.' 'But your dim eyes so thick with teares doe run,/ You cannot see from whence your comforts come.' 5.1.26-8; 33-4.

13. Murder of Lazarello, 4.2; Rodorique breaks into the forbidden vault, 5.1 and 5.2; death of Lothario, 5.3; flight of Rodorique, 5.4; torture and death of Jacinta and Julianus, 5.5.

14. 4.2.1-3; 5.1.35.

15. 4.3.53ff.

16. So much so that when Old Foster accuses Stephen of attacking Robert, he replies with a puzzled, 'Thou ravest.' 5.1.181.

17. Where Staines, in disguise, wins back with false dice some of the money extorted from him by a usurer and inherited by Bubble, once Staines' servant and now his master. The scene functions partly to illustrate Bubble's idiocy. It ends in a quarrel with Spendall.

18. _A Woman Killed with Kindness_ VIII.124-94; _Women Beware Women_ 2.2.

19. For a full discussion of Renaissance critical theory, see Madeleine Doran, _Endeavors of Art_, especially pp. 85-100 and 160ff.

20. See, e.g., Heywood's _Apology for Actors_, F3-3^{v}, (quoted by Madeleine Doran, p. 89):

> ...plays are writ with this aim, and carried with this method, to teach the subjects obedience to their king, to show the people the untimely ends of such as have moved tumults, commotions, and insurrections, to present them with the flourishing estate of such as live in obedience, exhorting them to allegiance, dehorting them from all traitorous and felonious stratagems.

Hamlet's remark on 'the mirror up to nature' (3.2.21) is only the most famous utterance of a critical common-place, that comedy is imitatio vitae, speculum consuetudinis, imago veritatis, 'the imitation of life, mirror of custom and image of truth'. (From Donatus, 'De tragoedia et comoedia', but attributed to Cicero; see Endeavors, p. 72 and n.47.)

21. Jonson's plays The Devil is an Ass and The Staple of News, both of which use interlude material, testify to the persistence of the tradition.

22. Rejected from the canon by Cyrus Hoy for linguistic reasons; SB 13 (1960).

23. A Woman Killed with Kindness is closest in tone to A Woman Never Vext; cf., e.g.,

> But this above the rest, in golden text,
> Shall be insculpt: A Woman never Vext.
>
> In golden letters shall these words be fill'd,
> 'Here lies she whom her husband's kindness kill'd'.

One could also add to the list I and II The Honest Whore and The Taming of the Shrew.

24. 1 Corinthians 13.11.

25. See Commentary, note to 1.1.170-2.

26. See, e.g., discussions of charity at 1.1.62-71; 1.1.168-76; 1.2.45-6; 3.3.141-6; 4.1.50-75; 4.2.89-157; 5.1.211-35; 5.2.15-28; 5.2.60-135; 5.2.152-93. The list is not exhaustive.

27. I am aware that Richard Levin has recently doubted the wisdom of the thematic approach; however, I believe that here it is a valid approach. (New Readings vs. Old Plays, chap. 1.)

28. See W.K. Jordan, Philanthropy in England 1480-1660.

29. See Certain Homilies appointed...to be...read...in Churches: 'A Sermon of good workes annexed unto faith', 'A Sermon of christian love and charity', 'A Sermon against contention and brawling'; The Second Tome of Homilies, 'An Homily of Alms deeds and mercifulness towards the poor and needy'.

30. II If You Know Not Me, C4-D1v.

31. See, e.g., The Triumphs of Truth, pp. 252 and 255; The Triumphs of Honour and Industry, pp. 304, 305, 306; The Sun in Aries, pp. 344-6; An Invention, p. 376; The Triumphs

of Integrity, pp. 389-91; The Triumphs of Health and Prosperity, p. 404 (ed. Bullen, Middleton, vol. 7); Munday's Chruso-thriambos, p. 39 (ed. J.H.P. Pafford).

32. See the dialogue between the Widow and Doctor in 1.2 especially 88-99. This is another passage with a Biblical source; see Commentary note.

33. II If You Know Not Me was reprinted in 1609, 1623 and 1633; The Shoemaker's Holiday in 1610, 1618, 1624, 1631. Stow's Survey had editions in 1598, 1603, 1618, 1633 and remained in print with revisions until 1754, showing the Londoners' interest in works about their city. Many plays refer to London and its environs, e.g., The Wise Woman of Hogsdon, A Chaste Maid in Cheapside, The Fair Maid of the Exchange, Bartholomew Fair, perhaps inevitably with London-based playwrights writing for a London audience. In the Caroline period, the expansion west-wards of the fashionable area was reflected in, e.g., Hyde Park, The Weeding of the Covent Garden.

34. See 1.1.62-4; 3.1.229-30; 3.1.242-6; 5.2.15-23.

35. 5.1.219-24.

36. Cf. Giraldi's dictum that young girls should be shamefast and timid and the character of Jane, of Dionysia and of Leodice. (See Endeavors of Art p. 221.)

37. With the exception of 4.3, which is a special case.

38. E.g. 4.1.191-6. It is of course a gross over-simplification to suppose that the confused state of such speeches is just the result of Rowley's inability to decide whether characters should speak verse or prose; technical inadequacy and the transmission of the text are also contributory factors.

39. Above, 'Structure'.

40. On a practical level, the rhyme gives a unity to the exchange and draws Robert's speech into the dialogue so that the effect verges on the choric; while the non-rhyming line 'Had you an ague then,' sets the Wife apart from Old Foster's sentiments.

41. See, e.g., Robert's speech 5.2.105-33.

42. E.g., 'Are dull and harsh; I joy to see so good a childe' (5.2.233).

43. A central point of Mrs. Sandeman's thesis is that Rowley's verse is professionally competent and would act well. For a more

detailed discussion of versification, see also Pauline Wiggin, An Inquiry into the Authorship of the Middleton-Rowley Plays.

44. In Dionysia's case, the result is to present her as a 'comic' rather than 'tragic' heroine; her fate - suicide over her husband's corpse - comes as more of a shock and this reversal of expectations possibly contributes to the uneasy tone of the last scene of All's Lost by Lust.

45. See Commentary, 3.1, 4.1, 4.3.

46. Yet another use of the rhymed couplet: here, to formalise the rules of a game. Cf. children's chanting games.

47. See Commentary 1.2.22-3.

48. 5.1.140.

Critical History

1. 2D6^{v}-2D7.

2. 1.2 (the Widow's discussion with the Doctor), 4.2 (Robert's first visit to Ludgate) and 5.1 (Robert's second visit).

3. Reprinted The Dramatic Essays of Charles Lamb, p. 210.

4. pp. 227-33.

5. See below, 'Stage History'.

6. Lectures on the Dramatic Literature of the Age of Elizabeth, 2nd ed., p. 78.

7. p. 94.

8. See above, 'Date'.

9. A Chronicle History of the English Stage, p. 403.

10. See above, 'Authorship'.

11. pp. 5, 14.

12. pp. 543-44.

13. The Age of Shakespeare, p. 184.

14. Ibid, p. 188.

15. Ibid.

16. Ibid, p. 189.

17. BL C.28.b.17, MS note to p. 127.

18. Elizabethan Drama, p. 262.

19. MLR XLV 1950, 129-41.

20. Unpublished doctoral thesis for London University, 1974.

Staging

1. A theory postulated in Shakespeare and the Rival Traditions, 1952.
2. Dramatic Records, June 22nd 1622, October 24th 1622 (p. 24).
3. There is no evidence at which theatre the play was produced; see above, 'The Title-page'.
4. Southern, p. 22.
5. Ibid, p. 23.
6. Ibid, p. 25.
7. See Southern's reconstruction, plate III, and Hosley, 'The Gallery over the Stage...' SQ Winter 1957.
8. In All's Lost by Lust Dionysia is doubled with Malena in the same way.
9. 2.3.4-6 New Arden ed.
10. Cf. the staging of The Fatal Dowry 4.2.50-86 (ed. Edwards and Gibson) and Antonio's Revenge 2.2.74ff. (ed. G.K. Hunter).
11. The dimensions of the gallery, which must necessarily affect any speculations on its use, are unknown.

Stage History and Adaptations

1. Sybil Rosenfeld, Theatre of the London Fairs in the 18th Century, p. 75, refers to 'playbills which must date before the death of Queen Mary in December 1694,' since they conclude "Vivant Rex et Regina." (This formula is also sometimes used during George III's reign, however; see the playbills in the Covent Garden scrapbook, BL Th. Cts. 39, untitled and unpaginated.)
2. Allardyce Nicoll, History of the English Drama, II.375. Neither of these drolls was published.
3. Nicoll, op. cit. IV.554.
4. J.R. Planché, Recollections, (1901) 42-43.
5. Old English Plays vol. 5, 227-33.
6. Planché, op. cit. 35-39.
7. By a delightful irony, a press cutting in BL Th. Cts. 39 preserves compositorial confusion over the date of the procession: 'the Lord Mayor's Show, as it passed through Cheapside in 1744.'
8. The Times Nov. 10th 1824.
9. Playbill for Nov. 19th 1824, BL Th. Cts. 39.

10. On Nov. 19th it was acted with The Irish Tutor and The Escapes (ibid). A play running for two or two and a half hours would have made a very long evening.
11. The Times Nov. 10th 1824.
12. Vol. IX, 299-301.
13. E.g., To hear a brother begging in a prison (gaol)
Who but ere while spread up a lofty sail... (p. 47.)
14. The Gentleman's Magazine vol. 94.
15. The Times Nov. 10th 1824.
16. Unidentified press cutting, Nov. 14 1824, BL Th. Cts. 39.
17. The Times Nov. 10th 1824.
18. p. 21. The offensive head-dress was of 'gold net and jewels' (costume list).
19. Genest, Some Account of the English Stage, IX.299-301, 342.
20. Nicoll, op. cit. IV.554.
21. Shirley S. Allen, Samuel Phelps and Sadler's Wells Theatre, p. 261.

[DRAMATIS PERSONAE

OLD FOSTER	a wealthy merchant
STEPHEN FOSTER	his younger brother
ROBERT FOSTER	his son
WALTER BRUYNE	merchant and alderman
SIR GODFREY SPEEDWELL) INNOCENT LAMBSKIN)	suitors to Jane Bruyne
RICHARD	Old Foster's factor
GEORGE	Bruyne's factor
CLOWN	the Widow's servant
KEEPER of Ludgate gaol	
HOST BOXALL	
DOCTOR of Divinity	
JACK) DICK) HUGH)	cheats
KING HENRY III	
MOUNTFORD	
ARUNDEL	

Bowlers, Pembroke, Cardinal, Lord Mayor.

WIDOW of Cornhill	afterwards Stephen's Wife
MISTRESS FOSTER	wife to Old Foster
JANE	Bruyne's daughter
JOAN	the Widow's maid.

The scene: the City of London.]

A NEW VVONDER A VVOMAN NEVER VEXT.

Actus Primus.

Enter OLD FOSTER, ALDERMAN BRUYNE and two Factors, RICHARD, and GEORGE.

OLD FOSTER This ayre has a sweet breath Master Bruyne.
BRUYNE Your partner Sir.
OLD FOSTER I, and in good I hope, this halcion gale
Playes the lewd wanton with our dancing sayles,
And makes'm big with vaporous envy.
BRUYNE Tis no more yet, but then our fraught is full
When shee returnes laden with merchandize
And safe deliver'd with our customage.
OLD FOSTER Such a delivery heaven send us,
But time must ripen it: are our accounts made even?
GEORGE To the quantity of a penny, if his agree with mine:
What's yours Richard?
RICHARD Five hundred sixty pounds;/read the grosse summe of A2[v]
your broade cloathes.
GEORGE 68. peices at B, ss, and l; 57. at l, ss, and o.
RICHARD Iust; leade, xix tunne.
OLD FOSTER As evenly we will lay our bosomes
As our bottomes with love as merchandise,
And may they both increase to infinites.
BRUYNE Especially at home; that golden traffique love
Is scantier far than gold; and one myne of that
More worth than twenty Argoseyes

Of the worlds richest treasure.
OLD FOSTER Here you shall dig, and finde your lading.
BRUYNE Here's your exchange; and as in love
So wee'le participate in merchandize.
OLD FOSTER The merchants casualty:
We alwayes venture on uncertaine ods,
Altho we beare hopes Embleme the anchor with us.
The winde brought it, let the wind blow't away agen;
Should not the Sea sometimes be partner with us
Our wealth would swallow us.
BRUYNE A good resolve: but now I must be bold
To touch you with somewhat that concernes you.
OLD FOSTER I could prevent you; is't not my unthrifty brother?
BRUYNE Nay, leave out the adjective (unthrifty,)
Your brother Sir, tis he that I would speake of.

OLD FOSTER He cannot be nam'd without unthrifty Sir, tis his proper Epithite, would you conceite but what my love has done for him so oft, so chargeable, and so expensive, you would not urge another addition.

BRUYNE Nay Sir, you must not stay at quantity till he forfeit the name of brother which is inseparable, hee's now in Ludgate Sir, and part of your treasure lyes buryed with him.

OLD FOSTER I, by vulgar blemish; but not by any good account;
There let him howle, tis the best stay he hath;
For nothing but a prison can containe him
So boundlesse is his ryot; twice have I raysde
His decayed fortunes to a faire estate A3
But with as fruitlesse charity, as if I had throwne
My safe landed substance backe into the Sea,
Or dressd in pitty some corrupted Iade,
And he should kick me for my courtesie.
I am sure you cannot but heare, what quicke-sands
He findes out, as Dice, Cards, Pigeon-holes,
And which is more, should I not restraine it,
Hee'd make my state his prodigality.
BRUYNE All this may be Sir, yet examples dayly shew
To our eyes, that Prodigalls returne at last

51 dressd] dresse Q

And the lowdest roarer, (as our Citty phrase is)
Will speake calme and smooth; you must helpe with hope Sir,
Had I such a brother, I should thinke
That heaven had made him as an instrument
For my best charity to worke upon;
This is a Maxime sure, Some are made poore,
That rich men by giving may encrease their store.
Nor thinke Sir,
That I doe tax your labors and meane my selfe
For to stand idlely by, for I have vowd
If heaven but blesse this voyage now abroad,
To leave some memorable relique after me,
That shall preserve my name alive till Doomesday.

OLD FOSTER I Sir, that worke is good, and therein could I
Ioyne with your good intents, but to releeve
A wast-good, a spendthrift.-

BRUYNE O no more, no more good Sir.

OLD FOSTER Sirra, when saw you my son Robert?

RICHARD This morning Sir, he said he would goe visit his Vncle.

OLD FOSTER I pay for their meetings I'me sure;
That boy makes prize of all his fingers light on
To releeve his unthrifty Vncle.

BRUYNE Does he rob, in troth I commend him.

OLD FOSTER Tis partly your fault, Sirra you see't, and suffer it.

RICHARD Sir, mine's a servants duty, his a sonnes,
Nor know I better how to expresse my love
Vnto your selfe, than by loving your son.

OLD FOSTER By concealing of his pilferings. A3v

RICHARD I dare not call them so; he is my second Master,
And methinkes tis far above my limits
Either to checke, or to complaine of him.

BRUYNE Gramercy Dick, thou mak'st a good construction,
And your son Robert a naturall Nephewes part
To releeve his poore Vncle.

OLD FOSTER Tis in neither well Sir;
For note but the condition of my estate;
I'me lately marryed to a wealthy Widow
From whom my substance chiefely does arise,

She has observed this in her Son in law,
Often complaines and grudges at it,
And what foule broyles such civill discords bring,
Few married men are ignorant of.

Enter MISTRIS FOSTER.

Nay will you see a present proofe of it?
MISTRIS FOSTER Shall I not live to breath a quiet houre?
I would I were a beggar with content
Rather than thus be thwarted for mine owne.
OLD FOSTER Why what's the matter Woman?
MISTRIS FOSTER I'le rowse'm up,
Tho you regard not of my just complaints
Neither in love to me, nor preserving me
From others injuries, both which y'are tyed to,
By all the rightfull lawes heavenly or humane,
But Ile complaine Sir, where I will be heard.
OLD FOSTER Nay, thou'lt be heard too farre.
MISTRIS FOSTER Nay Sir, I will be heard; some awkeward starre
Threw out his unhappy fire at my conception
And twill never quench while I have heate in me:
Would I were cold,
There would be bonefires made to warme defame,
My death would be a Iubilee to some.
OLD FOSTER Why Sir, how should I minister remedy and know not the cause?
BRUYNE Mother a pearle, woman, shew your husband the cause.
MISTRIS FOSTER Had he bin a husband Sir, I had had no cause to complaine, I threw down at his feete/the subjection of my whole A4 estate: he did not marry me for loves sake nor for pitty, but love to that I had,
He now neglects the love he had before;
A prodigall is suffer'd to lay waste
Those worldly blessings, which I long enclosde,
Intending for good uses.
OLD FOSTER That's my sonne.

121 my] his Q

MISTRIS FOSTER I, thou knowest it well enough, hee's the Conduit-pipe
That throwes it forth into the common shore.
OLD FOSTER And the other's my brother.
MISTRIS FOSTER You may well shame,
As I doe grieve the kindred, but I'de make
The one a stranger, the other a servant,
No son, nor brother;
For they deserve neither of those offices.
OLD FOSTER Why, did I ever cherish him, have not I threatned him
With disinheritance for this disorder?
MISTRIS FOSTER Why doe you not performe it?
OLD FOSTER The other's in *Ludgate*.
MISTRIS FOSTER No; hee's in my house, approving to my face
The charitable office of his kinde Nephew,
Who with his pilfering purloind from me,
Has set him at liberty; if this may be suffer'd
Ile have no eyes to see.
OLD FOSTER Prethee content thy selfe;
Ile see a present Remedy; sirra, go call'm in;
This worthy Gentleman shall know the cause,
And censure for us both with equity.
BRUYNE Nay good Sir, let not me be so imployd,

Enter ROBIN *and* STEPHEN FOSTER.

For I shall favour one for pitty,
The other for your loves sake.
OLD FOSTER Now Sir, are all my words with you so light esteem'd
That they can take no hold upon your duty?
ROBERT Misconster not, I beseech you.
MISTRIS FOSTER Nay, heele approve his good deeds I warrant you.
OLD FOSTER And you Sir.
STEPHEN Well Sir.
OLD FOSTER I had thought you had bin in *Ludgate* Sir. A4v
STEPHEN Why you see where I am Sir.
OLD FOSTER Why, where are you Sir?
STEPHEN In debt Sir, in debt.

OLD FOSTER Indeed that's a place you can hardly be remou'd from,
But this is not a place fit for one in Debt;
How came you out of prison Sirra?

STEPHEN As I went into prison Sirra, by the keepers.

OLD FOSTER This was your worke to let this bandog loose.

ROBERT Sir, it was my duty to let my Vncle loose.

OLD FOSTER Your duty did belong to me, and I did not command it.

ROBERT You cannot make a separation Sir,
Betwixt the duty that belongs to you,
And love unto my Vncle, as well you may
Bid me love my Maker, and neglect
The Creature, which he hath bid me love;
If man to man joyne not a love on earth,
They love not heaven, nor Him that dwells above it,
Such is my duty a strong Correlative
Vnto my Vncle: why, he's halfe your selfe.

BRUYNE Beleeve me Sir, he has answered you well.

OLD FOSTER He has not worthy Sir,
But to make voyde that false construction;
Here I disclayme the title of a brother;
And by that disclayme hast thou lost thy childes part;
Be thou engag'd for any debts of his,
In prison rot with him; my goods
Shall not purchase such fruitlesse recompence.

STEPHEN Then th'art a scurvy father, and a filthy brother.

MISTRIS FOSTER I, I, Sir, your tongue cannot defame his reputation.

STEPHEN But yours can, for all the City reports what an abominable scould he has got to his wife.

OLD FOSTER If ere I know thou keep'st him company,
Ile take my blessing from thee whil'st I live,
And that which after me should blesse thy estate.

STEPHEN And Ile proclayme thy basenesse to the world;
Ballads I'l make, and make'm Taverne musick B1
To sing thy churlish cruelty.

OLD FOSTER Tut, tut, these are bables.

STEPHEN Each Festivall day I'l come unto thy house,

169 you] me Q

And I will pisse upon thy threshold.
OLD FOSTER You must be out of prison first Sir.
STEPHEN If e'r I live to see thee Shreiffe of *London*,
I'l gild thy painted postes *cum privilegio*,
And kick thy Serjeants.
ROBERT Nay, good Vncle.
STEPHEN Why, I'l beg for thee, Boy;
I'l breake this leg, and binde it up againe,
To pull out pitty from a stony brest,
Rather than thou shalt want.
OLD FOSTER I, doe;
Let him seare up his arme, and scarfe it up
With two yards of rope; counterfeit two villaines;
Beg under a hedge and share your bounty:
But come not neare my house,
Nor thou in's company, if thou'lt obey;
There's punishment, for thee; for thee there's worse;
The losse of all that's mine, with my deare curse. *Exeunt.*

Manent STEPHEN *and* ROBIN.

STEPHEN Churle, Dog, you churlish rascally miser.
ROBERT Nay, good Vncle, throw not foule language;
This is but heate Sir, and I doubt not but
To coole this rage with my obedience:
But Vncle, you must not then heape on such fuell.
STEPHEN Cuz, I grieve for thee, that thou hast undergone
Thy fathers curse, for love unto thy Vncle.
ROBERT Tut, that bond shall ne'r be cancel'd, Sir.
STEPHEN I pitty that y'faith.
ROBERT Let pitty then from me turne to your selfe:
Bethinke your selfe Sir, of some course that might
Befit your estate, and let me guide it.
STEPHEN Ha, a course? sfoot I ha'te: Cuz, canst lend me 40. shillings? Could I but repaire this old decay'd Tenement of mine with some new playster; for alas, what can a man doe in such a case as this?
ROBERT I, but your course, Vncle.

STEPHEN Tush, leave that to me, because thou shalt wonder at it: If you should see me in a scarlet gowne within the compasse of a gold chaine, then I hope you'l say, that I doe keepe my selfe in good compasse: then Sir, if the Cap of Maintenance doe march before me, and not a Cap be suffer'd to be worne in my presence, pray doe not upbraide me with my former poverty: I cannot tell, state and wealth may make a man forget himselfe; but I beseech you doe not; there are things in my head that you dreame not of; dare you try me, Cuz?

ROBERT Why, forty shillings, Vncle, shall not keepe backe your fortunes.

STEPHEN Why gramercy Cuz; [Aside] now if the dice doe run right, this 40. shillings may set me up agen: To lay't on my backe, and so to pawne it, there's ne'r a damb'd Broker in the world will give me halfe the worth on't: No, whilst 'tis in ready cash, that's the surest Way; 7. is better than 11. a pox take the bones and they will not favour a man sometimes.

ROBERT Looke you Vncle, there's 40. shillings for you.

STEPHEN As many good Angells guard thee, as thou hast given me bad ones to seduce me, for these deputy divells dam worse than the old ones. Now Cuz, pray listen, listen after my transformation; I will henceforth turne an Apostate to prodigality; I will eate Cheese and Onions and buy lordships, and will not you thinke this strange?

ROBERT I am glad y'are merry, Vncle; but this is fixt
Betwixt an Vncle and a Nephewes love,
Though my estate be poore, revenewes scant,
Whil'st I have any left, you shall not want.

STEPHEN Why gramercy, by this hand Ile make thee an Alderman before I dye, doe but follow my steps. Exeunt.

[1.2] Enter WIDOW and CLOWNE. B2

WIDOW Sirra, will the Churchman come I sent you for?

CLOWNE Yes mistris, he will come: but pray resolve me one thing for my long service; What Businesse have you with the Churchman? Is it to make your Will, or to get you a new Husband?

WIDOW Suppose to make my Will, how then?

CLOWNE Then I would desire you to remember me, Mistris; I have serv'd you long, and that's the best Service to a woman: make a good Will if you meane to dye, that it may not be said, Though most women be long liv'd, yet they all dye with an ill-will.

WIDOW So Sir, suppose it be for marriage.

CLOWNE Why then remember your selfe mistris; take heede how you give away the head; it stands yet upon the shoulders of your widdowhood; the loving embracing Ivie has yet the upper place in the house; if you give it to the Holly, take heede, there's pricks in Holly; or if you feare not the pricks, take heede of the wands, you cannot have the pricks without the wands; you give away the sword, and must defend your selfe with the scabbard; these are pretty Instructions of a friend; I would be loth to see you cast downe, and not well taken up.

WIDOW Well Sir, let not all this trouble you; See, hee's come; Will you be gone?

Enter DOCTOR.

CLOWNE I will first give him a caveat, to use you as kindely as he can. If you finde my mistris have a minde to this coupling at barly-breake, let her not be the last couple to be left in hell.

DOCTOR I would I knew your meaning, Sir.

CLOWNE If she have a minde to a fresh husband, or, so, use her as well as you can; let her enter into as easie bands as may be. B2[v]

DOCTOR Sir, this is none of my traffique; I sell no husbands.

CLOWNE Then you doe wrong, Sir, for you take money for'm: What woman can have a husband, but you must have custome for him? and often the ware proves naught too, not worth the Impost.

DOCTOR Your mans pregnant, and merry, mistris.

WIDOW Hee's sawcy Sir. Sirra, you'l be gone.

CLOWNE Nay, at the second hand you'l have a fee too; you sell in the Church, and they bring'm againe to your Church-yarde, you must have tollage: me thinkes if a man dye whether you will or no, he should be buryed whether you would or no.

DOCTOR Nay now you wade too far, Sir.

WIDOW You'l be gone, Sirra.

CLOWNE Mistris make him your friend, for he knowes what rate good husbands are at; if there hath bin a dearth of women of late, you may chance picke out a good prize; but take heede of a Clerke.

WIDOW Will you yet Sir, after your needelesse trouble,

Be gone, and bid the maides dresse dinner.

CLOWNE Mistris, 'tis fasting day to day, there's nothing but fish.

WIDOW Let there be store of that; let bounty furnish the Table, and charity shall be the voyder. What fish is there, Sirra?

CLOWNE Marry there is Sammon, Pike, and fresh Cod, Soles, Maides, and Playce.

WIDOW Bid'm haste to dresse'm then.

CLOWNE Nay mistris, I'le helpe'm too; the maides shall first dresse the Pike, and the Cod, and then I'le dresse the maides in the place you wot on. <u>Exit</u> CLOWNE.

DOCTOR You sent for me Gentlewoman?

WIDOW Sir, I did, and to this end:
I have some scruples in my conscience;
Some doubtfull problemes which I cannot answer
Nor reconcile; I'de have you make them plaine.

DOCTOR This is my duty; pray speake your minde. B3

WIDOW And as I speak, I must remember heaven
That gave those blessings which I must relate:
Sir, you now behold a wondrous woman;
You onely wonder at the Epithete;
I can approve it good; Ghesse at mine age.

DOCTOR At the halfe way 'twixt thirty and forty.

WIDOW 'Twas not much amisse; yet nearest to the last;
How thinke you then; Is not this a wonder,
That a woman lives full seven and thirty yeares,
Mayde to a wife, and wife unto a widdow,
Now widdowed, and mine owne, yet all this while
From the extremest verge of my remembrance,
Even from my weaning houre unto this minute,
Did never taste what was calamity;
I know not yet what griefe is, yet have sought
A hundred wayes for its acquaintance; with mee
Prosperity hath kept so close a watch,
That even those things that I have meant a crosse,
Have that way turn'd a blessing; is it not strange?

DOCTOR Vnparaleld; this gift is singular,
And to you alone belonging; you are the Moone,

For there's but one, all women else are stars,
For there are none of like condition:
Full oft, and many have I heard complaine
Of discontents, thwarts, and adversities;
But a second to your selfe, I never knew
To groane under the superflux of blessings,
To have ever bin alien unto sorrow;
No trip of fate? Sure it is wonderfull.
WIDOW I, Sir, tis wonderfull; but is it well?
For it is now my chiefe affliction.
I have heard you say, that the child of heaven
Shall suffer many tribulations;
Nay, Kings and Princes share them with their subjects;
Then I that know not any chastisement
How may I know my part of childhood? B3v
DOCTOR 'Tis a good doubt; but make it not extreme,
'Tis some affliction, that you are afflicted
For want of affliction: Cherish that;
Yet wrest it not to misconstruction;
For all your blessings are free gifts from heaven;
Health, wealth, and peace; nor can they turne to Curses,
But by abuse. Pray let me question you:
You lost a husband, was it no griefe to you?
WIDOW It was; but very small; no sooner I
Had given it entertainement as a sorrow,
But straite it turn'd unto my treble joy;
A comfortable revelation prompts me then,
That husband whom in life I held so deare,
Had chang'd a frailty to unchanging joyes;
Me thought I saw him stellified in heaven,
And singing Hallelujahs 'mongst a quire
Of white Sainted soules: then againe it spake,
And said; It was a sinne for me to grieve
At his best good, that I esteemed best:
And thus this slender shadow of a griefe
Vanish't againe.
DOCTOR All this was happy;

Nor can you wrest it from a heavenly blessing.
Doe not appoint the rod: leave still the stroake
Vnto the Magistrate; the time is not past,
But you may feele enough.

WIDOW One taste more I had,
Although but little, yet I would aggravate
To make the most on't: thus 'twas; The other day,
It was my hap in crossing of the Thames,
To drop that wedlocke Ring from off my finger,
That once conjoyn'd me and my dead husband;
It sunke,
I pris'd it deare; the dearer, cause it kept
Still in mine eye the memory of my losse;
Yet I griev'd the losse, and did joy withall
That I had found a griefe; and this is all
The sorrow I can boast of. B4

DOCTOR This is but small.

WIDOW Nay sure I am of this opinion,
That had I suffer'd a draught to be made for it,
The bottome would have sent it up againe,
I am so wondrouslie fortunate.

DOCTOR You would not suffer it?

Enter CLOWNE.

WIDOW Not for my whole estate.

CLOWNE O mistris, where are you? I thinke you are the fortunat'st woman, that ever breath'd of two shoes: the thiefe is found.

WIDOW The thiefe; what thiefe? I never was so happy to be robb'd.

CLOWNE Bring him away Iug; nay, you shall see the strangest Piece of felony discover'd that ever you saw, or your great grandmothers Grandam before, or after, a pirate, a water thiefe.

WIDOW What's all this?

CLOWNE Bring him away Iug; yet the villaine would not confesse a word till it was found about him.

WIDOW I thinke the fellow's mad.

CLOWNE Did you not lose your wedding Ring the other day?

WIDOW Yes Sir, but I was not robb'd of it.

Enter IOANE *with a fish.*

CLOWNE No; well, thanke him that brings it Home then; and will aske nothing for his paines. You see this Sammon?

WIDOW Yes, what of it?

CLOWNE It cost but sixpence: but had the Fisher knowne the worth of it, 'twould have cost you forty shillings. Is not this your Ring?

WIDOW The very same.

CLOWNE Your maid *Ioane* examining this Sammon that shee bought in the Market, found that he had swallowed this Gudgeon.

WIDOW How am I vext with blessings? how thinke you/Sir, B4v
Is not this above wonder?

DOCTOR I am amaz'd at it.

WIDOW First that this fish should snatch it as a baite;
Then that my servant needes must buy that fish
Amongst such infinites of fish and buyers:
What fate is mine that runnes all by it selfe
In unhappy happinesse? My conscience dreads it:
Would thou hadst not swallowed it, nor thou not bought it.

CLOWNE Alas, blame not the poore fish, mistris, hee being a flegmatique Creature, tooke Golde for Restorative. He tooke it faire, and he that gets Gold, let him eate Gold.

WIDOW Nothing can hinder fate.

DOCTOR Seeke not to crosse it then.

WIDOW About your businesse, you have not pleas'd me in this.

IOANE By my maydenhead if I had thought you would have tane it no kindlier, you should ne'r have bin vext with sight on't; the garbidge should have bin the Cookes fees at this time. *Exit* IOANE.

CLOWNE Now doe I see the old proverbe come to passe; Give a woman lucke, and cast her into th'sea: There's many a man would wish his wife good Lucke, on that condition he might throw her away so. But mistris, there's one within would speake with you, that vexeth as fast against Crosses, as you doe against good lucke.

WIDOW I know her sure then, 'tis my gossip *Foster*:
Request her in, here's good company, tell her.

CLOWNE Ile tell her so for my owne credits sake. *Exit.*

WIDOW You shall now see an absolute contrary:

Would I had chang'd bosomes with her for a time,
'Twould make me better rellish happinesse.

Enter MISTRIS FOSTER and CLOWNE.

MISTRIS FOSTER O friend and gossip,
Where are you? I am o're loaden with my griefes,
And but in your bosome I know not where to ease me.

CLOWNE I had rather helpe you to a close-stoole,/and't please you. C1

MISTRIS FOSTER Ne'r had woman more sinister fate;
All ominous stars were in conjunction
Even at my birth, and doe still attend me.

DOCTOR This is a perfect contrary indeede.

WIDOW What ayles you Woman?

MISTRIS FOSTER Vnlesse seven witches had set spels about me,
I could not be so crost, never at quiet
Never happy houre, not a minutes content.

DOCTOR You hurt your selfe most with impatience.

MISTRIS FOSTER I, I, Physitions minister with ease,
Although the patient do receive in paine;
Would I could think but of one joyfull houre.

CLOWNE You have had two husbands to my knowledge; and if you had not one joyfull houre betweene both, I would you were hang'd i'faith.

MISTRIS FOSTER Full fourteene yeeres I liv'd a weary mayde,
Thinking no joy till I had got a husband.

CLOWNE That was a tedious time indeede.

MISTRIS FOSTER I had one lov'd me well, and then ere long
I grew into my longing peevishnesse.

CLOWNE There was some pleasure ere you came to that.

MISTRIS FOSTER Then all the kindenesse that he would apply,
Nothing could please; soone after it he died.

CLOWNE That could be but little griefe.

MISTRIS FOSTER Then worldly care did so o'reload my weakenesse,
That I must have a second stay; I chose againe,
And there begins my griefes to multiply.

WIDOW It cannot be, friend; your husband's kinde.

DOCTOR A man of faire condition, well reputed.

CLOWNE But it may be he has not that should please her.

WIDOW Peace Sirra: how can your sorrowes encrease from him?
MISTRIS FOSTER How can they but o'rewhelme me? he keepes a Son
That makes my state his prodigality;
To him a brother, one of the Citty scandals;
The tone the hand, the tother is the maw;
And betweene both my goods are swallowed up;
The full quantity that I brought amongst'm C1v
Is now consum'd to halfe.
WIDOW The fire of your spleene
Wasts it; Good sooth Gossip, I could laugh at thee,
And onely grieve I have not some cause of sorrow
With thee: Prethee be temperate, and suffer.
DOCTOR 'Tis good counsell mistris, receive it so.
WIDOW Canst thou devise to lay them halfe on me,
And Ile beare'm willingly.
MISTRIS FOSTER Would I could, that I might laugh another while:
But you are wise to heede at others harmes;
You'l keepe you happy in your widdowhood.
WIDOW Not I in good faith, were I sure marriage would make me unhappy.
MISTRIS FOSTER Try, try, you shall not neede to wish;
You'l sing another song, and beare a part
In my griefes descant, when y'are vext at heart:
Your second choyse will differ from the first:
So oft as widdowes marry they are accurst.
CLOWNE I, curst widdowes are; but if they had all stiffe husbands to tame'm, they'd be quiet enough.
WIDOW You'l be gone Sir, and see dinner ready.
CLOWNE I care not if I doe mistris, now my stomack's ready; yet Ile stay a little and be but to vex you.
WIDOW When goe you, Sirra?
CLOWNE I will not goe yet.
WIDOW Ha, ha, ha, thou makest me laugh at thee; prethee stay.
CLOWNE Nay then Ile goe to vex you. *Exit* CLOWNE.
MISTRIS FOSTER You have a light heart Gossip.
WIDOW So should you Woman, would you be ruld by me:
Come, we'l dine together, after walke abroad
Vnto my suburbe garden, where if thou'lt heare,

Ile read my heart to thee, and thou from thence
Shalt learne to vex thy cares with patience. *Exeunt.*

Actus Secundus C2

Enter HOST BOXALL, STEPHEN, IACKE, DICKE, HUGH.

HOST Welcome still my merchants of *bona Speranza*; what's your trafficke Bulleyes? What ware deale you in? Cards, Dice, Bowles, or Pigeon-holes; sort'm your selves; either Passage, Novum or Mumchance? Say my brave Bursmen, what's your recreation?

STEPHEN Dice mine Host: Is there no other roome empty?

HOST Not a hole unstopt in my house, but this my Thrifts.

IACK Miscall us not for our money, good mine Host, we are none of your thrifts; we have scap'd that scandall long agoe.

DICK Yes, his thrifts we are *Iacke*, though not our owne.

HOST Tush, you are young men, 'tis too soone to thrive yet: He that gathers young, spends when hee's old: 'Tis better to begin ill, and end well, than to begin well and end ill: Miserable fathers have for the most part unthrifty sons; leave not too much for your heires, Boyes.

IACK Hee sayes well i'faith; Why should a man trust to executors.

STEPHEN As good trust to hangmen as to executors: Who's in the bowling Alley mine Host?

HOST Honest traders, thrifty lads, they are rubbing on't; towardly Boyes, every one strives to lye nearest the Mistris.

STEPHEN Give's a bayle of Dice.

HOST Here my brave Wags.

STEPHEN We feare no Counters now mine Host, so long as we have your bayle so ready. Come, trip.

IACK Vp with's heeles.

DICK Downe with them. C2v

HUGH Now the dice are mine; set me now a faire Boord; a faire passage sweet bones. *Boreas.*

A noyse below in the bowling Alley, betting, rubbing and wrangling.

HOST How now my fine Trundletayles; my wodden Cosmographers:

My bowling Alley in an uprore? Is *Orlando* up in armes? I must be stickler; I am Constable, Iustice, and Beadle in mine owne house, I accuse, sentence, and punish: Have amongst you; looke to my box Boyes; he that breakes the peace, I breake his pate for recompence; looke to my box, I say. *Exit.*

STEPHEN A pox o'your box, I shall ne'r be so happy to reward it better; set me faire; aloft now.

IACK Out.

STEPHEN What wast?

DICK Two Trayes, and an Ace.

STEPHEN Seven still, pox on't; that number of the deadly sinnes haunts me damnably; Come sir, throw.

IACK Prethee invoke not so, all sinkes too fast already.

HUGH It will be found againe in mine hosts box.

IACK In still, two theeves and choose thy fellow.

STEPHEN Take the Miller.

IACK Have at them i'faith.

HUGH For a thiefe Ile warrant you, who'l you have next.

IACK Two Quaters and a Tray.

STEPHEN I hope we shall have good cheere, when two Caters, and a Tray goe toth' market.

Enter HOST.

HOST So all's whist; they play upon the still pipes now, the Bull-beggar comes when I shew my head, Silence is a vertue, and I have made'm vertuous, let'm play still till they be penny lesse; pawne till they be naked, so they be quiet, welcome, and welcome.

A noyse above at Cards.

How now, how now, my roaring *Tamberlaine*, take/heede the Soldan C3
comes; And 'twere not for proffit, who would live amongst such Beares? why *Vrsa Major* I say, what in *Capite Draconis*? is there no hope to reclayme you, shall I never live in quiet for you?

DICK Good mine Host still'm: civill Gamesters cannot play for'm.

HOST I come amongst you, you maledictious slaves; I'l utter you all; some I'l take ready money for, and lay up the rest in the stocks: looke to my box, I say. [*Exit.*]

STEPHEN Your box is like your belly mine Host, it drawes all; now for a suite of apparell.

IACK At whose suit I pray? y'are out againe with the threes.

STEPHEN Foote, I thinke my father threw three when I was begotten;

pox on't, I know now why I am so haunted with threes.

IACK Why, I prethee?

STEPHEN I met the third part of a knave as I came.

IACK The third part of a knave, s'foote what thing's that?

STEPHEN Why a Serjants Yeoman, man; the supervisor himselfe is but a whole one, and he shares but a groate in the shilling with him.

DICK That's but the third part indeed: but goes he no further?

STEPHEN No, he rests there.

HUGH Come, let's give o're.

STEPHEN I thanke you Sir, and so much a looser? there's but the wast-band of my suite left: now sweete bones.

HUGH Twelve at all.

STEPHEN Soft, this dye is false.

HUGH False? you doe him wrong Sir, hee's true to his Master.

STEPHEN Fullum.

DICK I'le be hang'd then: where's *Putney* then I pray you?

STEPHEN 'Tis false, and I'le have my money againe.

HUGH You shall have cold Iron with your silver then.

STEPHEN I, have at you Sir.

Enter HOST, *and* YOUNG FOSTER.

HOST I thinke hee's here, Sir.

YOUNG FOSTER *assists his Vncle and the* HOST, *beats* C3v
them off; Enter the Bowlers and steale away their Cloakes.

ROBERT I am sure hee's now, Sir.

HUGH Hold, hold, and you be Gentlemen hold.

ROBERT Get you gone Varlets, or there's hold to be taken.

HOST Nay sweete Sir, no bloodshed in my house; I am lord of misrule, pray you put up, Sir.

OMNES S'foote mine Host, where are our cloakes?

HOST Why, this is quarrelling; Make after in time: Some of your owne Crew, to try the weight has lifted them; looke out I say.

IACK There will ever be theeves in a dicing house till thou bee'st hang'd I'l warrant thee. *Exeunt Cheats.*

STEPHEN Mine Host, my Cloake was lin'd through with oringe tawney velvet.

85 S.D. Cheats] Cheat Q.

HOST How, your cloake? I ne'r knew thee worth one.

STEPHEN Y'are a company of Conycatching rascals; is this a suite to walke without a Cloake in?

ROBERT Vncle, is this the reformation that you promis'd mee?

STEPHEN Cuz, shall I tell thee the truth; I had diminish't but six pence of the forty shillings by chance meeting with a Friend, I went to a taylor, bargain'd for a suite, it came to full forty, I tender'd my xxxix and a halfe, and doe you thinke the scabby-wristed rascall would trust me for six pence.

ROBERT Your credit is the better, Vncle.

STEPHEN Pox on him, if the taylor had bin a man, I had had a faire suite on my backe, so venturing for the tother Tester-

ROBERT You lost the whole Bed-stead.

STEPHEN But after this day, I protest Cuz, you shall never see me handle those bones againe; this day I breake up schoole: if ever you call me unthrift after this day, you doe me wrong.

ROBERT I should be glad to wrong you so, Vncle.

STEPHEN And what sayes your father yet, Cuz?

ROBERT I'le tell you that in your eare. C4

Enter MISTRIS FOSTER, WIDDOW and CLOWNE.

MISTRIS FOSTER Nay, I pray you friend beare me company
A little this way, for into this dicing house
I saw my good Son in law enter, and 'tis ods
But he meetes his Vncle here.

WIDDOW You cannot tire me gossip in your company,
'Tis the best Affliction I have to see you impatient.

MISTRIS FOSTER I, I, you may make mirth of my sorrow.

CLOWNE We have hunted well, mistris; doe you not see the hare's in sight?

MISTRIS FOSTER Did not I tell you so; I, I,
There's good counsell betweene you, the tone would goe
Afoote to hell, the other the horseway.

ROBERT Mother, I am sorry you have trod this path.

MISTRIS FOSTER Mother? hang thee wretch, I bore thee not,
But many afflictions I have borne for thee;
Wert thou mine owne, I'd see thee stretcht a handfull,
And put thee a Coffin into the Cart, ere thou

Shouldst vex me thus.

ROBERT Were I your owne,
You could not use me worse than you doe.

MISTRIS FOSTER I'l make thy father turne thee out for ever,
Or else I'l make him wish him in his grave;
You'l witnesse with me Gossip where I have found him.

CLOWNE Nay, I'l be sworne upon a booke of Callico for that.

ROBERT It shal not neede,
I'l not deny that I was with my Vncle.

MISTRIS FOSTER And that shall disinherit thee, if thy father
Be an honest man; thou hadst bin better
To have bin borne a viper, and eate thy way
Through thy Mothers wombe into the world,
Than to tempt my Displeasure.

STEPHEN Thou lyest *Zantippe*; it had bin better thou hadst bin prest to death under two Irish Rugs, than to ride honest *Socrates* thy husband thus, and abuse his honest childe.

MISTRIS FOSTER Out Raggamuffin, dost thou talke?
I shall see thee / in *Ludgate* againe shortly. C4v

STEPHEN Thou lyest agen, 'twilbe at *More-gate*, Beldam, where I shall see thee in the Ditch dancing in a Cucking-stoole.

MISTRIS FOSTER I'l see thee hang'd first.

STEPHEN Thou lyest againe.

CLOWNE Nay Sir, you doe wrong to give a woman so many lies, shee had rather have had twice so many standings, than one lye.

MISTRIS FOSTER I'l lye with him I'l warrant him.

STEPHEN You'l be a whore then.

CLOWNE Little lesse I promise you, if you lye with him.

STEPHEN If you complaine upon mine honest Cuz,
And that his father be offended with him,
The next time I meete thee, though it be i'th'streete,
Ile dance i'th'durt upon thy velvet Cap;
Nay worse, I'le staine thy Ruffe; nay worse than that,
I'l doe thus: *Holds a wispe.*

MISTRIS FOSTER O my hart Gossip, do you see this? Was ever Woman thus abus'd?

WIDOW Me thinkes 'tis good sport y'faith.

MISTRIS FOSTER I, I am well recompenc'd to complaine to you,
Had you such a kindred-

WIDOW I would rejoyce in't Gossip.

MISTRIS FOSTER Do so; choose here then; Oh my hart! But Ile doe
Your errand; Oh that my Nayles were not par'd!
But I'l doe your errand; Will you goe Gossip?

WIDOW No, I'l stay awhile and tell'm out with patience.

MISTRIS FOSTER I cannot hold a joynt still; Dost wispe me,
Thou Tatterdemallion;
I'l doe your errands, if I have a Husband;
Oh that I could spit Wild-fire! My heart, Oh my heart!
If it does not goe pantle, pantle, pantle in my belly,
I am no honest woman: But I'l doe your errands. Exit MISTRIS FOSTER.

ROBERT Kinde Gentlewoman, you have some patience.

WIDOW I have too much Sir.

ROBERT You may doe a good office,
And make your selfe a peacefull moderator
Betwixt me and my angry / Father, whom his wife D1
Hath mou'd to spleene against me.

WIDOW Sir, I doe not disallow
The kindenesse your Consanguinity renders,
I would not teach you otherwise;
I'd speake with your Vncle, Sir, if you'l give me leave.

CLOWNE You may talke with me Sir, in the meane time.

Exit ROBERT and CLOWNE.

STEPHEN With me would you talke, Gentlewoman?

WIDOW Yes Sir, with you; you are a brave Vnthrift.

STEPHEN Not very brave neither; yet I make a shift-

WIDOW When you have a cleane shirt.

STEPHEN I'l be no Pupill to a woman; leave your discipline.

WIDOW Nay, pray you heare me Sir, I cannot chide.
I'l but give you good counsell; 'tis not a good Course
That you run.

STEPHEN Yet I must run to th' end of it.

WIDOW I would teach you a better, if you'd stay where you are.

STEPHEN I would stay where I am, if I had any money.

WIDOW In the dycing house?

STEPHEN I thinke so too, I have play'd at Passage all this while, now I'd go to Hazard.

WIDOW Dost thou want Money? Thou art worthy to be tatter'd. Hast thou no wit now thy Money's gone?

STEPHEN 'Tis all the portion I have; I have nothing to maintaine me but my wit; my Money is too little I'm sure.

WIDOW I cannot beleeve thy wit's more than thy Money: A fellow so well limb'd, so able to doe good service, and want.

STEPHEN Why Mistris, my shoulders were not made for a Frock and a Basket, nor a Coale-sacke neither, no nor my hands to turne a trencher at a tables side.

WIDOW I like that resolution well; but how comes it then, that thy wit leaves thy body unfurnisht? Thou art very poore?

STEPHEN The fortune of the Dice you see.

WIDOW They are the onely wizards, I confesse, D1v
The onely fortune-tellers; but he that goes
To seeke his fortune from them, must never hope
To have a good destiny allotted him:
Yet it is not the course that I dislike in thee,
But that thou canst not supply that course,
And out-crosse them that crosse thee; Were I as thou art -

STEPHEN You'd be as beggarly as I am.

WIDOW I'l be hang'd first.

STEPHEN Nay, you must be well hang'd e'r you can be as I am.

WIDOW So Sir, I conceite you; were I as well hang'd then as you could imagine, I would tell some rich widow such a tale in her eare.

STEPHEN Ha? Some rich widdow? By this pennilesse pocket, I thinke 'twere not the worst way.

WIDOW I'd be asham'd to take such a fruitlesse oath: I say, seeke me out some rich widow; promise her faire; shee's apt to believe a young man; marry her, and let her estate fly; no matter, 'tis charity; Twenty to one some rich Miser rak'd it together; this is none of *Hercules* labours.

STEPHEN Ha? let me recount these articles: Seeke her out; Promise her faire; Marry her; Let her estate fly: But where should I finde her?

WIDOW The easyest of all: Why man, they are more common than Taverne Bushes; two Fayres might be furnish'd every weeke in *London* with'm, though no Forrainers came in, if the Charter were granted once: Nay, 'tis thought, if the Horse-market be remov'd, that Smithfield shall be so imploy'd, and then I'l warrant you 'twill be as well furnish'd with widowes as twas with Sowes, Cowes, and old trotting Iades before.

STEPHEN S'foote, if it were, I would be a Chapman; I'd see for my pleasure, and buy for my love, for money I have none.

WIDOW Thou shalt not stay the Market; if thou'lt be rul'd, I'l 249
finde thee out a widdow, and helpe in some of the rest too; if thou'lt but promise me the last, but / to let her estate fly: for shee's D2
one I loue not, and I'd be glad to see that revenge on her.

STEPHEN Spend her estate, wer't five Aldermens; I'l put you in security for that, sfoote all my neighbours shall be bound for me, nay, my kinde Sister in law shall passe her word for that.

WIDOW Onely this I'l enjoyne you, to be matrimonially honest to her for you owne healthes sake: all other injuries shall be blessings to her.

STEPHEN I'l blesse her then; I ever drunke so much, that I was never great feeder; give me drinke, and my pleasure, and a little flesh serves my turne.

WIDOW I'l shew thee the party; What sayest thou to my selfe?

STEPHEN Your selfe, Gentlewoman, I would it were no worse; I have heard you reputed a rich widdow.

WIDOW I have a lease of thousands at least, Sir.

STEPHEN I'l let out your leases for you, if you'l allow me the power I'l warrant you.

WIDOW That's my hope Sir; but you must be honest withall.

STEPHEN I'l be honest with some; if I can be honest with all, I will too.

WIDOW Give me thy hand; goe home with me, I'l give the better clothes; and as I like thee then, we'l goe further, we may chance make a blinde Bargaine of it.

STEPHEN I can make no blind bargaine, unlesse I be in your bed, Widow.

WIDOW No, I bar that Sir, lets begin honestly, how e'r we end; marry for the waste of my estate spare it not; doe thy worst.

STEPHEN I'l doe bad enough, feare it not.

WIDOW Come, will you walk, Sir.

269b be honest] Dilke; he honest Q.

STEPHEN No Widow, I'l stand to no hazard of blinde Bargaines; either promise me marriage, and give me earnest in a handfast, or I'l not budge a foote.

WIDOW No Sir, are you growne so stout already?

STEPHEN I'l grow stouter when I am marryed. D2v

WIDOW I hope thou'lt vex me.

STEPHEN I'l give you cause I'l warrant you.

WIDOW I shall rayle, and curse thee I hope; yet I'd not have thee give over neither; for I would be vext; Here's my hand, I am thine, thou art mine, I'l have thee with all faults.

STEPHEN You shall have one with some, and you have mee.

Enter ROBIN and CLOWNE.

WIDOW Here's witnesse, come hither Sir. Cozin, I must call you shortly; and you Sirra, be witnesse to this match; here's Man and Wife.

ROBERT I joy at mine Vncles happinesse, Widdow.

CLOWNE I doe forbid the Banes: Alas poore Shagragge, my Mistris does but gull him; you may imagine it to be Twelfe-day at night, and the Beane found in the corner of your Cake, but 'tis not worth a fetch I'l assure you.

WIDOW You'l let me dispose of my selfe, I hope.

CLOWNE You love to be merry Mistris; Come, come, give him foure Farthings, and let him goe. He'l pray for his good Dame, and be drunke; why, if your blood does itch that way, we'l stand together; how thinke you? I thinke here is the sweeter bit, you see this Nap, and you see this Lowse, you may cracke o' your choyse, if you choose here.

WIDOW You have put me to my choyse then; see, here I choose. This is my Husband: Thus I begin the Contract. Kisse.

STEPHEN 'Tis seal'd, I am thine; now Cuz feare no blacke Stormes; If thy father thunder, come to me for shelter.

WIDOW His word is now a deede, Sir.

ROBERT I thanke you both.
Vncle, what my joy conceives, I cannot utter yet.

CLOWNE I will make blacke Munday of this: e'r I suffer this disgrace, the kennell shall run with blood and rags. [Draws his sword.]

ROBERT Sir, I am your opposite.

312 opposite] Dilke; apposite Q.

CLOWNE I have nothing to say to you, Sir; I ayme at your Vncle. D3

ROBERT He has no weapon.

CLOWNE That's all one, I'l take him as I finde him.

WIDOW I have taken him so before you, Sir; Will you be quiet.

STEPHEN Thou shalt take me so too *Hodge*, for I'l be thy fellow, though thy Mistrisses Husband. Give me thy hand. *Exeunt*.

CLOWNE I'l make you seeke your fingers among the Dogs, if you come to me; my Fellow? You lowsie Companion; I scorne thee. S'foote, is't come to this? Have I stood all this while to my Mistris, an honest, hansome, plaine-dealing, serving Creature; and she to marry a Worson Tittere Tu Tattere with never a good rag about him? [*Muffles the point of his sword with his cap.*] Stand thou to me, and be my friend; and since my Mistris has forsaken me; [*Prepares to stab himself with the blunted sword.*]

Enter ROBIN.

ROBERT How now? what's the matter?

CLOWNE 'Twas well you came in good time.

ROBERT Why man?

CLOWNE I was going the wrong way.

ROBERT But tell me one thing, I apprehend not;
Why didst lay thy Cap upon the swords point?

CLOWNE Do'st not thou know the reason of that? why, 'twas to save my belly: dost thou thinke I am so mad to cast my selfe away for e'r a woman of'm all, I'l see'm hang'd first.

ROBERT Come *Roger*, will you goe?

CLOWNE Well, since there is no remedy, Oh teares bee you my friend!

ROBERT Nay, prethee *Roger* doe not cry.

CLOWNE I cannot choose; nay I will steepe
Mine eyes in crying teares, and crying weepe. *Exeunt*.

Actus Tertius D3v

Enter ALDERMAN BRUINE, SIR GODFRY SPEEDWELL, INNOCENT LAMBSKIN, and MISTRIS IANE.

BRUYNE Gentlemen, y'are welcome; that once well pronounc'd
Has a thousand Ecchoes; Let it suffice,
I have spoke it to the full: here's your affaires,
Here's your merchandize, this is your prise,
If you can mix your names and gentle Bloods
With the poore Daughter of a Cittizen.
I make the passage free, to greete and court,
Traffique the mart of love, clap hands and strike
The bargain through, (she pleas'd) and I shall like.

SPEEDWELL 'Tis good ware believe me, Sir, I know that by mine owne experience; for I have handled the like many times in my first wives dayes, I, by Knighthood, sometimes before I was marryed too; therefore I know't by mine owne experience.

LAMBSKIN Well Sir, I know by observation, as much as you doe by experience; for I have knowne many Gentlemen have taken up such ware as this is, but it has lyen on their hands as long as they liv'd; this I have seene by observation.

IANE I am like to have a couple of faire Chapmen: If they were at my owne dispose, I would willingly rifle them both at twelve pence a share; they would be good foode for a new plantation; the tone might mend his experience; and the other his Observation very much.

SPEEDWELL Sir, let me advise you: I see you want experience, meddle no further in this case, 'twilbe the more credit for your observation; for I finde by my Experience, you are but shallow.

LAMBSKIN But shallow Sir? Your experience is a little wide; D4 you shall finde I wilbe as deepe in this case as your selfe; my observation has bin, where your Experience must waite at doore; yet I will give you the fore Horse place, and I wilbe in the Fill's, because you are the elder Tree, and I the young Plant; put on your experience, and I will observe.

SPEEDWELL Sweete Virgin, to be prolix and tedious, fits not Experience; short words and large deedes are best pleasing to women.

3.1

IANE So, Sir.

SPEEDWELL My name is *Speedwell*, by my fathers Coppy.

IANE Then you never serv'd for't it seemes.

SPEEDWELL Yes, sweete Feminine, I have serv'd for it too: for I have found my nativity suited to my name, as my name is *Speedwel*, so have I sped well in divers actions.

IANE It must needes be a faire and comely suit then.

LAMBSKIN You observe very well, sweete Virgine; for his Nativity is his Dublet, which is the upper part of his suite; and his name is in's breeches, for that part which is his name, he defiles many times.

SPEEDWELL Your observation is corrupt, Sir; Let me shew mine owne Tale; I say, sweete Beauty, my name is *Speedewell*, my God-father by his bounty being an old Souldiour, and having serv'd in the wars as far as *Bulloyne*, therefore cal'd my name *Godfry*; a Title of large renowne; my wealth and wit has added to those, the paraphrase of Knighthood; so that my name in the full longitude is cal'd *Sir Godfry Speedwell*, a name of good experience.

IANE If every quality you have be as large in relation as your name Sir, I should imagine the best of them, rather than heare them reported.

SPEEDWELL You say well, sweet Modesty, a good imagination is good,/ and shewes your good experience. D4v

LAMBSKIN Nay, if names can do any good, I beseech you observe mine; My name is *Lambskin*, a thing both hot and harmelesse.

IANE On Sir, I would not interrupt you, because you should be briefe.

LAMBSKIN My Godfather seeing in my face some notes of disposition, in my Cradle did give me the title of *Innocent*, which I have practis'd all my life time; and since my fathers Decease, my wealth has purchast me in the vanguard of my name, the paraphrase of gentility; So that I am cald Master *Innocent Lambskin*.

IANE In good time; and what Trade was your father, Sir?

LAMBSKIN My father was of an Occupation before he was a Tradesman; for, as I have observ'd in my fathers and mothers report, they set up together in their youth; my father was a Starch-maker, and my Mother a Laundresse; so being partners, they did occupy long together before they were marryed; then was I borne.

IANE What, before your father was marryed?

LAMBSKIN Truly a little after, I was the first fruits, as they say; then did my father change his Copy, and set up a Brewhouse.

IANE I, then came your wealth in, Sir.

LAMBSKIN Your observation's good; I have carryed the Tallyes at my girdle seven yeares together with much Delight and observation; for I did ever love to deale honestly in the Nick.

IANE A very innocent resolution.

SPEEDWELL Your experience may see his course education; but to the purpose, sweet Female; I doe love that Face of yours.

IANE Sir, if you love nothing but my face, I cannot sell it from the rest.

LAMBSKIN You may see his slender observation; sweet Virgin, I doe love your lower parts better than your face.

SPEEDWELL Sir you doe interrupt, and thwart my love.

LAMBSKIN I Sir, I am your Rivall; and I will thwart your love: for your love licks at the face, and my love shall be Arsy-Versy to yours.

IANE I would desire no better wooing of so bad suitors.

SPEEDWELL Mistake me not kinde Heart.

LAMBSKIN He cals you Tooth drawer by way of experience.

SPEEDWELL In loving your face, I love all the rest of your body, as you shall finde by experience.

IANE Well Sir, you love me then?

SPEEDWELL Let your experience make a tryall.

IANE No Sir, I'l beleeve you rather, and I thanke you for't.

LAMBSKIN I love you too, faire Maide, double and treble, if it please you.

IANE I thanke you too Sir; I am so much beholding to you both; I am affraid I shall never requite it.

SPEEDWELL Requite one, sweete Chastity, and let it be Sir Godfry, with the correspondencie of your Love to him; I will maintaine you like a Lady, and it is brave, as I know by experience.

LAMBSKIN I will maintaine you like a Gentlewoman: And that may be better maintenance than a Ladies, as I have found by observation.

SPEEDWELL How dare you maintaine that, Sir?

LAMBSKIN I dare maintaine it with my purse, Sir.

SPEEDWELL I dare crosse it with my sword Sir.

LAMBSKIN If you dare crosse my purse with your sword Sir, I'l lay an action of suspition of felony to you; that's flat, Sir.

IANE Nay, pray you Gentlemen doe not quarrell, till you know for what.

BRUYNE Oh, no quarrelling, I beseech you Gentlemen! The reputation of my house is soyld, if any uncivill noyse arise in't.

LAMBSKIN Let him but shake his blade at me, and I'l throw downe my purse, and cry a rape; I scorne to kill him, but I'l hang his knighthood,/ I warrant him, if he offer assault and battry on my purse. E1[v]

BRUYNE Nay, good Sir, put up your sword.

SPEEDWELL You have confinde him prisoner for ever, I hope your experience sees hee's a harmelesse thing.

Enter GEORGE *the Factor.*

GEORGE Sir, heres young Master *Foster* requests to speake with you.

BRUYNE Does he? Prethee request him. Gentlemen, please you taste the sweetenesse of my Garden awhile, and let my daughter beare you company.

SPEEDWELL Where she is leader, there will be followers.

IANE You send me to the Gallyes, Sir; pray you redeeme me as soone as you can; these are pretty Things for mirth, but not for serious uses.

BRUYNE Prethee be merry with them then awhile, if but for curtesie; thou hast wit enough; but take heede they quarrell not.

IANE Nay I dare take in hand to part'm without any danger; but I beseech you let me not be too long a prisoner. Will you walke Gentlemen?

LAMBSKIN If it please you to place one of us for your conduct, otherwise this old Coxcombe and I shall quarrell.

IANE Sir *Godfry*, you are the eldest; pray lead the way.

SPEEDWELL With all my heart, sweet Virgin; Ah, ha; this place promises well in the eyes of experience; Master *Innocent*, come you behinde.

LAMBSKIN Right Sir; but I put the Gentlewoman before, and that is the thing I desire and there your experience halts a little.

SPEEDWELL When I looke backe, Sir, I see your nose behinde.

LAMBSKIN Then when I looke backe, your nose stands here.

SPEEDWELL Sweet Lady, follow experience.

LAMBSKIN And let observation follow you. *Exeunt.*

BRUYNE So, now request you Master *Foster* in, *George*; but hark; Does that newes holde his owne still, that our ships are so neare returne, as laden on the Downes/with such a wealthy fraughtage? E2

GEORGE Yes Sir, and the next Tide purpose to put into the River: Master *Foster*, your partner, hath now receiv'd more such intelligence, with most of the particulars of your merchandize, your venture is return'd with trebble blessings.

BRUYNE Let him be ever blest that sent.
George now call in the young man; and hearke yee, *George*,
From him run to my Partner, and request him to me;
This Newes I'm sure makes him a joyfull Merchant;
For my owne part, I'l not forget my vow, *Exit* GEORGE.
This free addition heaven hath lent my state,
As freely backe to heaven I'l dedicate.

Enter ROBERT FOSTER.

I marry Sir, would this were a third Sutor
To my daughter *Iane*, I should better like him
Than all that's come yet. Now master *Foster*,
Are your father and your selfe yet reconcil'd?

ROBERT Sir, 'twas my businesse in your courteous tongue
To put the arbitration. I have againe
(Discover'd by my mother) reliev'd my poore Vncle,
Whose anger now so great is multiplyed,
I dare not venter in the eye of either,
Till your perswasions with faire excuse
Have made my satisfaction.

BRUYNE Mother a pearle, Sir, 'tis a shrewd taske;
Yet I'l doe my best; your father hath so good newes,
That I hope 'twill be a faire motive too't;
But womens tongues are dangerous stumbling blocks

Enter GEORGE.

To lye in the way of peace. Now *George*.

GEORGE Master *Foster*'s comming, Sir.

ROBERT I beseech you Sir, let not me see him,
Till you have confer'd with him.

BRUYNE Well, well, e'r your returne to Master *Foster*,
Call my Daughter forth of the garden. *Exit* GEORGE.

And how does your Vncle, Master Foster?
ROBERT Sir, so well, I'd be loth to anticipate the fame E2v
That shortly will o're-spread the city
Of his good fortunes.
BRUYNE Why I commend thee still,
He wants no good from thee, no not in report:
'Tis well done Sir, and you shew duty in't.

Enter IANE.

Now daughter, Where are your lusty Suitors?

IANE I was glad of my release, Sir: Suitors call you'm, I'd keepe dishwater continually boyling, but I'd seeth such Suitors; I have had much adoe to keepe'm from bloodshed; I have seene for all the world, a couple of cowardly Curs quarrell in that fashion, as t'one turnes his head, the other snaps behind; and as he turnes, his Mouth recoyles againe: but I thanke my paines for't, I have leagu'd with'm for a weeke without any farther entercourse.

BRUYNE Well daughter, well; say a third trouble come;
Say in the person of young Master Foster here
Came a third Suitor: how then?

IANE Three's the womans totall Arithmeticke in deede, I would learne to number no farther, if there was a good account made of that.

ROBERT I can instruct you so far, sweet Beauty.

IANE Take heede, Sir; I have had ill handsell to day; perhaps 'tis not the fortunate season, you were best adjourne your journey to some happier time.

ROBERT There shall no Augurisme fright my plaine Dealing: Sweete, I feare no houres.

IANE You'l not betray me with love-powder?

ROBERT Nor with Gun-powder neither ifaith; yet I'l make you yeeld if I can.

BRUYNE Goe, get you together; your father will be comming;
Leave me with your suite to him, ply this your selfe; and Iane,
Use him kindly, he shall be his Fathers heire
I can tell you.

175 fame] Dilke; Same Q.

IANE Never the more for that, Father; If I use him/kindely, it shalbe for something I like in him-selfe, and not for any good he borrowes of his father. But come Sir, will you walke into the Garden; for that's the field I have best fortune to overcome my Suitors in. E3

ROBERT I feare not that fate neither, but if I walke into your Garden, I shall be tasting your sweetes.

IANE Taste sweetely and welcome Sir; for there growes Honesty, I can tell you.

ROBERT I shall be plucking at your honesty.

IANE By my honesty but you shall not Sir: I'l hold you a hand full of Penny-royall of that y'faith, if you touch my honesty there, I'l make you eate Sorrill to your supper, though I eate Sullenwood my selfe: No Sir, gather first Time and Sage, and such wholsome Hearbes; and Honesty and Hearts-ease will ripen the whil'st.

ROBERT You have faire Roses, have you not?

IANE Yes Sir, Roses; but no Gillyflowers. *Exeunt Ambo.*

Enter Master FOSTER *and his wife.*

BRUYNE Goe, goe, and rest on *Venus* Violets;
Shew her a dozin of Batchelors Buttons Boy;
Here comes his father. Now my kind Partner, have we good newes?

OLD FOSTER Sir, in a word, take it; Your full lading and venture is return'd at sixty fold encrease.

BRUYNE Heaven take the glory; A wondrous blessing;
Oh keepe us strong against these flowing Tides!
Man is too weake to bound himselfe below,
When such high waves doe mount him.

OLD FOSTER O Sir, care and ambition seldome meete;
Let us be thrifty; Titles will faster come,
Than we shall wish to have them.

BRUYNE Faith I desire none.

OLD FOSTER Why Sir, if so you please, I'l ease your cares;
Shall I like a full adventurer now bid you
A certaine ready sum for your halfe traffique?

BRUYNE I, and I'd make you gainer by it too; E3v
For then would I lay by my trouble, and begin

A worke which I have promis'd unto heaven,
A house, a *Domus Dei* shall be rays'd,
Which shall to Doomesday be establish'd
For succour to the poore; for in all Ages
There must be such.

OLD FOSTER Shall I bid your venture at a venter?

BRUYNE Pray you doe Sir.

OLD FOSTER Twenty thousand pounds.

BRUYNE Nay, then you under-rate your owne value much; will you make it thirty?

OLD FOSTER Shall I meete you halfe way?

BRUYNE I meete you there Sir; for five and twenty thousand Pounds the full ventures yours.

OLD FOSTER If you like my payment, 'tis the one halfe in ready Cash, the other seal'd for six Monethes.

BRUYNE 'Tis Merchant like and faire; *George*, you observe this? Let the contents be drawne.

GEORGE They shall Sir.

OLD FOSTER Your hazard is now all past, Sir.

BRUYNE I rejoyce at it, Sir, and shall not grudge your gaines,
Though multiplyed to thousands.

OLD FOSTER Beleeve me Sir, I account my selfe a large Gainer by you.

BRUYNE Much good may it be to you, Sir; but one Thing
At this advantage of my love to you
Let me entreate.

OLD FOSTER What is it, Sir?

BRUYNE Faith my old suite, to reconcile those breaches
'Twixt your kinde son and you; Let not the love
He shewes unto his Vncle, be any more
A bar to sunder your blessings and his duty.

OLD FOSTER I would you had enjoyn'd me some great labour
For your owne loves sake, but to that my Vow
Stands fixt against I'm deafe; obdurat
To either of them.

MISTRIS FOSTER Nay Sir, if you knew all, you would not waste your Words E4
In so vaine expence: since his last Reformation,
He has flowne out againe, and in my sight

Relieved his Vncle in the Dicing house;
For which, either he shalbe no Father to him,
Or no husband to me.

BRUYNE Well Sir, go call my Daughter forth of the Garden,
And bid her bring her Friend along with her; [Exit GEORGE.]
Troth Sir, I must not leave you thus;
I must needes make him your son againe.

OLD FOSTER Sir, I have no such thing a kin to me.

Enter ROBIN and IANE. ROBIN kneels.

BRUYNE Looke you Sir, know you this duty?

OLD FOSTER Not I Sir; hee's a stranger to me,
Save your Knee, I have no blessing for you.

MISTRIS FOSTER Goe, goe to your Vncle Sir; you know
Where to finde him, hee's at his old haunt,
He wants more money by this time; but I thinke
The Conduitepipe is stopt from whence it ran.

OLD FOSTER Did he not say, hee'd beg for you, you'd best
Make use of's bounty.

BRUYNE Nay, good Sir.

OLD FOSTER Sir, if your daughter cast any eye of favour
Vpon this Vnthrift restrain't, hee's a beggar:
Mistris Iane, take heede what you doe.

MISTRIS FOSTER I, I, be wise Mistris Iane:
Doe not you trust to spleene in time worne to pitty,
You'l not finde it so; therefore good Gentlewoman
Take heede.

BRUYNE Nay then you are too impenitrable.

OLD FOSTER Sir, your money shall be ready, and your bills;
Other businesse I have none:
For thee, beg, hang, dye like a slave;
Such blessings ever thou from me shalt have. Exit FOSTER and his wife.

BRUYNE Well Sir: I'l follow you; and Sir, be comforted,
I will not leave till I finde some remorse;
Meane time let not want trouble you;/you shall not know it. E4v

ROBERT Sir, 'tis not want I feare, but want of blessing
My knee was bent for; for mine Vncles state,

296 in] Dodsley; and Q, Dilke.

Which now I dare say out-weighes my fathers farre,
Confirmes my hopes as rich, as with my fathers,
His love excepted onely.

BRUYNE Thy Vncles state, how for heavens love?

ROBERT By his late marriage to the wealthiest widow
That *London* had, who has not onely made him
Lord of her selfe, but of her whole estate.

BRUYNE Mother-a-pearle, I rejoyce in't: this newes is yet but young?

ROBERT Fame will soone speake it loud, Sir.

BRUYNE This may helpe happily to make all peace;
But how have you parly'd with my daughter, Sir?

IANE Very well Father: We spake something, but did nothing at all; I requested him to pull me a Catherin Peare, and had I not lookt to him he would have mistooke and given me a Popperin; and to requite his kindenesse, I pluck'd him a Rose, and he had almost prick'd my finger for my paines.

BRUYNE Well said Wag, are there sparkes kindled,
Quench'm not for me, 'tis not a fathers roughnesse,
Nor doubtfull hazard of an Vncles kindenesse
Can me deterre; I must to your father;
Where (as a chiefe affaire) I'l once more moue,
And if I can returne him backe to love. *Exeunt.*

[3.2] *Enter* DOCTOR *and* STEPHENS WIFE.

WIFE Sir, you see I have made a speedy choyse,
And as swift a marriage; be it as it will,
I like the man, if his qualities afflict me,
I shall be happy in't.

DOCTOR I must not distaste,
What I have help'd to make; 'tis I that joyn'd you.

WIFE A good bargaine, I hope.

Enter ROGER.

Roger, where's your Master?

CLOWNE The Good man of the house is within forsooth. F1

WIFE Not your Master, Sir?

CLOWNE 'Tis hard of digestion: Yes, my Master is within; hee masters you therefore I must be content: You have long'd for Crosses a good while, and now you are like to be farther off them than e'r you were; For I'm affraid, your good husband will leave you ne'r a crosse i'th'house to blesse you with.

WIFE Well Sir, I shall be blest in't: But where is he?

CLOWNE Where he has mistaken the place a little, being his wedding-day; He is in *nomine*, when he should be in *re*.

WIFE And where's that?

CLOWNE In your Counting-house; If he were a kinde Husband, he would have bin in another Counting-house by this time: hee's tumbling over all his money bags yonder; you shall heare of him in the bowling Alley againe.

WIFE Why Sir, all is his, and at his dispose;
Who shall dare to thwart him?

Enter STEPHEN *with bills and bonds.*

CLOWNE Looke where he comes.

WIFE How now, Sweete-heart? what hast thou there?

STEPHEN I finde much debts belonging to you, Sweete;
And my care must be now to fetch them in.

WIFE Ha, ha; prethee doe not mistake thy selfe,
Nor my true purpose; I did not wed to thrall,
Or binde thy large expence, but rather to adde
A plenty to that liberty; I thought by this,
Thou would'st have stuft thy pockets full of Gold,
And throwne it at a hazard; made Ducks and Drakes,
And baited fishes with thy silver flyes;
Lost, and fetcht more: why this had bin my joy;
Perhaps at length thou would'st have wast'd my store;
Why, this had bin a blessing to good for me.

STEPHEN Content thee, Sweete, F1v
Those daies are gone, I, even from my memorie;
I have forgot that e'r I had such follies,
And I'l not call'm backe: my cares are bent
To keepe your state, and give you all content.
Roger, goe, call your fellow-servants up to me,

41 cares] Dilke; eares Q.

And to my Chamber bring all bookes of debt;
I will o're-looke, and cast up all accounts,
That I may know the weight of all my cares,
And once a yeere give up my stewardship.

CLOWNE Now you may see what hastie matching is; You had thought to have bin vext, and now you cannot: You have marryed a husband, that, Sir reverence of the title, now being my Master in law, I doe thinke hee'l proove the miserablest, covetous Rascall, that ever beate beggar from his gate. But 'tis no matter; time was when you were fairely offered, if you would have tooke it; you might have had other matches y'faith, if it had pleas'd you; and those that would have crost you; I would have sold away all that ever you had had; have kept two or three Whores at liverie under your nose; have turn'd you out in your smocke, and have us'd you like a woman; where-as now, if you'd hang your selfe, you can have none of these blessings: but 'tis well enough, now you must take what followes. *Exit* CLOWNE.

WIFE I'm new to seeke for crosses, the hopes I meant
Turne to despaire, and smother in content.

Enter ROBERT.

STEPHEN O Nephew are you come? The welcom'st wish
That my heart has; This is my Kinsman, Sweete.

WIFE Let him be largely texted in your love,
That all the Citty may reade it fairely;
You cannot remember me, and him forget;
We were alike to you in poverty.

STEPHEN I should have beg'd that bounty of your love,
Though you had scanted me to have given't him;
For we are one, I an Vncle Nephew, F2
He a Nephew Vncle. But my Sweete selfe, 71
My slow request you have anticipated
With proffer'd kindenesse; and I thanke you for it.
But how, kinde Cozin, does your father use you?
Is your name found againe within his bookes?
Can he reade son there?

ROBERT 'Tis now blotted quite:
For by the violent instigation

Of my cruell Stepmother, his Vowes and Othes
Are stampt against me, ne'r to acknowledge me,
Ne'r to call, or blesse me as a childe;
But in his brow, his bounty, and behaviour
I reade it almost plainelie.

STEPHEN Cozin, grieve not at it;
That father lost at home, you shall finde here;
And with the losse of his inheritance,
You meete another amply profferd you;
Be my adopted son, no more my kinsman;
So that this borrowed bounty doe not stray
From your consent.

WIFE Call it not borrowed, Sir, 'tis all your owne;
Here 'fore this reverent man I make it knowne,
Thou art our childe as free by adoption,
As deriv'd from us by conception,
Birth, and Propinquitie; Inheritour
To our full substance.

ROBERT You were borne
To blesse us both, my knee shall practise
A sons duty even beneath sons,
Giving you all the comely dues of parents:
Yet not forgetting my duty to my father;
Where e'r I meet him, he shall have my knee,
Although his blessing ne'r returne to me.

STEPHEN Come then my dearest son, I'l now give thee
A taste of my love to thee; be thou my deputy,
The Factour and disposer of my businesse;
Keepe my accounts, and order my affaires;
They must be all your owne; for you, deere Sweet,
Be merry, take your pleasure, at home, abroad;
Visit your neighbours; ought that may seeme good F2v
To your owne will, downe to the Country ride;
For cares and troubles lay them all aside,
And I will take them up, it's fit that weight
Should now lye all on me: take thou the height
Of quiet and content, let nothing grieve thee;

I brought thee nothing else, and that I'le give thee.

Exit STEPHEN *and* ROBIN.

WIFE Will the Tide never turne? Was ever woman
Thus burden'd with unhappy happinesse?
Did I from Ryot take him, to waste my goods,
And he strives to augment it? I did mistake him.
DOCTOR Spoyle not a good Text with a false Comment;
All these are blessings, and from heaven sent;
It is your husbands good, hee's now transform'd
To a better shape, the prodigall's return'd.
Come, come, know joy, make not abundance scant;
You 'plaine of that which thousand women want. *Exeunt.*

[3.3] *Enter* ALDERMAN BRUINE, MASTER FOSTER *and* FACTORS *bearing o'r bags.*

BRUYNE So, so, haste home good Lads, and returne for the rest. Would they were cover'd, *George*, 'tis too Publicke Blazon of my estate; but 'tis no matter now; I'l bring it abroad againe e'r it be long. Sir, I acknowledge receit of my full halfe debt, twelve thousand five hundred pounds; it now remaines you seale those writings, as assurance for the rest, and I am satisfyed for this time.

OLD FOSTER Pray stay Sir, I have bethought me,
Let me once throw Dice at all, and either be
A compleate Merchant, or wracke my estate for ever:
Heare me Sir, I have of wares that are now vendible,
So much as will defray your utmost penny;
Will you accept of them, and save this charge
Of wax and parchment?
BRUYNE Be they vendible Sir?
I am your Chapman: What are they, Master *Foster*?
OLD FOSTER Broad clothes, Karsies, Cutchineale, such F3
As will not stay two dayes upon your hands.
BRUYNE I finde your purpose; you'd have your Ware-houses empty.
For the receit of your full fraught; I'l be your furtherer,
Make so your rates, that I may be no looser.

Enter GEORGE *and* RICHARD.

OLD FOSTER I have no other end, Sir; let our Factors
Peruse and deale for both.
BRUYNE Mine is return'd;
George, here's a new businesse; You and *Richard*
Must deale for some commodities betwixt us,
If you finde'm even gaine or but little losse,
Take carriage presently and carry'm home.
GEORGE I shall.
OLD FOSTER *Richard*, have you any further newes yet from our shipping?
RICHARD Not yet, Sir;
But by account from the last, when they put from *Dover*,
This Tide should bring them into Saint *Catharins* Poole;
The winde has bin friendly.
OLD FOSTER Listen their arrivall, and bid the Gunner speake it
In his lowd thunder all the Citty over;
Tingle the Merchants eares at the report
Of my abundant wealth; now goe with *George*.
RICHARD I shall doe both, Sir. *Exeunt* FACTORS.
OLD FOSTER I must plainely now confesse, Master Alderman,
I shall gaine much by you. The halfe of your Ship
Defrayes my full cost.
BRUYNE Beshrew me if I grudge it, being my selfe
A sufficient gainer by my venter, Sir.

Enter MISTRIS FOSTER.

MISTRIS FOSTER Still flowes the Tide of my unhappinesse,
The stars shoote mischiefe, and every houre
Is criticall to me.
OLD FOSTER How now woman?
Wrackt in the heaven of felicity? What ayl'st thou?
MISTRIS FOSTER I thinke the divel's mine enemy.
OLD FOSTER I hope so too; his hate is better than his friendship. F3[v]
MISTRIS FOSTER Your brother, your good brother, Sir.
OLD FOSTER What of him? hee's in *Ludgate* againe.
MISTRIS FOSTER No, hee's in *Hye-gate*;
He struts it bravely, an Aldermans pace at least.
OLD FOSTER Why, these are Oracles, doubtfull Enigmas!

MISTRIS FOSTER Why, I'm sure you have heard the newes; hee's marryed forsooth.

OLD FOSTER How, marryed? No woman of repute would choose so slightly.

MISTRIS FOSTER A woman, in whose brest, I had thought had liv'd
The very quintessence of discretion;
And who is't, thinke you? nay you cannot ghesse,
Though I should give you a day to riddle it;
'Tis my Gossip, Man, the rich Widdow of Cornehill.

OLD FOSTER Fye, fye, 'tis fabulous.

MISTRIS FOSTER Are you my husband? then is shee his wife·
How will this upstart beggar shoulder up,
And take the wall of you? his new found pride
Will know no eldership.

OLD FOSTER But wife, my wealth will five times double his,
E'r this Tide ebbe againe; I wonder I heare not
The Brazen Cannon proclame the Arrivall
Of my Infinite substance.

MISTRIS FOSTER But beggars will be
Proud of little, and shoulder at the best.

OLD FOSTER Let him first pay his old score, and then reckon;
But that shee:-

MISTRIS FOSTER I, that's it mads me too.
Would any woman, lesse to spite her selfe,
So much prophane the sacred name of wedlock:
A Dove to couple with a Storke, or a Lambe a Viper?

OLD FOSTER Content thee; Forgive her; shee'l doe so no more;
She was a rich widdow, a wife hee'l make her poore.

BRUYNE So Sir, you have clos'd it well; if so ill it prove,
Leave it to proofe, and wish not misery

Enter STEPHEN and ROBERT.

Vnto your enemy. Look, here he comes. F4

OLD FOSTER You say true, 'tis my enemy indeede.

STEPHEN Save you Master Alderman, I have some businesse with you.

BRUYNE With me, Sir, and most welcome, I rejoyce to see you.

MISTRIS FOSTER Doe you observe, Sir; he will not know you now?
Iockey's a Gentleman now.

OLD FOSTER Well fare rich widowes, when such beggars flourish;
But ill shall they fare, that florish o're such beggars.
STEPHEN Ha, ha, ha.
MISTRIS FOSTER He laughs at you.
OLD FOSTER No wonder, woman, he would doe that in Ludgate;
But 'twas when his kind Nephew did relieve him:
I shall heare him cry there againe shortly.
STEPHEN Oysters, new Walfleet Oysters.
OLD FOSTER The Gentleman is merry.
MISTRIS FOSTER No, no, no;
He does this to spight me; as who should say,
I had bin a fish-wife in my younger dayes.
BRUYNE Fye, fye, Gentlemen, this is not well;
My eares are guilty to heare such discords.
Looke, Master Foster; turne your eye that way;
There's duty unregarded, while envy struts
In too much state: believe me, Gentlemen,
I know not which to chide first. [ROBERT kneels.]
OLD FOSTER What Idoll kneeles that heretique too?
STEPHEN Rise Boy; thou art now my son, and owest no knee
To that unnaturall; I charge you rise.
OLD FOSTER Doe Sir, or turne your adoration that way;
You were kind to him in his tatter'd state;
Let him requite it now.
MISTRIS FOSTER Doe, doe, we have pai'd for't aforehand.
ROBERT I would I were divided in two halfes,
So that might reconcile your harsh division.
STEPHEN Proud Sir, this son which you have alienated
For my loves sake, shall by my loves bounty
Ride side by side in the best Equipage
Your scornes dare patterne him.
OLD FOSTER I, I, a beggars gallop up and downe. F4v
MISTRIS FOSTER I, 'tis up now, the next step downe.
STEPHEN Ha, ha, I laugh at your envy; Sir, my businesse is to you.
BRUYNE Good Sir, speake of any thing but this.
STEPHEN Sir, I am furnishing some shipping forth,
And want some English traffique, Broad-clothes, Karsies
Or such like; my voyage is to the Straites:

If you can supply me, Sir, I'l be your Chapman.
BRUYNE That I shall soone resolve you, Sir;

Enter FACTORS.

Come hither George.
OLD FOSTER This is the rich Merchant-man;
MISTRIS FOSTER That's neither grave nor wise;
OLD FOSTER Who will kill a man at Tiburne shortly;
MISTRIS FOSTER By Carts that may arise;
Or if the hangman dye, he may have his office.
BRUYNE Then you have bargain'd, George.
GEORGE And the Ware carryed home, Sir;
You must looke to be little gainer; but lose you cannot.
BRUYNE 'Tis all I desire from thence, Sir I can furnish you
With Wares I lately from your brother bought;
Please you goe see them, for I would faine divide you,
Since I can win no nearer friendship.
STEPHEN I'l goe with you, Sir. Exeunt ALDERMAN, STEPHEN and GEORGE.
OLD FOSTER Take your adoption with you, Sir.
ROBERT I crave but your blessing with me, Sir.
OLD FOSTER 'Tis my curse then; get thee out of mine eye.
Th'art a beame in't, and I'le teare it out
E'r it offend to looke on thee.
MISTRIS FOSTER Goe, goe, Sir; follow your Vncle-father,
Helpe him to spend, what thrift has got together;
'Twilbe charity in you to spend,
Because your charity it was to lend.
ROBERT My charity; you can a vertue name
And teach the use, yet never knew the same. Exit.

Enter RICHARD. G1

OLD FOSTER See wife, here comes Richard; now listen,
And heare me crown'd the wealthiest London Merchant.
Why dost thou looke so sadly?
MISTRIS FOSTER Why dost not speake; hast lost thy tongue?
RICHARD I never could speake worse.

125 nor] Dilke; not Q.

OLD FOSTER Why, thy voyce is good enough.
RICHARD But the worst accent Sir, that ever you heard,
I speake a Screechowles note. Oh you have made
The most unhappiest bargaine that ever Merchant did!
OLD FOSTER Ha? what can so balefull be, as thou would'st seeme
To make by this sad prologue? I am no traytor
To confiscate my goods: speake, what e'r it be.
RICHARD I would you could conceite it, that I might not speake it.
OLD FOSTER Dally not with torments, sinke me at once.
RICHARD Now y'ave spoke it halfe; 'tis sinking I must treate of;
Your ships are all sunke.
OLD FOSTER Hah!
MISTRIS FOSTER O thou fatall Raven; Let me pull thine eyes out
For this sad croake.
OLD FOSTER Hold woman; hold prethee;
'Tis none of his fault.
MISTRIS FOSTER No, no, 'tis thine, thou wretch;
And therefore let me turne my vengeance all on thee;
Thou hast made hot haste to empty all my Ware-houses,
And made roome for that the sea hath drunk before thee.
OLD FOSTER Vndone for ever! Where could this mischiefe fall?
Were not my ships in their full pride at *Dover*;
And what English *Carybdas* has the divell dig'd
To swallow nearer home.
RICHARD Even in the Mouth, and entrance of the *Thames*
They were all cast away.
OLD FOSTER Dam up thy Mouth
From any farther mischievous relation.
RICHARD Some men were sav'd, but not one penny-worth of goods.
OLD FOSTER Even now thy balefull utterance was chok'd, G1v
And now it runs too fast; thou fatall Bird no more.
MISTRIS FOSTER May Serpents breed, and fill this fatall Streame,
And poyson her for ever.
OLD FOSTER O curse not, they come too fast!
MISTRIS FOSTER Let me curse somewhere, Wretch, or else I'l throw
Them all on thee; 'tis thou, ungodly Slave,
That art the marke unto the wrath of Heaven:

I thriv'd e'r I knew thee.

OLD FOSTER I prethee split me too.

MISTRIS FOSTER I would I could; I would I had never seene thee;
For I ne'r saw houre of comfort since I knew thee.

OLD FOSTER Vndone for ever, my credit I have crackt,
To buy a Venture, which the Sea has sak'd;
What worse can woe report.

MISTRIS FOSTER Yes worse than all,
Thy enemies will laugh, and scorne thy fall.

OLD FOSTER Be it the worst then; that place I did assigne
My unthrifty brother, Ludgate, must now be mine.
Breake, and take Ludgate.

MISTRIS FOSTER Take Newgate rather.

OLD FOSTER I scorn'd my child, now he may scorne his father.

MISTRIS FOSTER Scorne him still.

OLD FOSTER I will; would he my wants relieve,
I'd scorne to take what he would yeeld to give:
My heart be still my friend, although no other;
I'l scorne the helpe of either son, or brother,
My portion's begging now; seldome before
In one sad houre, was man so rich and poore. Exeunt.

Actus Quartus G2

Enter MISTRIS IANE, GODFRY SPEEDWELL, and MASTER LAMBSKIN.

IANE Gentlemen, my Father's not within; please you to walke a turne or two in the garden, hee'l not be long.

LAMBSKIN Your father, Mistris Iane, I hope you have observation in you, and know our humours; we come not a wooing to your Father.

SPEEDWELL Experience must beare with folly; Thou art all innocent, and thy name is Lambskin; grave Sapience guides me, and I care not a pin for thy squibs, and thy Crackers; My old dry wood shall make a lusty bonefire, when thy greene Chips shall lye hissing in the Chimney-Corner. Remember Mistris, I can make you a Lady by mine owne experience.

LAMBSKIN Prethee doe not stand troubling the Gentlewoman with thy musty sentences, but let her love be laid downe betwixt us like a paire

190 sak'd] sok'd Q.

of Cudgells, and into whose hands she thrusts the weapons first, let him take up the Bucklers.

SPEEDWELL A match betweene us.

IANE Must I be stickler then?

LAMBSKIN We are both to run at the Ring of your setting up, and you must tell us who deserves most favour.

IANE But will you stand both at my disposing?

LAMBSKIN Else let me never stand but in a Pillory.

IANE You love me both you say?

SPEEDWELL By this hand-

LAMBSKIN Hand? Zoundes by the foure and twenty Elements.

IANE Pray spare your oathes; I doe believe you doe G2v
You would not else make all this stir to wooe.
Sir *Godfry*, you are a knight both tough and old,
A rotten building cannot long time hold.

LAMBSKIN *Speedewell*, live well, dye well, and be hang'd well, change your coppy well, your experience will not carry it else.

IANE Y'are rich too, at least your selfe so say;
What though? y'are but a gilded man of clay.

LAMBSKIN A man of Ginger-bread; y'faith I could finde in my heart to eate him.

IANE Should I wed you, the fire with frost must marry
Ianuary and *May*; I for a younger tarry.

LAMBSKIN That's I; in troth I'le be thy young *Lambskin*; thou shalt finde me as innocent as a sucking Dove: speake, Sweete Mistris, am I the youth in a basket?

IANE You are the sweete youth Sir, whose pretty eyes
Would make me love; but you must first be wise.

SPEEDWELL Ah, hah, is your coxcombe cut? I see experience must boord this faire Pinnace: a word in private.

LAMBSKIN I'l have no words in private, unlesse I heare too.

Enter MASTER BRUINE, STEPHEN *and* ROBIN.

BRUYNE Come Gentlemen,
We'l make few Words about it; Merchants in Bargaining
Must not, like Souldiors lying at a siege,
Stay Moneths, weekes, daies, but strike at the first parley.

Broad-clothes, and Woolls, and other rich Commodities,
I lately from your brother bought, are all your owne.
STEPHEN 'Tis well.
BRUYNE Then be not angry gentle Sir,
If now a string be touch'd, which hath too long
Sounded so harshly over all the Citty;
I now would winde it to a musicall height.
STEPHEN Good Master Alderman, I thinke that string
Will still offend mine eare; You meane the jarring
'Twixt me and my brother?
BRUYNE In troth the same.
STEPHEN I hate no poyson like that brothers name.
BRUYNE O Fye, not so.
STEPHEN Vncivill churle, when all his sailes were up, G3
And that his proud heart danc'd on golden waves:
BRUYNE As heaven be thank'd it still does.
STEPHEN Yet Sir, then I
Being sunke, and drown'd in mine owne misery,
He would not cast out a poore line of thred
To bring me to the shore; I had bin dead,
And might have starv'd for him.
BRUYNE A better fate Sir,
Stood at your elbow.
STEPHEN True Sir; this was he
That lifted me from want and misery,
Whose cruell father for that good
Cast him away; scorning his name and blood;
Lopt from his side this branch that held me deere;
For which hee's now my son, my joy, my heire.
But for his father hang him.
BRUYNE Fye, fye.
STEPHEN By heaven.
BRUYNE Come, come, live in more charity, he is your brother;
If that name offend, I'l sing that tune no more.
Yonder's my daughter busie with her suitors;
Wee'l visit them. Now Iane, bid your friends welcome.
IANE They must be welcome Sir, that come with you;

To thee ten thousand welcomes still are due.

ROBERT My sweete Mistris. [IANE] *kisse[s] him.*

LAMBSKIN Zounds Sir knight, we have stood beating the Bush and the bird's flowne away; this Citty Bowler has kist the Mistris at first cast.

BRUYNE How fare yee Gentlemen, what cheere Sir knight?

SPEEDWELL An adventurer still Sir, to this new found land.

LAMBSKIN He sayles about the point Sir, but he cannot put in yet.

BRUYNE The winde may turne Sir. A word Master *Foster*.

LAMBSKIN You see Sir *Speedwell*, what Card is turn'd up for trumpe; I hold my life this spruce Cittizen will forestall the market, Oh these briske factors, are notable firkers.

SPEEDWELL I doubt Sir, he will play the merchant with us.

BRUYNE They both are suitors Sir, yet both shoote wide;
My daughter sure must be your kinsmans bride. G3v

STEPHEN I'l give her a wedding Ring on that condition
And put a Stone in't worth a thousand pounde, Sir.

BRUYNE You have my hand and heart too't, be she pleas'd so.

LAMBSKIN S'foote, let's shew our selves Gallants, or Gallymawfryes; shall we be out-brav'd by a Cockney? A word my faire *Zenocrates*; Doe you see Sir, here be those that have gon a fishing, and can give you a Gudgion.

ROBERT You were best goe fish for better manners, or I shall bob for Eles with you. [*Trips up his heels.*]

LAMBSKIN Zoundes are you a striker? Draw, Sir knight.

BRUYNE Not in my house; I pray be quiet Gentlemen.

ROBERT He dares not doe't abroad believe me, Sir.

STEPHEN Now by my life my Boy, for this brave spirit
I hug thee in mine armes: lose life and limbes
E'r thou forsake thy love.

LAMBSKIN Hee's no Rivall here Sir; has struck me, and we are Gentlemen.

SPEEDWELL And heare yee, Sir, let him seeke out his equalls; for some of us are in danger to make her a Lady shortly; I know what I speake; what I speake, I'l doe; yet I'l doe nothing, but what comes from grave experience.

STEPHEN Speake what you please Sir, hee's a Gentleman
As good as either of you both, and shall

In lists of Love for such a bed-fellow,
Brave him that dares, and here lay downe more gold
To win her love, than both your states are worth.

SPEEDWELL Ha? doe you know us, Sir? You grow too bold; my experience now hath found you; you were once a tatter'd fellow, your name is *Foster*; have you such gold to give?

LAMBSKIN Yes, yes, has won it betting at the bowling Alleyes, or at the Pigeon-holes in the Garden Alleyes.

STEPHEN You are muddy Groomes to upbraid mee with that scorne,
Which vertue now gilds over; Pray yee Gentlemen G4
May I request your names.

LAMBSKIN Our names are in the Heralds bookes I warrant you;
My name is *Innocent Lambskin*; and this Knight,
Simply though he stands here, is knowne to be
Sir *Godfry Speedewell*.

STEPHEN Well may he Speede Sir; *Lambskin* and *Speedewell*; ha? Is't so? I thinke I shall give you a medicine to purge this itch of love, Sir.

LAMBSKIN No itch neither Sir, we have no scabs here, but your selfe and your Cozin.

STEPHEN Very good Sir, my little *Lambskin*. I have you here in Sheepeskin; looke you, 'tis so y'faith. See, Master Alderman, these two crackt Gallants are in severall bonds to my Predecessor for a debt of full two thousand apiece. Cozin, fetch me a Serjeant straite.

ROBERT Yes Sir.

SPEEDWELL O let him, I have a protection, Sir.

STEPHEN I'l try that, Sir.

SPEEDWELL A Serjeant? Nay, then
Experience must worke, Legs be strong and bold;
When Serjeants waite at feasts, the cheere's but cold.
I'l shift for one. *Exit.*

LAMBSKIN Knight, knight; S'foote if an errand Knight run away, I were an arrand Asse to tarry, and be catch'd in the lime-bush: I love the Wench well; but if they have no hole to place me in, but the hole in the Counter, I'l be gone and leave'm; that's flat. *Exit.*

BRUYNE You have scar'd the suitors from the marke, Sir.

STEPHEN I am glad on't, Sir; they are but such

As seeke to build their rotten state on you,
And with your Wealth to underprop their weakenesse;
Believe me, reverend Sir, I had much rather
You'd venter that my Cuz might call you father.

Enter STEPHENS WIFE.

BRUYNE We'l talke of that anon; See Sir, here comes your wife, G4v
The theame of all her time, with goodnesse mixt,
The happy Woman that was never vext;
Y'are welcome Mistris *Foster*.

WIFE I thanke yee Sir.

STEPHEN Wife, your two debtors were here but now; S. *Speedwell* and *Lambskin*; A Wolfe could not have torne poore *Lambskin* worse, than the bare name of a Serjeant: the very thought made them both to take their heeles and run away.

WIFE 'Las, they are poore and leane, and being so,
Kill them not till they are fatter.

STEPHEN At thy girdle, Sweete, hangs the keyes,
To lock the prison dores or let them loose:
'Twas my intent onely in way of mirth
To rid them from the presence of Mistris *Iane*,
That our adopted son might have no bar
Vnto his love.

WIFE The match is faire; and were that knot once tyed,
I'd send some Angels to attend the bride.

Enter GEORGE.

STEPHEN Sir, here's your factor.

BRUYNE Are the wares ready?

GEORGE Yes, and deliver'd Sir,
To Master *Foster's* servants, who conveyed them
In Carts to the Custome-house, there to be shipt;
But going with them, Sir, I met ill newes.

BRUYNE Ill newes? what ist?

GEORGE Old Master *Foster's* ships so richly laden,

159 theame] theame *Ent. Stepen's Wife* Q.

By strange misfortune, Sir, are cast away.

BRUYNE Now heaven forbid!

ROBERT Oh mee!

STEPHEN How? cast away; where?

BRUYNE 'Tis impossible; they rid at *Dover* safe,
When he out-bought my full share in the fraught,
And paid me downe neare thirty thousand pounds
In wares and money. H1

GEORGE Which had he not done, you had lost your venture:
By Master *Foster's* owne appointment Sir, they weighed
Their Anchors up, and so to come for *London*;
But by a mercilesse storme they all were swallowed,
Even in the *Theames* mouth; yet the men were sav'd,
But all the goods were lost.

ROBERT O my poore father!
This losse will breake his backe.

STEPHEN Ha? What's that to you?
If in my favour you'l sit warme, then bury
All love to him, nay duty, heare you Sir?
What shed'st thou teares for him, that had no care
To see thy heart drop Blood? he was unnaturall,
And heaven hath iustly now rewarded him.

BRUYNE 'Tis a most strange Fate;
He needes would buy my Part at any rate,
He car'd not what; and now all's lost.

STEPHEN Greedy desire
He swallowed, and now is swallowed; 'tis but his hyre;
And I'l not pitty it, no more than he,
In his abundance, did my misery.

WIFE I grieve for my poore Gossip, his good wife,
She never met good fortune all her life,
And this will breake her heart-strings: In good sooth
I'l goe and comfort her.

STEPHEN In good sooth you shall not,
Nor him, nor her at this time, gentle wife;
He scorn'd me in his height, now being poore,
If that he needes my helpe, he knowes my doore.

Sir, we'l for this time leave you, at fitter leasure,
We'l have this marriage talk't of.

BRUYNE At your owne good pleasure.

STEPHEN Come wife; Goe not to see your father, Sir, I charge you.

BRUYNE *Iane*, bring your friends to th'dore.

ROBERT I'l helpe my father, though my selfe grow poore. *Exeunt.*

BRUYNE Where's my Factor?

GEORGE Here Sir.

BRUYNE What, are the square stones, and timber brought as I appointed?

GEORGE Yes, Sir, and the workemen, that daily ply the Worke, H1v
are in number fourescore at least.

BRUYNE My vowes flew up to heaven, that I would make
Some pious worke in the brasse booke of Fame,
That might till Doomesday lengthen out my name.
Neare *Norton Folgate* therefore have I bought
Ground to erect this house, which I will call
And dedicate, *Saint Marie's Hospitall*;
And when 'tis finished, o'r the gates shall stand
In capitall letters, these words fairely graven
For I have given the worke and house to heaven
And cal'd it, *Domus Dei*, Gods house;
For in my zealous faith I know full well,
Where good deedes are, there heaven it selfe doth dwell. *Exeunt.*

[4.2] *Enter* OLD FOSTER, RICHARD *his factor, and the* KEEPER *of Ludgate.*

RICHARD Good Sir, resolve not thus; returne againe,
Your debts are not so great, that you should yeeld
Your body thus to prison unconstrain'd.

OLD FOSTER I will not trust the iron hearts of men;
My credit's lost, my wealth the Sea has swallowed,
Wrack'd at my dore, even in the mouth o'th' *Thames*;
Oh my misfortune! never man like me
Was so throwne downe, and cast to misery.

RICHARD Deare Sir, be patient.

OLD FOSTER I prethee get thee gone,

And with thy diligence assist thy Mistris
To keepe that little left, to helpe her selfe,
Whil'st here in Ludgate I secure my body
From Writs, Arrests, and Executions,
Which, well I know, my cruell Creditors
Will thunder on me. Goe, get thee gone;
If what is left they'l take, doe thou agree;
If not, I am here resolv'd to stay and dye.

RICHARD I'l doe my best Sir, to procure your peace. Exit.

OLD FOSTER Do so. Come Sir, I yeeld my selfe your prisoner;
You are the Keeper of this Ludgate.

KEEPER Yes Sir, your name is registred among the prisoners.

OLD FOSTER So, I have seene the faire outside of this tombe before;
This goodly apple has a rotten core. H2

KEEPER As all prisons have, Sir.

OLD FOSTER I prethee bar me of no priviledge
Due to a free Citizen; Thou knowest me well?

KEEPER Yes Master Foster, and I sorrow for your losses, yet doubt not but your son and brother-

OLD FOSTER O speake not of them! doe not kisse and kill me;
I have no son nor brother that esteemes me,
And I for ever hate their memory:
Prethee no more; I am come sicke into
A bad Inne, and looke for worse attendance,
I have taken a surfeit of misfortunes, and here
Must swallow pills with poyson to recure me:
I am sea-sicke, Sir, and heave my hands to heaven;
Ne'r to so low an ebbe was Foster driven.

KEEPER There be some Fees to pay, Sir, at your comming in.

OLD FOSTER So, so, if this old Wall-nut-tree, after all this cudgelling,
Have but one cluster left, thou shalt have that too;
If not, take off these leaves that cover me;
Pull off these white locks; rend them from my head,
And let me in my woes be buried.

KEEPER 'Las, Sir, this house is poore.

OLD FOSTER
I thinke no lesse;
For rich men seldome meete with such distresse,

Well, well, what booke must I reade over now?
What servile Oare must I be tyed to here,
Slave-like to tug within this christian Galley?
KEEPER Sir, being the youngest prisoner in the house,
You must beg at the iron grate above,
As others doe for your reliefe and their's.
OLD FOSTER For a beggar to beg, Sir, is no shame;
And for the iron grate, it beares an embleme
Of iron-hearted Creditors, that force men lye
In loathsome prisons thus to starve and die.

Enter ROBERT and kneeles.

KEEPER Who would you speake with, Sir?
Oh, cry you mercy; 'tis his sonne: I'l leave them. Exit. H2v
OLD FOSTER O torment to my soule! What mak'st thou here?
Cannot the picture of my misery
Be drawne, and hung out to the eyes of men,
But thou must come to scorne and laugh at it?
ROBERT Deare Sir, I come to thrust my backe under your loade,
To make the burden lighter.
OLD FOSTER Hence from my sight, dissembling villaine; goe,
Thine Vncle sends defiance to my woe,
And thou must bring it: Hence, thou Basyliske,
That kil'st me with thine eyes: nay, never kneele;
These scornefull mocks more than my woes I feele.
ROBERT Alas, I mocke yee not; but come in love,
And naturall duty Sir, to beg your blessing;
And for mine Vncle-
OLD FOSTER Him, and thee I curse,
I'l starve, e'r I eate bread from his purse,
Or from thy hand; Out villaine, tell that Cur,
Thy barking Vncle, that I lye not here
Vpon my bed of ryot, as he did,
Cover'd with all the villanies, which man
Had ever woven; tell him I lye not so,
It was the hand of heaven strucke me thus low,

67 thine] Lamb; mine Q.

And I doe thanke it. Get thee gone, I say,
Or I shall curse thee, strike thee; Prethee away;
Or if thou'lt laugh thy fill at my poore state,
Then stay, and listen to the prison grate,
And heare thy father, an old wretched man,
That yesterday had thousands, beg and cry,
To get a penny: Oh my misery!

ROBERT Deere Sir, for pitty heare me.

OLD FOSTER Vpon my curse I charge no nearer come,
I'l be no father to so vild a Son. Exit.

ROBERT O my abortive fate!
Why for my good am I thus pay'd with hate?
From this sad place of Ludgate here I freed
An Vncle, and I lost a father for it; H3
Now is my father here, whom if I succour,
I then must lose my Vncle's love and favour.
My Father once being rich, and Vncle poore,
I him relieving was thrust forth of dores;
Baffled, revil'd, and disinherited:
Now mine owne Father here must beg for bread,
Mine Vncle being rich, and yet if I
Feede him, my selfe must beg. Oh misery,
How bitter is thy taste! yet I will drinke
Thy strongest poyson; fret what mischiefe can,
I'l feede my Father, though, like the Pellican,
I pecke mine owne brest for him.

OLD FOSTER, and above at the grate, a box hanging downe.

OLD FOSTER Bread, bread, one penny to buy a Loafe of bread for the tender mercy!

ROBERT O me my shame! I know that voyce full well;
I'l help thy wants, although thou curse me still.

OLD FOSTER Bread, bread; some Christian man send back your charity to an number of poore prisoners; One penny for the tender mercy.

ROBIN puts in money.

The hand of heaven reward you, gentle Sir,
Never may you want, never feele misery;

Let blessings in unnumbred measure grow,
And fall upon your head where e'r you goe.
ROBERT O happy comfort! curses to the ground
First strucke me, now with blessings I am crown'd.
OLD FOSTER Bread, bread, for the tender mercy; one Penny for a loafe of bread.
ROBERT I'l buy more blessings; Take thou all my store,
I'l keepe no coyne, and see my father poore. [Puts in money.]
OLD FOSTER Good Angels guard you, Sir, my prayers shalbe
That heaven may blesse you for this charity.
ROBERT If he knew me, sure he would not say so;
Yet I have comfort if by any meanes
I get a blessing from my fathers hands:
How cheape are good prayers? A poore penny buyes
That, by which man up in a minute flies, H3v
And mounts to heaven.

Enter STEPHEN.

Oh me, mine Vncle sees me!
STEPHEN Now Sir, what make you here so neere the prison?
ROBERT I was going, Sir,
To buy meate for a poore bird I have,
That sits so sadly in the Cage of late,
I thinke he'l dye for sorrow.
STEPHEN So Sir, your pitty will not quit your paines, I feare me;
I shall finde that bird I thinke to be
That churlish Wretch, your father, that now has taken
Shelter here in Ludgate; Goe too, Sir, urge me not,
You'd best; I have given you warning: Fawne not on him
Nor come not neare him, if you'l have my love.
ROBERT 'Las Sir, that Lambe
Were most unnaturall that should hate the Dam.
STEPHEN Lambe me no Lambs, Sir.
ROBERT Good Vncle; 'las you know when you lay here
I succour'd you, so let me now helpe him.
STEPHEN Yes, as he did me,

134 your paines] Dilke; you paines Q.

To laugh and triumph at my misery;
You freed me with his gold, but 'gainst his will:
For him I might have rotted, and laine still;
So shall he now.

ROBERT Alack the day!

STEPHEN If him thou pitty, 'tis thine owne decay.

OLD FOSTER Bread, bread; some charitable man remember the poore prisoners; bread for the tender mercy, one penny.

ROBERT O listen Vncle; that's my poore father's voyce.

STEPHEN There let him howle;
Get you gon, and come not neare him.

ROBERT O my soule!
What tortours dost thou feele? Earth neare shall find,
A son so true, yet forc'd to be unkind. Exit.

STEPHEN Well, go thy waies, thou patterne of true vertue;
My heart is full, I could even weepe,
And much ado I had to forbeare,
To heare a brother begging in a Iayle, H4
That but e'r while spred up a lofty sayle
As proudly as the best: Oh, 'twere a sin
Vnpardonable in me, should I not succour him?
Yes, I will doe't, yet closely it shalbe done,
And he not know from whence his comforts come.
What ho, Keeper there, a word I praye.

Enter KEEPER.

KEEPER What's your pleasure, Sir.

STEPHEN What's he that at the grate there beg'd even now?

KEEPER One Master Foster, Sir, a decayed Citizen new come in. Cry you mercy Sir, you know him better than my selfe, I thinke.

STEPHEN I should doe, knew he me as I would know him:
Prethee take him from the grate, and that no more
He stand to beg, there's ten pound to pay his score,
And take off all his wants; if he demand
Who sends it, tell him, 'tis thine owne free Hand
To lend him money.

KEEPER Well Sir, I shall.

STEPHEN Spend what he will, my purse shall pay it all;
And at his parting hence, the poorest prisoner,
And all free Citizens that live in *Ludgate*,
Shall blesse his comming in; I'l for his sake
Doe something now, that whil'st this Citty stands,
Shall keepe the *Fosters* name engraven so high,
As no blacke storme shall cloud their memory.
KEEPER Heaven blesse your purpose, Sir. *Exeunt.*

[4.3] *Enter* STEPHENS WIFE, *and her sister* OLD FOSTERS WIFE.

WIFE Sister, there's no way to make sorrow light
But in the noble bearing; be content;
Blowes given from heaven are our due punishment;
All shipwracks are no drownings, you see buildings
Made fairer from their Ruines; he that I married,
The brother to your husband, lay, you know,
On the same bed of misery, yet now H4v
Hee's ranckt with the best Citizens.
MISTRIS FOSTER O you were borne
To wealth and Happinesse; I, to want and scorne!
WIFE Come, I will worke my husband; stay this griefe.
The longest sorrow findes at last reliefe.

Enter CLOWNE.

Now Sir, your businesse.
CLOWNE Marry mistris here are two creatures scarce able to make one man, desires to speake with you.
WIFE What are they, know their names.
CLOWNE Nay, I know that already; the one is a Thing that was pluc'd into the World, by the head and shoulders to be wondered at, and 'tis cald a knight; the other is a coach-horse of the same over-ridden race; and that's a foolish Gentleman.
WIFE O, they are my old debtors, *Speedwell* and *Lambskin*.
Goe call them in, and my gentle sister
Comfort your selfe and my imprison'd brother,
To whom commend me, give to him this gold,
What good I can, I'l doe for him be bold.

MISTRIS FOSTER May heavenly blessings guard you from all ill:
Never was woman vext as I am still. *Exit.*

Enter SPEEDEWELL *and* LAMBSKIN.

WIFE Now good Sir *Godfry* and Master *Innocent*.

LAMBSKIN I put my innocent case into your hands Mistris, as a simple country Clyent thrusts his money into a Lawyers, who stands upon no great Tearmes to take it.

SPEEDWELL We come about the old businesse, the sicknesse of the purse Lady.

CLOWNE And they'd be loth to keepe their beds i'th'counter Mistris; they are affraid of Serjeants, Master *Lambskin* knowes that Mace is a binder.

LAMBSKIN No truly it makes me loose for I never smell it, though it be two streetes off, but it gives me a stoole presently. I1

CLOWNE I, you have bin a loose liver alwayes, 'tis time to looke to you.

SPEEDWELL Fayre Lady, we are your debtors, and owe you mony,
Experience tels us that our bonds are forfeit,
For which your husband threatned to arrest us;
My Shoulders love no such clappings, I love Tobacco,
But would be loth to drinke in *Woodstreet*-Pipes;
Some money we will pay ere we goe hence:
I speake you see with grave experience.

WIFE I know it well, Sir.

LAMBSKIN Had not your husband (when we went about fowling
For the Aldermans daughter) driven away the Bird
We might have bidden you to a better breakefast;
But now you must take what we can set before you.

Enter ROBERT.

WIFE I am content to doe so: you shall finde
Nor me nor my husband carry a griping minde.
Now Cuz, where's your Vncle?

ROBERT He's hard at hand,
I saw him comming with the Lord Maior and Aldermen.

LAMBSKIN Zoundes Knight, if the Maior come the shoulder clappers are not farre off.

WIFE O feare not, I'l be your surety Sir.

CLOWNE Doe you not smell Poultry ware, Sir *Godfry*?

SPEEDWELL Most horribly, I'l not endure the sent on't.

WIFE Vpon my trust none here shall doe you wrong;
What is his businesse with the Aldermen?

ROBERT About the entertainment of the King
That meanes to visit *London*.

WIFE Saw you your sad father?

ROBERT I did; would I might never see man more
Since he so hates my sight; the prison doore,
Which gapes for commers in, that mouth of hell,
Shut me out with a churlish cold farewell;
After my fathers most unnaturall part
Was plaid on miseries stage, mine Vncle comes
In thunder on me, threatning with blacke stormes I1v
To nayle me to the earth, if I releeved
My poore old father.

Enter STEPHEN.

CLOWNE Here's my master now Gentlemen.

STEPHEN O Gentlemen, y'are both welcome,
Have you paid this money on your bonds yet?

WIFE Not yet Sir,
But here they come like honest Gentlemen
To take some order for it: good Sweetheart
Shall it be put to me?

STEPHEN Doe as you please;
In all thy deeds th'rt govern'd with good starres,
Therefore if thou cry'st peace, I'le not raise warres.
E'ne order it how thou wilt.

WIFE I thanke ye Sir;
Then tell me Gentlemen, what present money
Can you pay?

62 Aldermen?] Dilke; Alderman? Q.

To see the dedication of my House,
Built for the weary travellers to rest in;
Where stands three hundred beds for their releefe,
With meat, drinke, and some money when they part,
Which I'l give freely with a willing heart.

STEPHEN A pious, worthy, and religious act:
Come Sir, to th'Guildhall; Wife, looke to your Kinsman,
Watch him neare; but doe not hinder him
If he releeve his father: Come Master Alderman,
With such sweet incense up your offerings flye,
I'l build one Altar more to charity. Exeunt.

Actus Quintus

Enter OLD FOSTER, his Wife, and KEEPER.

KEEPER Come, come, be merry Sir; doe as mourners doe at Funerals,
weare your Hat in your eyes, and / laugh in your heart. I3

OLD FOSTER I have no such fat legacie left me,
To teach me how to play the hypocrite.

KEEPER No? Why looke yee Sir, you shall want neither Meate, drinke, money, nor any thing that the House affords, or if any thing abroad like yee, Sir, here's money, send for what you will Sir: Nay, you shall beg no more at the Grate neither.

OLD FOSTER Ha? Is not this Ludgate?

KEEPER Yes Sir.

OLD FOSTER A Iayle, a prison,
A tombe of men lock'd up alive and buryed?

KEEPER 'Tis what you please to call it.

OLD FOSTER O, at what crevice
Then hath comfort like a Sun-beame crept?
For all the doores and windowes are of Iron,
And barr'd to keepe her out; I had a limbe
Cut from my body deare to me as life;
I had a son and brother too; Oh griefe,
They both would give me poyson first in gold,
Before their hollow palmes ten Drops should hold
Of natures drinke, cold water, but to save

My life one minute; whence should pitty come,
When my best friends doe beate it from this roome.

KEEPER No matter Sir, since you have good meat set before you, never aske who sent it; if heaven provide for you, and make the fowles of the Ayre your Cators, feed you fat, and be thankefull, and so I leave you. Exit.

MISTRIS FOSTER The Keeper is your friend, and powres true balme
Into your smarting wounds; therefore deare Husband
Endure the dressing with patience.

OLD FOSTER O wife, my losses are as numberlesse
As the Sea's sands that swallowed them. And shall I
In reckoning them, my sad griefes multiply?

MISTRIS FOSTER You may Sir,
But your dim eyes so thick with teares doe run,
You cannot see from whence your comforts come. I3v
Besides your debts being truly counted cannot be great.

OLD FOSTER But all my wealth and state lyes
In the seas Bottome.

MISTRIS FOSTER It againe may rise.

OLD FOSTER Oh never.

MISTRIS FOSTER Good Sir, so hope, for I from heaven espy
An arme to plucke you from this misery.

Enter KEEPER.

KEEPER Sir, there's one without desires to speake with you.

OLD FOSTER Goe send him in; none comes to doe me good
My wealth is lost, now let them take my blood.

Enter ROBERT. He kneeles to OLD FOSTER.

Ha? what art thou? Call for the Keeper there
And thrust him out of doores, or locke me up.

MISTRIS FOSTER O 'tis your son, Sir.

OLD FOSTER I know him not:
I am no King, unlesse of scorne and woe,
Why kneel'st thou then; why dost thou mock me so?

ROBERT O my deare father, hither am I come

Not like a threatning storme to encrease your wrack
For I would take all sorrowes from your backe
To lay them all on my owne.
OLD FOSTER Rise mischiefe, rise, away and get thee gone.
ROBERT O if I be thus hatefull to your eye
I will depart, and wish I soone may dye;
Yet let your blessing, Sir, but fall on me.
OLD FOSTER My heart still hates thee.
MISTRIS FOSTER Sweet husband.
OLD FOSTER Get you both gon;
That misery takes some rest that dwells alone;
Away thou villaine.
ROBERT Heaven can tell,
Ake but your finger, I to make it well,
Would cut my hand off.
OLD FOSTER Hang thee, hang thee.
MISTRIS FOSTER Husband.
OLD FOSTER Destruction meete thee, turne the key there ho. I4
ROBERT Good Sir: I'm gone, I will not stay to grieve you:
Oh knew you (for your woes) what paines I feele,
You would not scorne me so. See Sir, to coole
Your heate of burning sorrow I have got
Two hundred pounds and glad it is my lot
To lay it downe, with reverence at your feete;
No comfort in the world to me is sweet,
Whil'st thus you live in moane.
OLD FOSTER Stay.
ROBERT Good troth Sir, I'l have none on't back,
Could but one penny of it save my life.
MISTRIS FOSTER Yet stay and heare him; Oh unnaturall strife,
In a hard fathers bosome.
OLD FOSTER I see mine error now: oh can there grow
A Rose upon a Bramble? did there e'r flow
Poyson and health together in one tide?
I'm borne a man; reason may step aside,
And leade a father's love out of the way:
Forgive me, my good Boy, I went astray;

Looke, on my knees I beg it; not for joy
Thou bringst this golden rubbish, which I spurne
But glad in this, the heavens mine eye balls turne,
And fixe them right to looke upon that face
Where love remaines with pitty, duty, grace.
Oh my deare wronged boy!
ROBERT Gladnesse o'rwhelmes my heart with joy,
I cannot speak.
MISTRIS FOSTER Crosses of this foolish world
Did never grieve my heart with torments more
Than it is now growne light,
With joy and comfort of this happy sight.
OLD FOSTER Yet wife, I disinherited this boy.
ROBERT Your blessings all I crave.
OLD FOSTER And that enjoy
For ever, evermore; my Blessings fly,
To pay thy vertues, love and charity.

Enter STEPHENS WIFE.

MISTRIS FOSTER Here comes your brothers wife, / welcome deare sister. I4v
WIFE I thanke you; how fare you brother?
OLD FOSTER Better than your husband's hate could wish me,
That laughes to see my backe with sorrowes bow:
But I am rid of halfe my ague now.
WIFE Had you an ague then?
OLD FOSTER Yes, and my heart had every houre a fit.
But now 'tas left me well, and I left it.
WIFE O, 'tis well Cozin, what make you heare I pray?
ROBERT To support a weake house falling to decay.
WIFE 'Tis well, if you can doe't, and that the timber
You under-prop it with be all your owne.
Hearke Cuz, where's your Vncles mony?
ROBERT Faith Aunt 'tis gone,
But not at dice, nor drabbing.
WIFE Sir, I believe
With your Vncles gold your father you relieve.

ROBERT You are sav'd believing so, your beliefe's true.
WIFE You cut large thongs of that's another's due
And you will answer't ill: [Aside] now in good troth
I laugh at this jest, much good doe them both:
My wager I had won, had I but layd.
OLD FOSTER What has my poore boy done, that you have made
So much blood rise in's cheekes?
WIFE Nothing deare brother,
Indeed all's well: The course that he has runne
I like and love, let him hold on the same;
A sons love to a father none can blame;
I will not leave your brother's iron heart
Till I have beate it soft with my intreates.
OLD FOSTER 'Twill ne'r be musick 'tis so full of frets.
WIFE Frets make best musike: strings the higher rack'd
Sound sweetest.
OLD FOSTER And sound nothing when they are crackt,
As is his love to me, and mine to him.
WIFE I hope you both in smoother streames shall swim:
Hee's now the Sheriffe of London, and in counsell
Set at the Guildhall, in his scarlet Gowne K1
With Maior and Aldermen, how to receive the King,
Who comes to see Master Bruines Hospitall
To morrow consecrated by th'Cardinall,
And old Saint Marie's Spittle, here by Shoreditch.
MISTRIS FOSTER I sister, he and you may sit
'Bout what you will; Heaven I'm sure prospers it,
But I am ever crost; you have bin bound
For three great voyages, yet ne're run a ground;
Maid, wife, and widdow, and wife agen; have spread
Full and faire sayles, no wracks you e're did dread,
Nor e're felt any; but even close a shore,
I'm sunke, and midst of all my wealth made poore.
WIFE You must thanke heaven.
MISTRIS FOSTER I doe indeed, for all.
WIFE Sister, that hand can raise that gives the fall.

Enter KEEPER.

140 three] Dilke; thee Q.

KEEPER Master *Foster*, the new Sheriffe your brother is come to *Ludgate*, and I am come in haste to know your pleasure, if you would see him.

OLD FOSTER I'l see a fury first, hence, clap to the doore I prethee.

WIFE Why, 'tis your brother Sir.

ROBERT Father let's flye
The thunder of his rage.

WIFE Stand valiantly,
And let me beare the storme, all hurts that are,
And ruines in your bosomes I'l repayre.

Enter STEPHEN FOSTER.

STEPHEN Where's the Keeper, goe Sir, take my Officers,
And see your prisoners presently convey'd
From *Ludgate* unto *Newgate*, and the Counters.

KEEPER I shall Sir.

STEPHEN Let the Constables of the Wards assist you, goe, dispatch and take these with you;
How now, what mak'st thou here thou Catiffe? ha!
Com'st thou to stitch his wounds that seekes to cut
My Throate, dar'st thou in dispight
Releeve this Dotard?

OLD FOSTER Get thee from my sight, K1v
Thou divell in red; com'st thou in scarlet pride
To tread on thy poore Brother in a Iayle,
Is there but one small conduit-pipe that runs
Could water to my comfort, and wouldst thou
Cut off that thou cruell man?

STEPHEN Yes, I'l stop that pipe that thou maist pining sit,
When drops but fell on me, thou poysond'st it:
Thou thrust'st a sonnes name from thy cruell brest,
For cloathing of his Vncle; now that Vncle
Shall thrust him naked forth for clothing thee,
Banisht for ever from my wealth and me.

OLD FOSTER Thou canst not be to nature so uneven,
To punish that which has a pay from heaven;
Pitty I meane, and duty; Wouldst thou strike?

Wound me then, that will kill thee if I can,
Th'art no brother, and I'le be no man.
STEPHEN Thou ravest.
OLD FOSTER How can I choose? thou makest me mad,
For shame thou shouldst not make these white haires sad;
Churle, beat not my poore boy, let him not lose
Thy love for my sake, I had rather bruise
My soule with torments for a thousand yeeres,
Could I but live them, rather than salt teares
Thy malice draw from him; see here's thy gold,
Tell it, none's stole, my woes can ne'r be told.
ROBERT O misery! Is nature quite forgot?
OLD FOSTER Choke with thy dung-hill muck, and vex me not.
STEPHEN No, keepe it, he perhaps that money stole
From me, to give it thee, for which to vex thy Soule,
I'l turne him forth of doores, make him thy heire,
Of Iayles, miseries, curses, and dispaire;
For here I disinherit him of all.
OLD FOSTER No matter, lands to him in heaven will fall.
WIFE Good Husband.
MISTRIS FOSTER Gentle brother.
ROBERT Deare Vncle.
STEPHEN I am deafe.
OLD FOSTER And damn'd, the divels thumbs stop thine eares.
STEPHEN I'l make thee wash those curses off with teares. K2
Keeper, away with him out of my sight,
And doe Sir, as I charg'd you.
KEEPER Yes Sir; I will.
OLD FOSTER Poore tyranny; when Lions weake Lambs kill.
Exeunt [OLD FOSTER, ROBERT and KEEPER.]
STEPHEN How now wife, art vext yet?
WIFE Never so well content, beleeve me Sir;
Your mildnesse weares this maske of cruelty well.
STEPHEN I'm glad th'are gone, mine eyes with raine did swell,
And much adoe they had from powring downe:
The Keeper knows my minde, Wife I have paid
My brothers debts; and when he's out of doore

To march to Newgate, he shall be set free.
WIFE O let me kisse thee for this charity;
But for your Cozin Sir.
STEPHEN He's my lives best health,
The Boy shall not miscarry for more wealth
Than London Gates locke safe up every night,
My breath in blacke clouds flyes, my thoughts are white.
WIFE Why from Ludgate doe you remove prisoners?
STEPHEN This is my meaning wife;
I'l take the prison downe and build it new,
With Leads to walke on, Roomes large and faire:
For when my selfe lay there, the noysome ayre,
Choakt up my spirits, and none better know,
What prisoners feele, than they that taste the woe.
The workmen are appointed for the businesse,
I will ha't dispatcht before 'tis thought on.
WIFE In good deeds I will walke hand in hand with you,
There is a faire tenement, adjoyning
Close to the Gate that was my fathers,
I'l give it freely, take it downe, and adde
So much ground to the worke.
STEPHEN 'Tis fairely given.
Thy soule on prisoners prayers shall mount to heaven:
The Plummers and the Workemen have survey'd
The ground from Paddington; whence I'l have laid
Pipes / long to London to convey K2v
Sweet water into Ludgate from fresh Springs:
When charity tunes the pipe, the poore man sings.

Enter KEEPER.

How now Keeper.
KEEPER The prisoners are remov'd Sir.
STEPHEN What did you with my brother?
KEEPER As you commanded Sir, I have discharged him.
STEPHEN How did he meet that unexpected kindnesse?

232 Paddington; whence] Dilke; Paddington; from whence Q

KEEPER Troth Sir, as a man or'ecome'twixt griefe and gladnes,
But turning to his sonne, he fetcht a sigh
So violent, as if his heart would breake,
And silent, wept, having no power to speake.
WIFE 'Las good old man, some sweet bird must sing,
And give his sorrowes present comforting.
STEPHEN Not yet, I'l wracke his sorrowes to the height,
And of themselves they'l then sinke softly downe;
Keeper, goe thou agen after my brother,
Charge in my name him and his sonne to appeare
Before the King, to whom I will make knowne
Their wrongs against me; shewing just cause
To disinherit both by course of law. Be gone.
KEEPER I am gone Sir. Exit.
STEPHEN Come Wife.
WIFE What's your meaning Sir?
STEPHEN Thou shall know that anon.
The heavens oft scowle, clouds thicken, winds blow high,
Yet the brightest Sunne cleares all, and so will I. Exeunt.

[5.2] Enter, HENRY THE THIRD, MOUNTFORD, PEMBROKE, ARUNDELL, LORD MAIOR, SHERIFFE FOSTER, CARDINALL, BRUINE, &c.

KING O! welcome is all love, our peoples shouts
In their hearts language, make our benvenues,
Most high and soveraigne; we returne all thankes
Vnto our loving Cittizens, chiefely to you Sir,
Whose pious worke invites our Majesty
To royallize this place with our best presence,
Accompanied with this Reverend Cardinall;
Would we might, after many broyles,
End our dayes in these religious toyles;
We would worke most faithfully; but bounteous Sir, K3
How doe you call your buildings? 11
BRUYNE Vnlesse it please your Majesty to change it,
I call it, Domus Dei.
KING The house of God,

It is too good to change, pray you proceede.
BRUYNE These are my ends: to all distressed Christians,
Whose travailes this way bends the hospitall,
Shall free souccour be, for three dayes, and three nights
Sojourne, for dyet, and lodging, both sweet, and satisfying;
And if their neede be such, as much in Coyne,
As shall for three dayes more defray their further travaile;
This unto heaven, be you Testator, good my Liege,
And witnesse with me, noble Gentlemen,
Most free and faithfully, I dedicate.
KING An honourable worke, and deserves large memory.
MOUNTFORD 'Tis a good example, 'tis pitty 'tis no better followed.
ARUNDELL But say Sir, now in some future age,
Perhaps some two or three hundred yeere behinde us,
This place intended for a use so charitable,
Should bee vnhallowed agen, by villanous inhabitants;
Say whores, in the stead of christians,
And your hospitable Tenements, turn'd into stewes;
Would not this grieve you in your grave?
BRUYNE If my grave were capable of griefe:
Sure it would Sir.
KING Prethee be a false Prophet.
ARUNDELL I will, if I can, my Lord.
KING Let now our Heraulds in the streets proclaime,
The title, and office, of this hospitall;
Make knowne to all distressed travellors,
That we'le accept this charitable house,
This Domus Dei, shall be their free sojourne,
As is propos'd.

Enter the one way, Stephens WIFE, the other, MISTRIS FOSTER, IANE, OLD FOSTER, ROBERT and KEEPER. All kneele.

What are these peticioners?
ROBERT Each hath a knee for duty, the other for petition.
KING Rise, your dutie's done, your petitions K3v
Shall neede no knees, so your intents be honest,

Does none here know them?
STEPHEN Yes my good Lord, there's now a wonder in your sight.
KING A wonder, Master Sheriffe, you meane for beauty.
STEPHEN No my Lege, I would not so boast mine owne wife,
But 'tis a wonder that excels beauty.
KING A wonder in a woman; What is't I prethee?
STEPHEN Patience my Leige, this is a woman
That was never vext.
KING You may boast it largely;
'Tis a subjects happinesse above a Queenes;
Have you suites to us?
ROBERT I am the suppliant plaintiffe, royall _Henry_
From me their griefes take their originall.
KING What art thou?
ROBERT Even what your Grace shall please to make of me;
I was the son to this distressed father,
Vntill he tooke his paternity off,
And threw me from his love, then I became
Son to mine Vncle by adoption,
Who likewise that hath tane away againe,
And throwne me backe to poverty; never was Son
So tost betwixt two fathers, yet knowes not one,
For still the richest does despise his heire,
And I am backe expulst into despaire.
KING This may your vices cause.
ROBERT For that I come
To your impartiall censure for a doome.
KING We heare, speake on,
We know the parties, each one relate his griefe,
And if it lye in us, we'l yeeld reliefe;
'Tis first requisite that we know of you Sir,
The cause of this your Sonnes disinheritance.
OLD FOSTER Before I understood his vertuous minde,
Or weighed his disposition to be kind,
I did that froward worke; This now great man,
Was an unthrifty wretch, a prodigall then,
And I disdain'd to know his brotherhood,

Denyed reliefe to him; this childe kinde and good
Against my contradiction, did him releive,
As his / distressed Vncle, at this K4
I chide; forbade, still hee holds on his course,
He growes more kinde, and he in wasting worse;
My rage continued as it had begun,
And in that rage I threw away my sonne.
  STEPHEN The like plead I, my Lord: for when my state
Had rais'd it selfe by an uncertaine fate,
I tooke this out-cast childe, made him my owne,
As full and free, as I my selfe had sowne
The seede that brought him forth; for this my loue,
His oblieg'd duty presently did prove
A traytor to my trust, against my will,
Succouring that foe, which I did love so ill,
Onely for hating him; my charity
Being thus abus'd, and quit with injurie,
What could I then
But as his father erst, so I agen
Might throw him from my love? for worse is love abus'd
Then new borne hate, and should be soe refus'de:
I did a fathers part, if it were bad,
Blame him for both, there I my patterne had.
  KING You fall betwixt two pillars Sir, is't not so?
  ROBERT Vnhappy fate, my Lord, yet thus I pleade:
For this my fathers hate I might deserve,
I broke his precepts, and did unchildly swerve
From his commission, I to my Vncle gave
What was my fathers, striving thereby to save
His falne repute; he rag'd, I did it still,
Yet must confesse as it was well, twas ill,
Well in my love, me thought, ill to my fate:
For I thereby ruin'd my owne estate,
But that mine Vncle throwes me forth of doore
For the same cause he tooke me in before,
Beats sorest, gainst my bosome; if twere good
To take from a father for an Vncles foode,

In lawes of love and nature, how much rather
Might I abridge an Vncle for a father?
Charitie's a vertue generally stands,
And should dispersed be through all mens hands. K4v
Then would you keep't alone; for when your heire
I first adopted was, charity was there:
How errs your judgement then? seeing you see
What was good in you, makes sin in mee;
You'l say my father did it, oh throw away
That foule excuse; let not discretion stray
So farre a side; if custome lawfull make,
Then sin were lawfull for example sake;
Nor were those wasted goods only your owne,
Since part was mine having adoption;
Then doe me right, my Lord, yet doe no wrong,
For where my duty fail'd my love was strong.
  KING With an impartiall eare we have heard
Your loving story, 'tis both fayre and honest.
  STEPHEN O let me now anticipate your Grace,
And casting off the shadow of a face,
Shew my hearts true figure, how have I striv'd
To make this forc't counterfeit long liu'd,
And now it bursts; come into my heart,
I have two iewells here shall never part
From my loves eye watch, two worthy to be fil'd,
On times best record; a woman and a child,
Now Sir, to you I come, we must be friends,
Though envie wils not so, yet love contends
Gainst envy and her forces; my young yeares
Say I must offer first, a peace in teares.
  OLD FOSTER O let my shame my bosomes center breake!
Love is so young it coyes, but cannot speake.
  KING You blesse mine eyes with objects that become
The theater of Kings to looke upon.
  STEPHEN The keeper is discharg'd Sir, your debts are paid,
And from the prison y'are a new free man made:

132 me]Dilke; him Q.

Theres not a Creditor can aske you ought,
As your sonne did for me, so have I bought
Your liberty with mine, and to encrease it more,
Because I know bare liberty is poore
Without assistance: to raise your state agen, L1
The thirds of mine are yours, say you Amen.
WIFE No, not to that, you are kind brothers now,
Divide by halfes that love, and I'l allow.
STEPHEN Thou art onely wise in vertue, as thou setst downe,
So let it be, halfe my estate's your owne.
OLD FOSTER It whole redownes agen, for I am yours;
Forget this minute my forgetfull houres.
STEPHEN O, they are buried all Sir.
KING This union's good,
Such league should ever be in brotherhood.
STEPHEN Yet without boast, my Leige, let me relate
One small thing more, remorse of my owne state,
And my deare brothers worse succession;
For that we both have prisoners been in one
Selfe-same place of woe, and felt those throwes
That Ludgate yeelds; my charity bestowes
Some almes of comfort: Keeper you can speake it.
KEEPER And many hundreds more Sir, you have reedified
And built it faire, adding more ground to it,
And by pipes of lead from Paddington,
Drawne Water thither, free for all prisoners,
Lodgings likewise free, and a hundred pounds
Yearely, to make them fires for better comfort:
All this is almost finisht.
KING A worthy work, the better being done
In the Founders eie, not left unto succession.
STEPHEN O my good Lord, I ever keep in mind
An English Sentence, which my tutor is,
And teaches me to act my Charity
With mine owne hands, so doubtfull is Performance,
When the Benefactor's dead.
KING What is't I prethee?

STEPHEN This my good Lord,
Women are forgetfull, Children unkind,
Executors covetous, and take what they find,
If any man aske where the deads goods became,
The Executor sweares he dyed a poore man.
KING You have prevented well, so has this good Alderman,
I wish you many Schollers.
WIFE You make some doubt of me in this Sir;
Did you not say that women were forgetfull? L1v
KING You have vext her now Sir, how doe you answer that?
STEPHEN No my Lord, she's exempt from the proverbe.
WIFE No my Lord, I'l helpe it better, I doe confesse
That women are forgetfull, yet ne'r the lesse
I am exempt, I know my fate, and finde
My deare husband must not leave me behind,
But I must goe before him, and 'tis said,
The grave's good rest when women goe first to bed.
STEPHEN Thankes for thy excuse good wife, but not thy love
To fill my grave before me, I would not live
To see that day.
WIFE Prethee no more, I had rather be angry than flatter'd.
KING You have a wonder Master Sheriffe, a prizelesse jewell.
STEPHEN Many jewels my good Lord; a brother, wife, and child,
For this I would have strove even with a father,
How ere rough stormes did in my brows appeare,
Within my bosome it was alwaies cleare.
OLD FOSTER I give him to you now Sir.
STEPHEN I take him, and to him backe doe give,
All that my selfe behind in state shall leave.
OLD FOSTER And all that you gave me, I doe bestow,
So in one houre become full heire to two.
BRUYNE I claime a third by this bonds vertue, see
As a third father, thou art heire to me.
IANE I will not goe to him father on any of these conditions.
ROBERT You shall have love to boote too, sweet Iane.

221 me] those Q.

IANE Nay, and you play booty, I dare not trust you.

ROBERT What shall I say, except my hand and heart,
Ty'de in a True-loves Knot, ne'r to part.

IANE I marry Sir, these are better conditions than the inheritance of three fathers; let me have Love in *Esse*, let lands follow in *Posse*: now I'l have thee as fast as the Priest can dispatch us, let him read as fast as he can.

KING The liveliest harmony that ere I heard:
All instruments compar'd to these sweet tunes,
Are dull and harsh; I joy to see so good a childe,
A woman wonder, brothers reconcil'd; L2
You worthy Sir, did invite us to a feast,
Wee'l not forget it, but will bee your guest,
Because wee'l veiw these wonders o're agen,
Whose records doe deserve a brazen Pen,
But this above the rest, in golden text,
Shall be insculpt; *A Woman never Vext.*   *Exeunt.*

FINIS

Press Variants

Sheet A

Outer forme

A1 Title-page ROWLEY,] ROWLEY Bodl.[2]

A3 fruitlesse] fr uitlesse Bodl.[2] (1.1.49)

Inner forme

A2 it:] it? Ashley, Bodl.[2], Worc.[2], Keynes, Hunt. (1.1.10)

Sheet B

Outer forme

B2[v] then] hen Worc.[2] (1.2.49)

Clowne.] Clownr. Bute (1.2.52 S.D.)

B3 selfe,] selfe BL[2], Bodl.[3] (1.2.84)

Inner forme

B3[v] heaven;] hea ven Worc.[1], Worc.[2]; hea even BL[1], BL[2], Ashley, Dyce, Bodl.[1], Bodl.[2], Keynes, Bute, Hunt. (1.2.99)

turne to] turn e to Worc.[1]; tu rnto BL[1], BL[2], Ashley, Dyce, Keynes, Bute, Hunt., Bodl.[1], Bodl.[2] (1.2.100)

Sheet C

Outer forme

C4[v] In Ludgate] n Ludgate BL[1], BL[2], Ashley, Dyce, Worc.[1], Worc.[2], Bodl.[1], Bodl.[2], Bodl.[3], Bute (2.1.151)

Sheet D

Inner forme

D4 tedious,] ted ious Worc.[1], Bute, Hunt, BL[2], Bodl.[1], Bodl.[3] (3.1.31)

Sheet E

Outer forme

E1 soyld] solyd BL[1], BL[2], Ashley, Worc.[2], Bodl.[1], Bodl.[2], Bodl.[3], Hunt. (3.1.110)

E2[v] handsell] handfell Keynes, (3.1.194)

shall] shall (a inverted) BL[1], BL[2], Ashley, Worc.[2], Bodl.[1], Bodl.[2], Bodl.[3], Hunt. (3.1.204)

E3 sum] some BL[1], BL[2], Ashley, Worc.[2], Bodl.[1], Bodl.[2], Bodl.[3], (3.1.238)

E3] E5 BL[1], Bodl.[2]

Inner forme

E1[v] him] hi m BL[1], Bodl.[2] (3.1.113)

Additional Collations

Sheet A

Outer forme

A4^{v} Correlative] Corelative BL1, Ashley, Bodl.^{1}, Bodl.^{2}, Worc.^{1}, Worc.^{2}, Keynes, Hunt. (1.1.175)
reputation.] reputation‸ BL^{1}, BL^{2}, Ashley, Bodl.^{1}, Bodl.^{2}, Worc.^{1}, Worc.^{2}, Keynes, Hunt. (1.1.186)
world;] world‸ Bodl.^{2} (1.1.192)

Sheet F

Inner forme

F1^{v} smother] smoother BL[1], Bodl.[2], Keynes, Hunt. (3.2.61)

Kinsman] hinsman BL[1], Bodl.[2], Keynes, Hunt. (3.2.63)

F2 a] an Bodl.[2], Hunt., BL[1], Keynes (3.2.70)

Vncle; but] Vncle. But BL[1], Bodl.[2], Keynes, Hunt. (3.2.71)

F3^{v} good brother] goodbrother BL[1], Bodl.[2], Keynes, Hunt. (3.3.48)

O. Fost.] O, Fost. BL[1], Bodl.[2], Keynes, Hunt. (3.3.51 speech prefix; this text, OLD FOSTER)

Enigma's!] Enigmaes! BL[1], Bodl.[2], Keynes, Hunt. (3.3.51; this text, Enigmas!)

wife.] wife; BL[1], Bodl.[2], Keynes, Hunt. (3.3.60)

F4 enemy. Look,] enemy looke, BL[1], Bodl.[2], Keynes, Hunt. (3.3.78)

true, 'tis] true ‸'tis BL[1], Bodl.[2], Keynes, Hunt. (3.3.79)

Iockey's] Iockeye's BL[1], Bodl.[2], Keynes, Hunt. (3.3.83)

laughs] laughes BL[1], Bodl.[2], Keynes, Hunt. (3.3.87)

divided] devided BL[1], Bodl.[2], Keynes, Hunt. (3.3.108)

division] devision BL[1], Bodl.[2], Keynes, Hunt. (3.3.109)

Sheet G

Outer forme

G1 accent Sir, that] accent that BL[2], Ashley, Bodl.[3], Worc.[1], Worc.[2] (3.3.153)

G2^{v} say] say (a inverted) Ashley, Bodl.[3], Worc.[1], Worc.[2] (4.1.30)

Ste. 'Tis well. Bru.] Bru. 'Tis well. Ste. BL[2], Ashley, Bodl.[3], Worc.[1], Worc.[2] (4.1.50; this text, speech prefixes expanded.)

Inner forme

G2 our] ora Bodl.[3], Worc.[1], Worc.[2] (4.1.4)

Sheet I

Outer forme

I2^{v} tends] tend s BL[1], BL[2], Ashley, Bodl.[1], Bodl.[2], Worc.[2], Keynes, Hunt. (4.3.135)

Sheet K

Inner forme

K2 Woman] Woman (m inverted) BL[2], Ashley, Bodl.[1], Keynes, Hunt.

(running title)

K4 Vext.] Vext, BL^{2}, Ashley, Bodl.^{1}, Keynes (running title)
Him] H turned BL^{1}, Dyce, Bodl.^{2}, Bodl.^{3}, Worc.^{1}, Worc.^{2}, Bute,
(5.2.100; this text, him.)

Sheet L

Outer forme

L1 Paddington,] Paddingtun, Keynes, Hunt. (5.2.177)

Inner forme

L2 Worc.^{2}, Keynes, Hunt. lack centre ornament.

Emendation of Accidentals

1.1

6 fraught] fraHght

42 *Ludgate*] Ludgate

81 in troth] introth

100 of.] of:

101 it?] it.

118 cause?] cause.

135 Why,] Why

138 *Ludgate*.] Ludgate.

157 *Ludgate*] Ludgate

186 reputation.] reputation ‸

199 *London*,] London,

225 ha'te] hate

251 Cheese and] Cheeseand

1.2

122 *Thames*,] Thames,

2.1

5 Host:] *Host*:

72 further?] further.

80 Fullum.]Fullum:

81 *Putney*]Putney

you?]you:

109 Tester -]Tester ‸

151 *Ludgate*]Ludgate

152 *More-gate*] More-gate

195 shift -] shift ‸

200 to ‸] to'

206 tatter'd.] tatter'd ‸

224 art -] art ‸

241 *London*] London

244 *Smithfield*] Smithfield

288 with all] withall

304 choose.] choose?

311 blood and] bloodand

313 Vncle.] Vncle ‸

315 him.] him:

318 hand. *Exeunt.*] 319 Dogs, *Exeunt*‸

3.1

46 *Bulloyne*,]Bulloyne,

48 Knighthood;] Kinghthood;

127 Gentlemen?] Gentlemen.

131 With all]Withall

141 fraughtage?] fraughtage.

E2]E3

156 and]annd

193 sweet] sweeet

200 love-powder?] love-powder

238 traffique?] traffique.

246 venter?] venter.

293 restrain't,] restraint,

309 fathers farre] fathersfarre

312 love?] love.

314 *London*] London

317 Sir.] Sir‸

319 Sir?] Sir.

328 father;] father.

3.2

3 afflict] affiict (foul case)

6 *Roger*, where's]*Roger*. Where's

8 Sir?]Sir.

23 thwart] twhart

121 shape] shade (turned letter)

3.3

13 parchment?] parchment.

29 *Dover*,] Dover,

46 enemy.] enemy ‸

49 *Ludgate*] Ludgate

Hye-gate]Hye-gate

51 Enigmas!]Enigma's (corrected state)

58 *Cornehill*.] Cornehill.

88 *Ludgate*;] Ludgate;
91 *Walfleet*] Walfleet
116 envy;] envy ^
126 shortly;] shortly.
145 name] name.
146 same.] same ^
148 *London*] London
171 *Dover*;] Dover;
172 *Carybdas*] *Carybda's*
195 *Ludgate*,] Ludgate,
196 *Ludgate*.] Ludgate.
Newgate] Newgate

4.1

15 us.] us^
28 live well] livewell
36 in troth] introth
thou shalt] thoushalt
71 deere;] deere.
98 Cockney?] Cockney.
151 flat.] flat^
166 so,] so;
177 ready?] ready.
187 *Dover*] Dover
193 *London*;] London;
195 *Theames*] Theames
205 lost.]lost,
219 to th'dore]toth' dore
220 *Exeunt.*] Q places at 221.
229 *Norton Folgate*] Norton Folgate

4.2

6 *Thames*;] Thames;
12 *Ludgate*] Ludgate
20 *Ludgate*.] Ludgate.
28 brother -]brother.
74 barking] barkiug (turned letter)
91 *Ludgate*] Ludate

101 taste!] taste!

106 mercy!] mercy!

115 comfort!] comfort!

137 Ludgate;] Ludgate;

143 here^] here.

155 him.] him^

169 now?] now.

180 Ludgate,] Ludgate,

183 Fosters] Foster's

4.3

9 scorne!] scorne!

20 Lambskin.] Lambskin^

23 me,] me

34 Lambskin] Lambskin,

54 Vncle?] Vncle.

81 me?] me.

89 you.] you,

96 content?] content.

110 me?] me.

111 feet?] feet:

127 might.] might:

128 right.] right^

134 agree^] agree.

155 to th'] toth'

5.1

9 Ludgate?] Ludgate?

33 run,] run.

34 come.] come,

79 aside,] aside.

88 joy,] joy^

89 speak.] speak^

90 world^] world.

131 London,] London,

135 by th'] by'th

178 Pitty] Pirty (foul case)

180 Th'art] Tha'rt

210 *Newgate*,] Newgate,

229 STEPHEN] Q omits speech prefix

234 *Ludgate*^] *Ludgate*;

235 the pipe,] the, pipe

5.2

15 ends:] ends.^

33 capable of]capableof

41 *Dei*,] *Dei*:

sojourne,] fojourne, (foul case)

43 petition.]petition,

75 disinheritance.]disiuheritance^ (turned letter)

79 then,] then.

120 Charitie's^] Charitie's,

124 errs]er'rs

133 fail'd] fai'ld

139 counterfeit] co unterfeit

153 y'are] yare

154 ought,] onght, (turned letter)

155 for me,] forme,

190 forgetfull,]forgetfull.

197 forgetfull?]forgetfull,

Alterations to Lining

1.1

13-14 Dilke; Q:Five...pounds;/Read...cloathes.

17-19 Dilke; Q:As...bottomes/With...increase/To infinites.

38-40 Q:He...Sir,/Tis...conceite/But...him/So...expensive,/You... addition.

41-43 Q:Nay...quantity/Till...brother/Which...Sir,/And...him.

53-54 Dilke; Q:I...quicke-/Sands...Pigeon-holes,

61-71 Dilke; Q:Had...had/Made...charity/To...Some/Are...may/Encrease ...doe/Tax...stand/Idlely...blesse/This...some/Memorable... shall/Preserve...Doomesday.

78-79 Q:I...boy/Makes...on

93-98 Q:Tis...the/Condition...marryed/To...substance/Chiefely... her/Son...it,

105-10 Dilke; Q:Why...Woman?/I'le...complaints/Neither...others/ Injuries,...rightfull/Lawes...complaine/Sir,...heard.

115-17 Q:Would...made/To...some.

120-25 Q:Had...to/Complaine,...feete/The...estate:/He...pitty,/ But...love/He...waste

128-29 Dilke; Q prints as prose.

130-34 Q:You...kindred,/But...servant,/No...neither/Of those offices.

135-36 Dilke; Q:Why...threatned/Him...disorder?

144-47 Q:Prethee...present/Remedy,...worthy/Gentleman...censure/ For...equity.

149-50 Dilke; Q prints as one line.

151-52 Q:Now...you/So...can/Take...duty?

161-63 Q:Indeed...remou'd/From,...in/Debt;...Sirra?

168-76 Dilke; Q:You...betwixt/The...unto/My...my/Maker,...he/Hath ...not/A...nor/Him...duty/A...unto/My...selfe.

178-84 Q:He...voyde/That...disclayme/The...disclayme/Hast...engag'd/ For...him;/My...such/Fruitlesse recompence.

187-88 Dilke; Q:But...what/An...wife.

205-10 Q:I,...up/With...villaines;/Beg...come/Not...obey;

223-24 Dilke; Q:Bethinke...course/That...it.

225-28 Dilke; Q:Ha,...me/40....Tenement/Of...what/Can...this?

230-37 Dilke; Q:Tush,...wonder/At...gowne/Within...I/Hope...in/

Good...Maintenance/Doe...suffer'd/To...upbraide/Me...state/ And...himselfe;/But...my/Head...Cuz?

238-39 Q:Why...backe/Your fortunes.

240-45 Dilke; Q:Why...right,/This...backe,/And...Broker/In...on't:/ No,...surest/Way;...bones/And...sometimes.

247-51 Dilke; Q:As...given/Me...divells/Dam...listen,/Listen... henceforth/Turne...eate/Cheeseand...will/Not...strange?

256-57 Dilke; Q:Why...make/Thee...but/Follow my steps.

1.2

2-4 Dilke; Q:Yes...resolve/Me...What/Businesse...Churchman?/ Is...new/Husband?

6-9 Dilke; Q:Then...Mistris;/I...best/Service...you/Meane... Though/Most...dye/With an ill-will.

11-18 Dilke; Q:Why...mistris;/Take...head;/It...of/Your...Ivie/ Has...house;/If...heede,/There's...not/The...you/Cannot... wands;/You...defend/Your...pretty/Instructions...to/See...up.

19-20 Dodsley; Q:Well...you;/See,...gone?

21-23 Dilke; Q:I...you/As...mistris/Have...barly-breake,/Let...hell.

25-26 Dilke; Q:If...or/So...enter/Into...be.

28-30 Dilke; Q:Then...for'm:/What...must/Have...proves/Naught... Impost.

33-36 Dilke; Q:Nay,...too;/You...againe/To...tollage:/Me...no,/ He...no.

39-41 Dilke; Q:Mistris...rate/Good...dearth/Of...picke/Out...Clerke.

45-46 Q:Let...the/Table...voyder./What...Sirra?

47-48 Dilke; Q:Marry...Cod,/Soles...Playce.

50-52 Dilke; Q:Nay...first/Dresse...dresse/The...on.

76-77 Lamb; Q:That...meant/A...blessing;/Is...strange?

100-101 Dilke; Q:Health...to/Curses,...you:

115-19 Q:All...it/From...appoint/The...the/Magistrate;...but/You ...enough.

119-26 Q:One...little,/Yet...most/On't:...hap/In...Thames,/To... finger,/That...husband;/It...kept

136-37 Dilke; Q:O...fortunat'st/Woman...is/Found.

138 Dilke; Q:The...happy/To be robb'd.

139-41 Dilke; Q:Bring...strangest/Piece...saw,/Or...after,/A...thiefe.

143-44 Dilke; Q:Bring...not/Confesse...him.

148-49 Dilke; Q:No;...it/Home...paines./You...Sammon?

151-52 Dilke; Q:It...knowne/The...shillings./Is...Ring?

154-55 Dilke; Q:Your...shee/Bought...swallowed/This Gudgeon.

164-66 Dilke; Q:Alas,...fleg-/matique/Creature...faire,/And...Gold.

170-72 Dilke; Q:By...would/Have...ne'r/Have...should/Have...time.

173-77 Dilke; Q:Now...passe;/Give...sea:/There's...good/Lucke,... her/Away...would/Speake...against/Crosses,...lucke.

184-86 Q:O...am/O're...bosome/I...me.

187 Dilke; Q:I...close-stoole,/And't please you.

200-201 Dilke; Q:You...knowledge;/And...betweene/Both,...i'faith.

224-26 Q:The...it;/Good...grieve/I...thee:

234 Q:Not...marriage/Would...unhappy.

240-41 Dilke; Q:I,...husbands/To...enough.

243-44 Q:I...ready;/Yet...you.

2.1

1-4 Dilke; Q:Welcome...*Speranza*;/What's...in?/Cards,...sort'm/ Your...Mumchance?/Say...recreation?

7-8 Dilke; Q:Miscall...are/None...agoe.

10-14 Dilke; Q:Tush,...yet:/He...old:/'Tis...to/Begin...have/For ...not/Too...Boyes.

15 Dilke; Q:Hee...trust/To executors.

16-17 Dilke; Q:As...executors:/Who's...Host?

18-19 Dilke; Q:Honest...on't;/Towardly...Mistris.

22-23 Dilke; Q:We...so/Long...ready./Come, trip.

26-27 Dilke; Q:Now...faire/Boord;...*Boreas*.

28-33 Dilke; Q:How...Trundletayles;/My...Cosmographers:/My...uprore?/ Is...stickler;/I...mine/Owne...punish:/Have...Boyes;/He... pate/For...say.

34-35 Dilke; Q:A...to/Reward...now.

36-37 Dilke; Q prints as one line.

39-40 Dilke; Q:Seven...the/Deadly...throw.

48-49 Dilke; Q:I...two/Caters,...market.

50-57 Dilke; Q:So...now,/The...head,/Silence...vertuous,/Let'm... pawne/Till...welcome,/And welcome./How...take/Heede...proffit,/ Who...*Vrsa/Major*...there/No...quiet/For you?

59-61 Dilke; Q:I...I'l/Vtter...lay/Vp...say.

62-63 Dilke; Q:Your...it/Drawes...apparell.

65-66 Dilke; Q:Foote,...was/Begotten;...so/Haunted with threes.

70-71 Dilke; Q:Why...himselfe/Is...the/Shilling with him.

75-76 Dilke; Q:I...but/The...bones.

89-90 Dilke; Q:Nay...lord/Of...Sir.

92-93 Dilke; Q:Why,...time:/Some...has/Lifted...say.

94-95 Dilke; Q:There...house/Till...thee.

96-97 Dilke; Q:Mine...with/Oringe tawney velvet.

99-100 Dilke; Q:Y'are...rascals;/Is...in?

102-106 Dilke; Q:Cuz,...diminish't/But...a/Friend,...it/Came... halfe,/And...would/Trust...pence.

108-109 Dilke; Q:Pox...had/Had...for/The tother Tester

111-13 Dilke; Q:But...never/see...I/Breake...after/This...wrong.

117-20 Q:Nay,...little/This...good/Son...his/Vncle here.

121-22 Q:You...best/Affliction...impatient.

124-25 Dilke; Q:We...see/The...sight?

126-28 Q:Did...counsell/Betweene...hell,/The...horseway.

130-34 Q:Mother?...but/Many...thou/Mine...and/Put...vex/Me thus.

134-35 Dodsley; Q prints as one line.

136-38 Dilke; Q:I'l...else/I'l...witnesse/With...him.

140-41 Q prints as one line.

142-46 Dilke; Q:And...father/Be...have/Bin...thy/Mothers...my/ Displeasure.

147-49 Q:Thou...hadst/Bin...to/Ride...his/Honest childe.

150-51 Q:Out...thee/In shortly.

156-57 Dilke; Q:Nay...lies,/Shee...than/One lye.

167-68 Q:O...ever/Woman...abus'd?

174-75 Q:Your...doe/Your...Gossip?

176-82 Q:I...thou/Tatterdemallion;...a/Husband;...Wild-fire!/My... pantle,/Pantle,...woman:/But...errands.

185-88 Q:You...a/Peacefull...angry/Father,...spleene/Against me.

188-90 Q:Sir,...your/Consanguinity...teach/You...Sir,/If...leave.

199-200 Q:I'l...good/Course...run./Yet...it.

204-205 Dilke; Q:I...all/This...Hazard.

208-209 Dilke; Q:'Tis...have;/I...wit;/My...sure.

210-11 Dilke; Q:I...Money:/A...service,/And want.

212-14 Dilke; Q:Why...Frock/And...nor/My...side.

215-16 Dilke; Q:I...it/Then,...unfurnisht?/Thou...poore?

219-24 Dilke; Q:The...to/Seeke...hope/To...is/Not...that/Thou... out-/Crosse...art

228-29 Dilke; Q:So...then/As...widow/Such...eare.

232-36 Dilke; Q:I'd...oath:/I...promise/Her...man;/Marry...matter,/ 'Tis...rak'd/It...labours.

238-39 Dilke; Q:Promise...fly:/But...her?

240-46 Dilke; Q:The...common/Than...be/Furnish'd...no/Forrainers... once:/Nay,...that/Smithfield...I'l/Warrant...as/Twas...before.

247-48 Dilke; Q:S'foote,...for/My...none.

249-52 Dilke; Q:Thou...rul'd,/I'l...of/The...but/To...and/I'd...her.

253-55 Dilke; Q:Spend...you/In...bound/For...word/For that.

256-58 Dilke; Q:Onely...honest/To...injuries/Shall...her.

259-61 Dilke; Q:I'l...much,/That...drinke,/And...turne.

263-64 Dilke; Q:Your...worse;/I...widdow.

266-67 Dilke; Q:I'l...me/The...you.

271-73 Dilke; Q:Give...give/The...we'l/Goe...blinde/Bargaine of it.

274 Dilke; Q:I...be/In...Widow.

275-76 Dilke; Q:No,...how/E'r...estate/Spare...worst.

279-81 Dilke; Q:No,...blinde/Bargaines;...give/Me...budge/A foote.

286-88 Dilke; Q:I...I'd/Not...would/Be...mine,/I'l...faults.

290-92 Dilke; Q:Here's...Sir./Cozin,...you/Sirra,...Wife.

293-96 Dilke; Q:I...Shagragge,/My...may/Imagine...the/Beane...but/ 'Tis...you.

299-303 Dilke; Q:You...come,/Give...goe./He'l...drunke;/Why,...we'l/ Stand...here/Is...you/See...choyse,/If...here.

306-307 Q:'Tis...blacke/Stormes;...shelter.

308-309 Q:I...conceives,/I...yet.

310-311 Dilke; Q:I...suffer/This...rags.

317-18 Dilke; Q:Thou...fellow,/Though...hand.

319-25 Dilke; Q:I'l...Dogs,/If...lowsie/Companion;...this?/Have... honest,/Hansome,...to/Marry...rag/About...since/My...me:

330-31 Q:But...didst/Lay...point?

332-34 Dilke; Q:Do'st...'twas/To...to/Cast...all,/I'l...first.

3.1

2-6 Q:Has...spoke/It...merchandize,/This...gentle/Bloods... Cittizen.

10-13 Dilke; Q:'Tis...mine/Owne...like/Many...Knighthood,/Sometimes ...I/Know't...experience.

14-17 Dilke; Q:Well...doe/By...Gentlemen/Have...lyen/On...I/Have ...observation.

18-21 Dilke; Q:I...Chapmen:/If...would/Willingly...they/Would... the/Tone...his/Observation very much.

22-24 Dilke; Q:Sir,...experience,/Meddle...the/More...my/Experience, ...shallow.

25-30 Dilke; Q:But...wide;/You...as/Your...your/Experience...will/ Give...the/Fill's,...the/Young...will/Observe.

31-32 Dilke; Q:Sweete...not/Experience;...are/Best...women.

36-38 Dilke; Q:Yes,...too:/For...name,/As...sped/Well...actions.

40-42 Dilke; Q:You...his/Nativity...part/Of...for/That...times.

43-49 Dilke; Q:Your...mine/Owne...is/*Speedwell*,...on/Old...as/ Bulloyne,...a/Title...has/Added...Kinghthood;/So...cal'd/ *Sir*...experience.

50-52 Dilke; Q:If...as/Your...rather/Than...reported.

53-54 Dilke; Q:You...good,/And...experience.

55-56 Dilke; Q:Nay,...observe/Mine;...harmelesse.

57 Dilke; Q:On...you/Should be briefe.

58-62 Dilke; Q:My...disposition,/In...I/Have...fathers/Decease,... vanguard/Of...that/I...*Lambskin*.

64-68 Dilke; Q:My...a/Tradesman;...fathers/And...in/Their...my/ Mother...did/Occupy...marryed;/Then...borne.

70-71 Dilke; Q:Truly...say;/Then...up/A Brewhouse.

73-75 Dilke; Q:Your...Tallyes/At...much/Delight...to/Deale...Nick.

77-78 Dilke; Q:Your...to/The...that/Face of yours.

79-80 Dilke; Q:Sir,...it/From the rest.

81-82 Dilke; Q:You...Virgin,/I...face.

84-85 Dilke; Q:I...love:/For...love/Shall...yours.

89-90 Dilke; Q:In...body,/As...experience.

94-95 Dilke; Q:I...treble,/If...you.

96-97 Dilke; Q:I...beholding/To...it.

98-100 Dilke; Q:Requite...be/Sir...your/Love...Lady,/And...experience.

101-102 Dilke; Q:I...And/That...Ladies,/As...observation.

106-107 Dilke; Q:If...Sir,/I'l...you;/That's flat, Sir.

108 Dilke; Q:Nay,...quarrell,/Till...what.

109-10 Dilke; Q:Oh,...Gentlemen!/The...any/Vncivill...in't.

111-13 Dilke; Q:Let...I'l/Throw...I/Scorne...knighthood,/I...on/My purse.

115-16 Dilke; Q:You...ever,/I...thing.

117 Dilke; Q:Sir,...requests/To...you.

118-20 Dilke; Q:Does...Gentlemen,/Please...Garden/Awhile,...company.

122-23 Dilke; Q:You...redeeme/Me...pretty/Things...uses.

124-25 Dilke; Q:Prethee...awhile,/If...enough;/But...not.

126-27 Dilke; Q:Nay...without/Any...not/Be...Gentlemen.

131-32 Dilke; Q:Withall...place/Promises...Master/Innocent,...behinde.

133-34 Dilke; Q:Right...that/Is...desire/And...little.

140-41 Dilke; Q:Does...ships/Are...Downes/With...fraughtage.

142-45 Dilke; Q:Yes...River:/Master...more/Such...particulars/Of...return'd/With trebble blessings.

146-49 Q:Let...call/In...him/Run...this/Newes...Merchant;

154-55 Q:To...better/Like...Foster,

170-71 Dilke; Q:I...you/Have...him.

172-73 Q:Well,...my/Daughter...garden.

175-77 Q:Sir,...the/Same...fortunes.

181-87 Dilke; Q:I...you'm,/I'd...I'd/Seeth...to/Keepe'm...all/The ...quarrell/In...the/Other...his/Mouth...paines/For't,...without/Any farther entercourse.

191-92 Dilke; Q:Three's...in/Deede,...farther,/If...that.

194-95 Dilke; Q:Take...day;/Perhaps...were/Best...time.

196-97 Dilke; Q:There...plaine/Dealing:...houres.

200-201 Dilke; Q:Nor...I'l/Make...can.

203-205 Q:Leave...selfe;/And...his/Fathers...you.

206-10 Dilke; Q:Never...him/Kindely,...him-/Selfe,...father./But ...for/That's...overcome/My Suitors in.

211-12 Dilke; Q:I...walke/Into...sweetes.

213-14 Dilke; Q:Taste...growes/Honesty,...you.

216-20 Dilke; Q:By...hold/You...y'faith,/If...eate/Sorrill...selfe:/No...wholsome/Hearbes;...ripen/The whil'st.

223-25 Dilke; Q:Goe,...her/A...comes/His...we/Good newes?

226 Dilke; Q;Sir,...venture/Is...encrease.

243-45 Dilke; Q:Which...to/The...such.

247 Q:Pray...Sir./Twenty thousand pounds.

248-49 Dilke; Q:Nay,...much;/Will...thirty?

251-52 Dilke; Q:I...thousand/Pounds...yours.

253-54 Dilke; Q:If...ready/Cash,...Monethes.

255-56 Q:'Tis...you/Observe...drawne./They shall Sir.

260 Dilke; Q:Beleeve...large/Gainer by you.

261-63 Dilke; Q:Much...one/Thing...you/Let me entreate./What...Sir?

266-67 Q:He...bar/To...duty.

269-71 Dilke; Q:For...my/Vow...deafe,/Obdurat...them.

272-77 Q:Nay...your/Words...last/Reformation,...againe,/And...the/ Dicing...no/Father...me.

278-80 Q:Well...the/Garden...along/With...thus;

284-85 Dilke; Q:Not...your/Knee,...you.

286-89 Q:Goe,...to/Finde...wants/More...the/Conduite...ran.

292-94 Q:Sir,...upon/This...Mistris/Iane,...doe.

295-97 Q:I,...trust/To...you'l/Not...Gentlewoman

300-302 Q:Sir,...bills;/Other...thee,/Beg...slave;

306 Q:Meane...you;/You...it.

316 Q:Mother...newes/Is...young?

320-24 Dilke; Q:Very...did/Nothing...me/A...him/He...Popperin;/ And...Rose,/And...paines.

325-26 Dilke; Q:Well...quench/'M...roughnesse

3.2

4-5 Q:I...make;/'Tis...you

6 Q:A...hope./Roger,...Master?

9-13 Dilke; Q:'Tis...within;/Hee...be/Content:...good/While,... be/Farther...For/I'm...leave/You...with.

15-16 Q:Where...little,/Being...nomine,/When...re.

18-21 Dilke; Q:In...kinde/Husband,...another/Counting-house... tumbling/Over...shall/Heare...againe.

22-23 Dilke; Q:Why...his/Dispose;...him?

36-37 Dilke; Q:Perhaps...wast'd/My...to/Good for me.

38-39 Q:Content...gone,/I,...memorie;

48-59 Dilke; Q:Now...is;/You...now/You...husband,/That,...law,/ I...covetous/Rascall,...But/'Tis...fairely/Offered,...had/ Other...those/That...away/All...three/Whores...out/In...where-/ As...of/These...must/Take what followes.

75-76 Dodsley; Q:'Tis...instigation

82-84 Q:Cozin,...home,/You...inheritance,

92-94 Dilke; Q:As...and/Propinquitie;...substance.

94-98 You...both,/My...duty/Even...all/The...not/Forgetting... father;

3.3

2-6 Q:Would...Publicke/Blazon...now;/I'l...belong./Sir,...debt,/ Twelve...remaines/You...rest,/And...time.

7-9 Q:Pray...once/Throw...compleate/Merchant,...ever:

13-14 Q:Be...Chapman:/What...*Foster*?

17-19 Q:I...Ware-/Houses...fraught;/I'l...that/I...looser.

20-21 Q:I...our/Factors...both.

21-25 Q:Mine...businesse;/You...commodities/Betwixt...but/Little ...home.

28-31 Q:Not...they/Put...into/Saint...friendly.

38-39 Dilke; Q:I...your/Ship...cost.

40-41 Dilke; Q:Beshrew...a/Sufficient...Sir.

44-45 Dilke; Q:How...felici-/ty?/What ayl'st thou?

49-50 Q:No...bravely,/An...least.

52 Q:Why,...newes;/Hee's marryed forsooth.

53 Dilke; Q:How,...choose/So slightly.

54-58 Q:A...liv'd/The...is't,/Thinke...give/You...rich/Widdow of Cornehill.

64-67 Dilke; Q:But...e'r/This...the/Brazen...my/Infinite substance.

67-68 Q prints as prose.

92-94 Q:No,...who/Should...dayes.

108-109 Dilke; Q:I...that/Might...division.

116 Q:Ha,...businesse/Is to you.

127-28 Dilke; Q:By...dye,/He...office.

129-30 Q:Then...*George*./And...looke/To...cannot.

139-40 Dilke; Q:Th'art...it/Offend...thee.

147-48 Dilke; Q:See...*Richard*;/Now...crown'd/The...Merchant.

164-65 Dilke; Q:O...for/this/Sad croake.

165-66 Q prints as one line.

166-69 Q:No,...therefore/Let...thou/Hast...Ware-houses,/And...before/ Thee.

175-76 Dilke; Q:Dam...farther/Mischievous relation.

4.1

1-2 Dilke; Q:Gentlemen,...please/You...garden,/Hee'l...long.

3-4 Dilke; Q:Your...observation/in you,/And...Father.

5-10 Dilke; Q:Experience...inno-/cent,/And...me,/And...Crackers;/ My...when/Thy...Chimney-/Corner....by/Mine owne experience.

11-14 Dilke; Q:Prethee...Gentlewoman/With...laid/Downe...into/ Whose...him/Take...Bucklers.

17-18 Dilke; Q:We...setting/Vp,...favour.

28-29 Dilke; Q:Speedwell,...well,/Change...else.

32-33 Dilke; Q:A...in/My...him.

36-38 Dilke; Q:That's...shalt/Finde...Sweete/Mistris,...basket?

41-42 Dilke; Q:Ah,...must/Boord...private.

44-49 Q:Come...few/Words...in/Bargaining...stay/Moneths,...parley./ Broad-clothes,...I/Lately...owne.

54-55 Dilke; Q:Good...still/Offend...jarring

62-66 Q:Yet...mine/Owne...line/Of...bin/Dead,...him.

66-67 Dilke; Q prints as one line.

67-70 Dilke; Q:True...want/And...that/Good...blood;

77 Dilke; Q:Wee'l...friends/Welcome.

81-83 Dilke; Q:Zounds...Bush/And...Citty/Bowler...cast.

88-90 Dilke; QYou...turn'd/Vp...spruce/Cittizen...Oh/These...firkers.

97-100 Dilke; Q:S'foote,...Gallymaw-fryes;/Shall...word/My...those/ That...a/Gudgion.

101-102 Dilke; Q:You...I/Shall...you.

109-10 Q:Hee's...me;/And...Gentlemen.

111-14 Dilke; Q:And...equalls;/For...her/A...what/I...but/What... experience.

115-19 Dilke; Q:Speake...as/Good...of/Love...dares,/And...love,/ Than...worth.

120-22 Dilke; Q:Ha?...bold;/My...you;/You...is/Foster;...give?

123-24 Dilke; Q:Yes,...Alleyes,/Or...Alleyes.

132-34 Dilke; Q:Well...Speedwell;/Ha?...medicine/To...Sir.

135-36 Q:No...here,/But...Cozin.

137-40 Q:Very...you/Here...y'faith./See,...Gallants/Are...Predecessor/For...apiece./Cozin,...straite.

144-46 Dilke; Q:A...worke,/Legs...waite/At...cold.

147-51 Dilke; Q:Knight,...Knight/Run...tarry,/And...the/Wench...to/Place...Counter,/I'l...flat.

153-55 Q:I...seeke/To...your/Wealth...weakenesse;

158-61 Dilke; Q:We'l...Sir,/Here...theame/Of...happy/Woman...welcome/Mistris Foster.

162-65 Q:Wife,...Speedwell/And...torne/Poore...name/Of...both/To...away.

168-71 Dilke; Q:At...to/Lock...loose:/'Twas...to/Rid...Iane,

177-80 Q:Yes,...servants,/Who...Custome-/House,...them,/Sir,...newes.

194-96 Dilke; Q:But...were/Swallowed,...yet/The...lost.

196-97 Q:O...backe.

197-202 Q:Ha?...you'l/Sit...him,/Nay...teares/For...drop/Blood?...hath/Iustly...him.

203-205 Q:'Tis...my/Part...lost,

205-208 Q:Greedy...swallowed;/'Tis...more/Than...misery.

211-212 Q:And...heart-strings:/In...her.

223 Dodsley; Q:What,...timber/Brought...appointed?

224-25 Dilke; Q:Yes,...the/Worke,...least.

4.2

9-17 Dilke; Q:I...diligence/Assist...to/Helpe...secure/My...Executions,/Which,...will/Thunder...what/Is...agree;/If...dye.

25-26 Dilke; Q:I...free/Citizen;...well?

27-28 Q:Yes...losses,/Yet...brother.

32-33 Q:Prethee...a/Bad...attendance,

35-37 Dilke; Q:Must swallow pills/With...Sir,/And...so/Low...driven.

39-43 Q:So,...this/Cudgelling,...shalt/Have...that/Cover...from/My...buried.

57 Q:Oh,...sonne:/I'l leave them.

105-106 Lamb; Q:Bread,...a/Loafe...mercy!

109-10 Q:Bread,...back/Your...prisoners;/One...mercy.

117-18 Lamb; Q:Bread,...one/Penny...bread.

130-31 Lamb; Q prints as one line.

134-39 Q:So...me;/I...churlish/Wretch,...taken/Shelter...me/Not, ...warning:/Fawne...him,/If...love.

151-52 Dilke; Q:Bread,...remember/The...mercy,/One penny.

154-55 Dilke; Q prints as one line.

155-57 Lamb; Q:O...feele?/Earth...true,/Yet...unkind.

159-60 Dilke; Q prints as one line.

170-71 Dilke; Q:One...new/Come...him/Better...thinke.

172-74 Q:I...know/Him...grate,/And...beg,/There's...and/Take... demand.

4.3

8-9 Q:O...and/Happinesse;...scorne!

13-14 Dodsley; Q:Marry...creatures/Scarce...speake/With you.

16-19 Dilke; Q:Nay,...a/Thing...the/World,...be/Wondered...other/ Is...race,/And...Gentleman.

28-30 Dilke; Q:I...hands/Mistris,...money/INto...great/Tearmes...it.

33-35 Dilke; Q:And...counter/Mistris;...Lambskin,/Knowes...binder.

36-37 Dilke; Q:No...though/It...presently.

38-39 Dilke; Q:I...alwayes,/'Tis...you.

42-45 Dilke; Q:For...my/Shoulders...love/Tobacco,...Woodstreet-/ Pipes;...hence:

54-55 Q:He's...comming/With...Aldermen.

56-57 Q:Zoundes...come/The...off.

73-74 Dilke; Q:To...my/Poore old father.

78-79 Q prints as one line.

84-86 Q:I...Gentlemen,/What...pay?

87-89 Dilke; Q:And...knew/Where...case:/Mistris,...the/Skin...you,

93-95 Q:All...quit,/For...to/My...canceld:

98 Q:Goe...their/Money,...drinke.

99-102 Dilke; Q:I'le...come/Gallants...bumbast/Your...lookes/As ...could/Take...into/The dog-house.

103 Dilke; Q:How...thou/Musing on?

104-105 Q:I...Sir./A...what?/For...unmeet

110-11 Q:Wouldst...me./Would...feet:/Doe...ill.

112-13 Dilke; Q:Thy...wings/I'l...heaven.

155-57 Dilke; Q:Come...your/Kinsman,...hinder/Him...Alderman,

5.1

1-2 Dilke; Q:Come,...at/Funerals,...and/Laugh...heart.

5-8 Dilke; Q:No?...neither/Meate,...the/House...yee,/Sir,...Sir:/ Nay,...neither.

9-10 Q:Ha?...Ludgate?/Yes Sir./A...up/Alive and buryed?

11-21 Q:O,...comfort/Like...doores/And...keepe/Her...body/Deare... too;/Oh...first/In...ten/Drops...water,/But...whence/Should... doe/Beate...roome.

22-25 Dilke; Q:No...set/Before...heaven/Provide...the/Ayre...thankefull,/ And...you.

27-28 Dilke; Q:The...balme/Into...deare/Husband...patience.

29-31 Dilke; Q:O...the/Sea's...shall/I...multiply?

32-33 Dilke; Q prints as one line.

35 Q:Besides...cannot/Be great.

36-37 Q:But...seas/Bottome./It...rise.

60-62 Lamb; Q:Heaven...it/Well,...off.

88-89 Q prints as one line.

95-97 Dilke; Q:And...my/Blessings...charity

98 Q:Here...wife,/Welcome deare sister.

111-12 Dilke; Q:Faith...dice,/Nor drabbing.

112-13 Dilke; Q:Sir,...father/You relieve.

119-20 Dilke; Q:What...have/Made...cheekes?

120-22 Dilke; Q:Nothing...well:/The...love,/Let...same;

127-28 Dilke; Q:Frets...higher/Rack'd...sweetest.

137-44 Dilke; Q:I...will;/Heaven...crost;/You...voyages,/Yet... widdow,/And...sayles,/No...any;/But...of/All...poore..

147-49 Q:Master...brother/Is...haste/To...him.

151-52 Q:Father...rage.

152-54 Dilke; Q:Stand...hurts/That...repayre.

155-57 Dilke; Q:Where's...take/My...prisoners/Presently...unto/ *Newgate*,...Counters.

159-64 Q:Let...you,/Goe,...now,/What...com'st/Thou...cut/My...this/ Dotard?

164-69 Dilke; Q:Get...red;/Com'st...poore/Brother...conduit-/pipe... and/Wouldst...man?

185-87 Dilke; Q:My...could/I...thy/Malice...gold,

192-95 Dilke; Q:From...thy/Soule,...him/Thy...dispaire;

215 Dilke; Q:My...thoughts/Are white.

226-29 Dilke; Q:There...Gate/That...downe,/And...worke.

231-35 Dilke; Q:The...ground/From...pipes/Long...Ludgate;/From... the/Poore man sings.

5.2

5-8 Dilke; Q:Whose...royallize/This...this/Reverend...broyles,

13-14 Dilke; Q prints as prose.

18-23 Dilke; Q:Sojourne,...and/Satisfying;...in/Coyne,...their/ Further...you/Testator,...noble/Gentlemen,...dedicate.

26-32 Q:But...some/two...place/Intended...bee/Vnhallowed...whores,/ In...hospitable/Tenements,...grieve/You...grave?

33-34 Q prints as one line.

39-42 Dilke; Q:Make...that/We'le...Dei:/Shall...propos'd.

44-46 Dilke; Q:Rise...neede/No...does/None...them?

49-50 Dilke; Q:No...mine/Owne...beauty.

52-53 Q:Patience...that/Was never vext.

53-55 Q:You...happinesse/Above...us?

60-63 Dilke; Q:I...he/Tooke...love,/The...adoption,

65-68 Dilke; Q:And...was/Son...knowes/Not...heire,/And...despaire.

69-70 Dilke; Q prints as one line.

71-75 Dilke; Q:We...parties,/Each...us,/We'l...we/Know... disiuheritance.

82-84 Dilke; Q:Against...his/Distressed...forbade,/Still...course,

96-100 Q:Onely...thus/Abus'd,...then/But...throw/Him...abus'd

166-67 Dilke; Q:This...brotherhood.

177-81 Q:And...drawne/Water...lodgings/Likewise...make/Them...finisht.

182-83 Dilke; Q:A...eie,/Not...succession.

184-88 Dilke; Q:O...English/Sentence,...my/Charity...is/Performance, ...dead.

189-91 Dilke; Q:This...forgetfull./Children...find,

207-208 Q prints as one line.

227-30 Dilke; Q:I...the/Inheritance...have/Love...Posse:/Now... Priest/Can...can.

Commentary

Dramatis Personae

INNOCENT LAMBSKIN: Innocent: a) foolish; b) guiltless. Lambskin: parchment, thus debtors' bonds and by extension a euphemism for 'to be in debt'. Cf. *The Compter's Commonwealth*, F2:

> Now my young Gallant (that neuer before this time was lapped vp in Lambskinne...)

The Shoemaker's Holiday, I4^{v}: (ed. Bowers, 5.4.8-10.)

> ...let wine be plentiful as beere, and beere as water, hang these penny pinching fathers, that cramme wealth in innocent lamb skinnes.

Brewer, *The Love-Sick King*, B4^{v}:

> Thorn. This Halfpenny, and this Millan Needle, shall I multiply to a Million of Halfpence, and this innocent Lamb-skin to a Magnificent Lordship.

CLOWN: also called 'Roger' or 'Hodge'. Hodge: familiar form of Roger. Both forms are typical names for stage servants and clowns; see, e.g., *Gammer Gurton's Needle*, *A Warning for Fair Women*, *Thomas Lord Cromwell*, *The Shoemaker's Holiday*, *The English Traveller*.

HOST: called 'Boxall' in the entry for Act 2 only.

HENRY III: according to Dilke, printer's error for Henry VI. Walter Bruine lived during Henry III's reign, Stephen Foster in Henry VI's. There seems no reason to suppose a misprint: Henry III was famous for his piety and also as the chief builder of Westminster Abbey. He is thus easily identifiable with the play's King.

Pembroke, Cardinal, Lord Mayor: 'ghost' characters, listed in Henry III's entry but not mentioned again. Possibly present to fill out the scene, or an indication that 5.2 was partially revised.

1.1

3 in good: a) to good effect, successfully; b) in merchandise. halcion gale: favourable breeze. halcion:

> A little birde that layeth hir egges on the sea sandes. when she layeth, be the sea neuer so troublous, it becommeth sodenly calme vntil the yonge be hatched.

(Cooper, *Thesaurus*, F6, 'Alcedo'.) Thus: calm, peaceful. gale: strong, but not tempestuous wind.

4-5 *Playes...makes'm big*: a common image. Cf., e.g., *A Midsummer Night's Dream*, 504-5 (2.1.128-9):

> When we haue laught to see the sailes conceiue,
> And grow big bellied with the wanton winde.

Day, *Isle of Gulls*, $C4^v$:

> *Basil* My thoughts come like a saile afore the wind, swolne big with newes, and thine eares the midwife must deliuer me of this burden.

Heywood, *The Brazen Age*, I1:

> *Phoebus* There see I Marchants trading and their sayles
> Big bellied with the wind.

Dick of Devonshire, fol. 31:

> the Brasille fleete
>
> ...Is putting into harbour, and aloud
> calls for a Midwife, she is great wth gold
> & longs to be delivered.

5 *envy*: Hazlitt emends to 'embryo' but Q's reading is possible. The ships are 'pregnant' with the envy they will cause when they land; 'vaporous' a) because dependent on the wind; b) borne on the breath (of rumour).

6 *Tis no more yet*: taking 'vaporous' as b). 'It's all still in the wind', or, 'don't count your chickens'.

fraught: a) cargo of ship; b) burden, load; c) used fig. of a woman in childbirth. Cf. C. Brooke, *The Ghost of Richard III*, xii:

> ...shee long'd to see
> Her burth'nous fraught: at last she brought forth me.

(Quoted *OED* *sb*. 3.)

15 *B, ss and l...l, ss, and o*: merchants' marks attached to cloth to show its value, as price-tags. Cf. Middleton, *Anything for a Quiet Life*, C4:

> *Frank*: The price? *Cham*. Look on the mark, *George*.
> *George*: *O* *Souse* and *P*, by my facks, sir.
> *Cham*: The best sort then, sixteen a yard, nothing

to be bated.

Ibid, D1:

> George: but for the Stuff Sir, 'tis L. ss and K.

Heywood, The Fair Maid of the Exchange, B1^{v}:

> Phil: Stay Vrsula, haue you those sutes of Ruffes,
> Those stomachers, and that fine peece of Lawne
> Marck'd with the Letters CC and S.

17 lay: load with cargo.

18 bottomes: ships; used as an extended metaphor of the ship's loading.

27 the merchants casualty: the merchant is liable to chance or to suffer accidents. casualty: 'state of subjection to change; liability to accident; precariousness, uncertainty.' (OED 3.)

29 hopes Embleme the anchor: cf. Hebrews 6.19, 'Which hope we haue as an anker of the soule, both sure and stedfast...' The anchor is often used as an emblem in, e.g., printers' devices; see McKerrow 164, 170, 192, 195, 210, 222, 232, 233. Cf. also the punning emblem to 'January' in The Shepherd's Calendar:

> Emblem: Anchora speme. Gloss:...the meaning wherof is, that notwithstanding his extreme passion and lucklesse loue, yet leaning on hope, he is some what recomforted.

Killigrew, Claracilla, E7^{v}:

> And dee heare let him be broke upon an Anchor,
> That on hopes emblem the wretch may meete
> His despairing crosse.

31 Should not the Sea: ironic anticipation. Cf. Old Foster's reaction at 3.3.170ff.

38 proper: a) belonging peculiarly to himself; b) fit, suitable.

39 conceite: imagine.

40 chargeable: demanding a) much expense; b) responsibility.

inseparable: cannot be cast off.

42 Ludgate: debtors' prison at the Ludgate, west of St. Paul's, for freemen of the City.

43 part of your treasure: echoing Matt. 6.20-21, 'But lay vp for your selues treasures in heauen...For where your treasure is, there will your heart be also.'

44 vulgar blemish: common slur.

51 dressd: the compositor mis-read terminal d to produce Q's 'dresse'; see G.R. Proudfoot,

> ...one of the most common of all confusions to which English secretary hand is liable, that of *e* and *d*, particularly in final position.

('Dramatic Manuscripts and the Editor', *Editing Renaissance Dramatic Texts*, p. 31.)

54 Pigeon-holes: out-door game, the rules of which are obscure. See J.O. Halliwell, *A Dictionary of Archaic and Provincial Words*:

> A game like our modern *bagatelle*, where there was a machine with arches for the balls to run through, resembling the cavities made for pigeons in a dove-house.

56 prodigality: foolish, wasteful excess; cf. Rowlands, *Diogenes' Lantern*, $A2^v$:

> Stay, let me see, what is he? O, tis Prodigalitie and his whore...walking towards the suburbs to a bawdy house for their recreation.

59 roarer: noisy, quarrelsome bully, a fashionable affectation. Chough and Kastrel come to London to learn to 'roar' in *A Fair Quarrel* and *The Alchemist* respectively.

64-65 Some...store: proverbial; see Ray, *Proverbs*, $G8^v$, 11:

> Giving much to the poor, doth increase a mans store.

91 naturall: acting a) as nature prompts; b) as befits one related by blood.

97 Son in law: step-son.

101 present: immediate.

103 content: 'contented condition'. (*OED* $sb.^2$)

112 awkeward starre: star in an unfavourable position astrologically, thus affecting her adversely. (Referring to the belief that the position of the stars at birth influences the character; cf. *Much Ado About Nothing*, 728-31 (2.1.299-303):

> ...to be merry, best becomes you, for out of question, you were born in a merry howre.
> Beatr. No sure my Lord, my Mother cried, but then there was a starre daunst, and vnder that was I borne.)

116 bonefires: usually lit to celebrate an event of national rejoicing especially the birth of a royal child.

to warme defame: to encourage slander.

119 Mother a pearle: a coinage; bowdlerization of 'Mother a God' (the King's oath in Samuel Rowley's *When You See Me You Know Me*) to conform with the prohibition against stage blasphemy. See Sir Henry Herbert's note for August 1623:

> For the Company at the Curtain; A Tragedy of the Plantation of Virginia; the profaneness to be left out, otherwise not tolerated.

120 husband: a) spouse; b) one who is careful of resources.

128 Conduit-pipe: channel to convey water or refuse.

129 shore: sewer.

130 shame: be ashamed of.

139 approving: displaying, making proof of.

147 censure: judge.

153 Misconster: misconstrue.

163 Sirra: used to inferiors of either sex; here, an insult, returned by Stephen at 164, showing increasing ill-feeling.

170-72 as well...me love: cf. the biblical 'loue thy neighbour as thy selfe', *Matt.* 22.39, *Lev.* 19.18; 'Loue your enemies', *Matt.* 5.44, Luke 6.27; 'loue one another', *John* 15.12. See also the prayer-book reading for April 27th (*I John* 3.10-11):

> ...whosoeuer doeth not righteousness is not of God,
> neither he that loueth not his brother.
> For this is the message that ye heard from the
> beginning, that we should loue one another...

175-76 my duty...My Vncle: my duty is inseparable from my relationship with my uncle. Correlative: 'each of two things having a reciprocal relation such that the one necessarily implies, or is complementary to, the other; something normally related to, or occurring with, something else; used of persons: A relative.' (*OED* B *sb.* 1, 2a, c.)

176 why...selfe: cf. Middleton, *The Phoenix*, $E4^v$:

> ...Vncles are halfe Fathers,
> Why they come so neare our bloods th' are ene part
> of it.

180 Here...brother: prodigals could legally be disowned; see

Donne's 'Sermon preached at Greenwich April 30 1613' (*Sermons*, X3):

> The third Incommodity that a Prodigal incurrs by the Law, is, *Exhaeredatus creditur*, He is presum'd to be disinherited by his father.

182-83 *Be thou...him*: Robert would be liable for any debt of Stephen's for which he stood surety if Stephen defaulted. Cf. the case of John Shakespeare, prosecuted for his brother's debts (quoted by Schoenbaum, *Shakespeare's Lives*, p. 17).

195 *bables*: foolish prating.

200 *painted postes*: placed outside the home of a sheriff or Lord Mayor to show an official lived there. Cf. *Twelfth Night* 440-41 (1.5.139-40): 'hee sayes hee'l stand at your doore like a Sheriffes post.' Nashe writes of, 'cheeks sugar-candied and cherry blusht so sweetly, after the colour of a newe Lord Mayors postes. ('Pierce Penniless', *Works*, I.180.)

cum privilegio: Latin tag, *cum privilegio* (*ad imprimendum solum*), used commonly on books such as the Bible for which a printer had been awarded sole rights of printing by the Stationers' Company; here, used to continue the thought of 197: 'I'l befoul your posts, with impunity'.

203 *I'l breake this leg*: beggars were supposed to fake injuries to arouse sympathy; see, e.g., Dekker's *O per se O!*, 'Their Making of their Sores'.

220 *bond*: a) the natural tie between father and son; b) a deed by which a person binds himself to pay a certain sum of money to his heirs.

225 *ha'te*: have it.

227 *case*: a) appearance, clothes; b) situation.

231 *compasse*: circumference.

233 *compasse*: moderation.

Cap of Maintenance: for ceremonial use. 'A Sword, a Cap of maintenance, a Mace...Are borne before the Maior, and Aldermen.' (John Taylor, 'A Very Merry Wherry Ferry Voyage', *Works*, 2B2, col. 2, 18-20.)

244 *7. is better than 11.*: the odds in the dice-game hazzard favour a throw of seven; a player throwing eleven when his opponent has thrown five, six, eight or nine loses the throw.

(Cotton, Complete Gamester, $M4^v$-7.)

bones: dice (made of bone or ivory). Cf. Diogenes' Lantern, A3:

> ...the Canniball should neuer feed more vpon poore men, and play the Dice-maker with their bones.

247 Angells: gold coins, so called because of the impression of St. Michael killing the dragon on the obverse, and worth ten shillings. Cf. Brewer, The Country Girl, F4:

> Lad. These be good Angels, I can tell you. - Looke,
> Mar. Thy Angels are all Devils; and such gold,
> But golden Fetters.

250-51 eate...lordships: save money by a frugal diet and invest in land. Cheese and Onions: thought to be the favourite food of the Welsh, popularly supposed to be miserly. lordships: the territory belonging to a peer's estate.

1.2

4 Will: sexual desire.

7 serv'd...Service: OED records no use of 'serve' as it is used of stud animals before 1844, but it seems clear that this meaning was available to Rowley; the Clown puns on 'serve' a) as a servant; b) as a lover. Cf. Beaumont, Philaster, 2nd Folio, E4:

> King: Put him away, h'as done you that good service,
> Shames me to speak of.

Middleton and Dekker, The Roaring Girl, ed. Bowers, 2.1.324-28:

> Moll: What parts are there in you for a gentlewoman's service?
> Trapdoor: Of two kinds, right worshipful, moveable and immoveable - moveable to run of errands, and immoveable to stand when you have occasion to use me.

See also Christopher Ricks, Essays in Criticism 10, 1960, p. 296: 'the cruder sexual sense, linked as it is with the farmyard sense, is also very frequent in Shakespeare and in Middleton.'

8-9 though...ill-will: proverbial; 'Give a woman her will and she will live the longer.' (Tilley W626.)

9 dye: reach sexual orgasm.

12 *head*: usually maidenhead (inappropriate for a widow); here, chastity.

13 *Ivie*: traditionally female.

has yet...house: is still in control; 'you can still look after your own affairs'.

14 *Holly*: traditionally male.

pricks: male sexual organs.

15 *wands*: made of holly and sometimes used for punishment. See *Five Hundred Points of Good Husbandry*, H8^{v}, 7:

> *Let holliwand threat,*
> *Let fizgig be beat.*
>
> A wand in thine hand, though ye fight not at all,
> make youth to their businesse better to fall.

A Woman Killed with Kindness, C1^{v}:

> *Ienk*. 'Tis no boot for me to deny it, my Maist. hath giuen me a coat here, but he takes paines himselfe to brush it once or twice a day with a holly-wand.

To be under the wand = to be liable to corporal punishment.

15-16 *cannot...wands*: 'you cannot have (sexual) pleasure without paying for it'. Cf. *The Anatomy of Absurdity*:

> In some Countries therefore, the Bride at the day of her mariage, is crowned by the Matrons with a Garland of prickles, and so deliuered to her husband, that he may know he hath tyed himselfe to a thornie pleasure. (Nashe, *Works*, I.15-16.)

sword: a) symbol of authority; b) phallic symbol.

17 *scabbard*: female sexual organs. Cf. *The Maid in the Mill*, Fletcher and Rowley, S2:

> *Bust*. It was a Miller and a Lord
> That had a scabbard and a sword,
> He put it up in the Country word
> The Miller and his daughter.

Nixon, *A Strange Foot-Post*, G4:

> For he that strikes with Sword, it is decreed
> Shall be restruck with Scabberd, till he bleed.

Also, possibly referring to stage-business (in *A Midsummer Night's Dream*?); see Sharpham, *The Fleer*, E1^{v}:

> Fle: Faith like Thisbe in the play, a has almost kil'd himself with the scabberd.

18 cast downe: for intercourse.

taken up: sexual innuendo, with the suggestion of 'taking up' a woman's linen.

21 use: in the sexual sense.

22 coupling: mating.

22-23 barly-breake: a game.

> Then couples three be streight allotted there,
> They of both ends the middle two doe flie,
> The two that in mid place, Hell called were,
> Must strive with waiting foot, and watching eye
> To catch of them, and them to Hell to beare,
> That they, as well as they, Hell may supplie.

(Sidney, Works, II.220.)

last...hell: a) loser at barley-break; b) left unmarried, an 'old maid' (who according to tradition leads apes in hell); c) sexually unsatisfied. Cf. The Decameron, tenth story, third day, in which a monk teaches a naive would-be hermit to let him put his 'devil' in her 'hell'.

26 bands: bonds.

27 traffique: a) merchandise; b) sexual dealings.

29 custome: a) tax, the Church's fees; b) habitual sexual intercourse. The Clown suggests that the Doctor sleeps with women as his payment for the marriage ceremony.

30 Impost: custom duty.

31 pregnant: full of ideas.

33-35 you sell...tollage: referring to fees charged by the clergy for marriages and funerals. tollage: a) charge paid for travelling on a road; b) sound of the passing-bell at a funeral.

35-36 dye...buryed: a) 'you can't control death so why should you control burial?' b) 'if a man will have intercourse without your leave, he should be successful without your leave'. dye: see above, n. 9; buryed: in a woman's sexual parts.

41 Clerke: churchman.

44 fasting day: Friday. See The Inner Temple Mask, Middleton, A3, B1:

> Fast. ... No-body minds Fasting day, I haue scarce bin thought vpon a' Fryday nights;...

> Plum. ... I was borne an Anabaptist, a fell foe, to fish and Fridayes.

(There were also fasting days in Lent, but Rowley is unlikely to have set the play then because of the prohibition on marriage.)

46 voyder: tray or basket used in cleaning the table to remove scraps and dishes.

51 dresse: a) prepare, cook; b) fondle.

Pike,...Cod: phallic symbols ('Cod' implying 'codpiece').

64 halfe way 'twixt thirty and forty: Planché kept the character of the Widow almost unchanged but made her ten years younger (27). See Introduction, 'Stage History'.

93 Then I that know not: Hebrews 12,6-8:

> For whom the Lord loueth he chasteneth, and scourgeth euery sonne whom hee receiueth. If yee endure chastening, God dealeth with you as with sonnes: for what sonne is he whom the father chasteneth not? But if yee bee without chastisement, whereof all are partakers, then are yee bastards, and not sonnes.

106 comfortable: comforting.

109-11 Me thought...soules: cf. Brewer, *The Country Girl*, D4:

> Sir Oli. I must tell you Lady,
> I thought the Musick of your husbands end,
> Those heavenly Notes he entertain'd it with,
> Taught him by Angels, had instructed you,
> To looke upon that Being that he has,
> As hee's a glorious Chorister with them!

112-13 It was a sinne...esteemed best: cf. *Twelfth Night* 362-63 (1.5.65-6):

> Clo. The more foole (Madona) to mourne for your Brothers soule, being in heauen.

117 Doe not appoint: referring to the proverb, 'to make a rod for one's own back'? (Tilley R153, *ODEP* p. 681.)

139 Iug: familiar form of Joan; used of servant girls, sometimes implying immoral character; cf. *The Birth of Merlin*, where Iug is the Clown's name for his sister (who has a child by the devil).

154 Your maid Ioane: see Introduction, 'Sources', for the origins of this incident.

155 Gudgeon: bait.

156 How...blessings: cf. A Shoemaker, a Gentleman, Rowley, $D3^{v}$:

> Al. I am blest in curses.

165 flegmatique: having too much phlegm in his body, thus having a cold, moist humour appropriate to a fish.

Golde: used in medicines. Cf. II Henry IV 2694-96 (4.1.61-63):

> Therefore, thou best of Gold, art worst of Gold.
> Other, lesse fine in Charract, is more precious,
> Preseruing life, in Med'cine potable.

166 he that gets Gold: inversion of the proverb, 'If she would eat gold he would give it her'. (ODEP p. 214.)

173-74 Give a woman lucke: adaptation of, 'Give a man luck and cast him into the sea'. (Tilley M146, ODEP, p. 302.)

182 bosomes: hearts, thus natures, thoughts.

186 ease: a) unburden my sorrows; b) experience a motion of the bowels.

189 All ominous stars: cf. 1.1.112.

216 please her: i.e. sexually.

219 That makes my state: cf. 1.1.56.

240 stiffe: sexually demanding.

252 suburbe garden: kept by a citizen on the outskirts of the City. Suburb gardens acquired a reputation as meeting places for unfaithful wives and their lovers, but Rowley does not suggest anything unseemly about the Widow's garden. It provides a reason for her to be in the same area as Stephen in Act 2.

2.1

1 bona Speranza: Cape of Good Hope, here used metaphorically. Cf. Mynshul, $A5^{v}$-6: 'Being once arrived [in prison] there is few can come neere to touch at the Cap of Bona Speranza.'

3 Passage: see Cotton, The Complete Gamester, M4:

> Passage is a Game at Dice to be play'd at but by two, and it is performed with three Dice. The Caster throws continually till he hath thrown Doublets under ten, and then he passeth and wins.

The function of the third die is not clear.

Novum: dice-game played by five or six, the two principal throws in which are nine and five.

4 Mumchance: one player shuffles, the other cuts the cards. Each player names a card; whichever comes first off the pile, wins. See Greene's A Notable Discovery of Cozenage, B3.

Bursmen: traders. The Royal Exchange, built by Sir Thomas Gresham in 1566, was known as The Burse; Britain's Burse was built in 1609.

10-14 Tush...heires, Boyes: this passage is based on proverbs.

10 'tis too soone to thrive: referring to, 'Who spends before he thrives will beg before he thinks'. (Tilley S740.) The Host is advising the young men to ignore this proverbial wisdom - they are too young to worry about such things.

11 He that gathers: 'He that spares when he is young may the better spend when he is old.' (Tilley S710.)

'Tis better...end ill: 'A hard beginning has a good ending.' (Tilley B260.)

12-13 Miserable...sons: 'A sparing father and a spending son.' (Tilley F91.)

16 As good...executors: alluding to the saying,

> Women are forgetfull, children unkind,
> Executors covetous, and take what they find,

quoted by Stephen, 5.2.190-93. Also a play on 'hangman' and 'executors' as 'those who perform executions'. Cf. Dekker, Old Fortunatus, ed. Bowers, 2.2.356-9:

> ...for by this meanes the charges of a Tombe is sau'd, and you being heyres, may doe as many rich Executors doe, put that money in your purses, and giue out he dyed a begger.

The Honest Man's Fortune, 1.1.78-79:

> Dubois: how, is yor law as bad. I rather wish the hangman thy executor.

18 rubbing: a bowl 'rubs' when it hits an obstacle lying in its path.

19 Mistris: jack. See Taylor, 'Wit and Mirth', Works, 2R3:

> The marke which they ayme at hath sundry names and epithites, as a Blocke, a Iacke, and a Mistris... But I hold a Mistresse to be the fittest name for it, for there are some that are commonly termed Mistresses, which are not much better then mine Aunts;

> and a Mistris is oftentimes a marke for every knaue to haue a fling at, euery one striues to come so neere her that hee would kisse her.

Cf. also Every Woman in her Humour, D1^{v}:

> ...Sirra, these bowles which we roule and turn in our lower spher, are by vse made wodden worldlings right for euery one striues who shal lye neerest the mistris.

20 Bayle: bale, set of dice.

22-23 Counters...bayle: playing on double meanings. Counters: a) debtors' prisons; b) tokens used in games. Bayle: a) surety; b) dice.

23ff. The game which is being played is apparently passage, although this normally involves only two players. See n. 2.1.3. 36 Stephen is out because he has thrown doublets (two threes) which, including the ace, total less than ten. 47 Jack wins; 4+4+3 = 11, a winning throw. 64 Stephen loses. The chances of winning with threes are less than with a higher number; 'high runners are most requisite for this Game, such as will rarely run any other chance than four, five, or six, by which means if the Caster throws Doublets he scarcely can throw out.' (Cotton, M4.) 77 Hugh wins.

27 Boreas: north wind. Presumably Hugh is blowing on the dice and continuing the idea of wind and sailing suggested by 'a faire passage'.

28 How now my fine Trundletayles: the Edict and Severe Censure against Private Combats and Combatants, 1613, obliged gaming-house keepers to stop any arguments in their houses in case they led to duels. Failure to do so incurred three months' imprisonment and prohibition from keeping a gaming-house for at least three years (O4-4^{v}). This may explain the Host's anxiety to keep the peace, as well as his natural desire to prevent damage to his house.
Trundletayles: mongrel, curly-tailed dogs; the term is used as an insult.
wodden Cosmographers: cosmography: the science which maps the physical features of the universe and the earth. The bowlers are using wooden bowls or 'globes'. Cf. Every Woman in her Humour, quoted n. 19 above.

29 Orlando: an allusion to Orlando Furioso implying madness. The Host several times uses exotic names with only a superficial relevance to what he is saying for the sake of word-play. See also n. 54, 56 below. Cf. Middleton and Rowley, The Changeling, 3.3.112-14:

> Lol. Must I come amongst you there? Keep you the fool, mistress; I'll go up and play left-handed Orlando amongst the madmen.

30 stickler: official whose job it was to part the combatants in a contest or, e.g., keep spectators out of the way.

32-33 looke to my box: dicing-house owners took a percentage of the winnings, put into the box. Cf. Taylor, Wit and Mirth, 2Q2^{v}-3:

> One asked a fellow what Westminster Hall was like; marry, quoth the other, it is like a Butlers Box at Christmas amongst gamesters, for whosoever loseth, the Box will be sure to bee a winner.

36 out: see n. 23ff.

38 Trayes,...Ace: two threes and one.

41 sinkes: with a play on 'sinck' = five on a die.

43 In still: Jack has thrown two dice over ten and the third die is unimportant.

43 choose thy fellow: referring to, 'Ask my Fellow, if I be a thief' (Tilley F177)? Perhaps Jack is suggesting that his fellows and he are thieves - a suggestion taken up by Stephen in the next line. Also, referring to the dice-game and the possibility that one die is superfluous?

44 Take the Miller: continuing the allusion of 43. Cf. 'Put a Miller, a weaver and a tailor in a bag and shake them, the first one that comes out will be a thief'. (Tilley M957.) The three dice represent the three thieves in the bag; not only are they shaken like the thieves, but they are also robbing Stephen. Miller: proverbially dishonest; see, e.g., Fletcher and Rowley, The Maid in the Mill, Q1^{v}:

> Fra. Are you a thief?
> Bust. So far forth as the Son of a Miller.

47 Two Quaters and a Tray: two fours and a three. Stephen puns (48) on Quater (four) and Cater (one who provides food).

51 Bull-beggar: bogey-man.

Silence is a vertue: proverbial; a variation on 'Silence does seldom harm'. (Tilley S445, ODEP p. 733.)

54-55 Tamberlaine,...Soldan comes: misquotation of, 'Now Tamberlaine the mightie Souldan comes,' (I Tamberlaine 1633). Tamberlaine is the type of a ranting, powerful conqueror. The reference is not entirely appropriate; Marlowe's Sultan is defeated by Tamberlaine.

55 Beares: rough, noisy people.

56 Vrsa Major: the Great Bear, a constellation; an image naturally suggested by 'Beares'.

Capite Draconis: dragon's head, the constellation Draco; associated, like the bear, with lechery. See, e.g., King Lear 1.2. 457-59:

> My father compounded with my mother vnder the Dragons taile, and my Natiuity was vnder Vrsa Maior, so that it followes, I am rough and Leacherous.

Ursa Major and Capite Draconis are probably the names of rooms in the inn; the Host moves between at least two locations off-stage. Cf. the staging of Lollio's mad-house scene, The Changeling 3.3.

57 reclayme: redeem, reform, in the sense 'to save someone's soul'.

59 maledictious: a coinage, from maledict = accursed.

utter: offer for sale.

64 suit: legal action.

y'are out: see n. 23ff.

65 my father...begotten: the child was supposed to be influenced by the father's circumstances at the time of procreation; cf. The Puritan, B2:

> ...I was borne a Begger, for if the truth were knowne, I thinke I was begot when my Father had neuer a penny in his purse.

threw three: performed the sexual act three times.

70-71 Serjants Yeoman...with him: a Serjeant can be bribed for a shilling, his yeoman for fourpence. Yeomen arrested debtors and were notoriously corrupt; see, e.g., Nixon, A Strange

Foot-Post, $C1^{v}$-2:

> [A Sargeant] is an Officer, whose office I disallow not, but dislike some of his fraternitie in their extreame executing of their duties, which will fawne like Spaniels, on such as bribe them, and will be inquisitiue after them, where they are sure they are not: But mercilesse Furies to haunt out poore men, which are disable to fee, and feed them with rewards.

71 groate: silver coin worth 4d.

77 Twelve at all: see n. 23ff.

80 Fullum: a) Fulham, west of the City; b) false die, loaded so that it always falls showing a low value. It is 'palmed' by the cheaters and exchanged either for a genuine die or one loaded to show high values when anyone except Stephen is playing.

81 Putney: on the south bank of the Thames, opposite Fulham.

109 Tester: a) 6d; b) covering for a bed.

132 stretcht a handfull: hanged.

133 the Cart: the tumbril which took the condemned to the gallows with their coffins.

139 booke of Callico: obscure. An account book recording dealings in callico cloth (a luxury item)?

144 viper: see Topsell, The History of Serpents, F3:

> ...the female departeth and conceiueth hir young in hir belly, who euery day...grow to perfection and ripenesse, and at last...doe likewise destroy their mother, for they eate out her belly.

Topsell refutes the story, which he traces to a misreading of Aristotle, but it remained a common source of imagery. Cf., e.g., Dekker, The Bellman of London, F4:

> Thus the Common wealth is dishonoured by feeding such Vipers in her wombe, that can not liue but by gnawing out of her bowels.

147 Zantippe: wife of Socrates, notorious for her shrewish temper.

147-8 prest to death: punishment for those refusing to plead in a court (who thus were not convicted and whose estates escaped confiscation). Mistress Foster should keep silent.

148 Irish Rugs: coarse, heavy lengths of material.

153 Cucking-stoole: used especially for scolds and gossips.

Cf. Deloney, John Winchcomb, L3:

> She would be so mad and furious...as if she strove for the best game at the cucking-stoole.

157 standings: 'she would rather have been sexually satisfied'.

160 lye with him: a) match him in accusations of lying; b) sleep with him.

166 SD wispe: 'A twist or figure of straw for a scold to rail at; also a badge of ignominy with which a scold was taunted or presented.' (Wilson, note to Nashe, Works, I.299.34.) Stephen offers Mistress Foster a piece of straw as an insult.

173-74 I'l doe your errand: possibly referring to the ironic proverb, 'I will go twenty Miles on your errand,' meaning, 'I'll do anything rather than what you want me to'. (Tilley M927, ODEP p. 308.) Cf. Measure for Measure 1524-26 (3.1.31-34):

> The Deputy cannot abide a Whore-master: if he be a Whore-monger, and comes before him, he were as good go a mile on his errand.

195 make a shift: a) to make do, get by; b) shift = undershift.

204 Passage: see n. 3 above.

205 Hazard: a dice-game, very complex, and more than usually dependent on luck. See Cotton, M4v:

> Hazzard is a proper name for this Game; for it speedily makes a man or undoes him.

Stephen is willing to gamble his future.

211 service: a) as a servant; b) in a sexual sense.

212-13 Frock...Coale-sacke: distinguishing marks of workmen. Frock: smock, worn by peasant labourers and porters. Coale-sacke: carried by colliers who sold coal in the streets of London.

227 well-hang'd: a) efficiently and thoroughly hanged (executed); b) equipped with male sexual organs. The pun on 'hang-' is not uncommon; see, e.g., The Birth of Merlin, B3:

> Clown: Pox on his Hangers, would he had bin gelt for his labor.

241 Taverne Bushes: of ivy, hung outside to indicate the trade. See Middleton and Rowley, The Spanish Gipsy, G4v:

> Ro. I sit like an Owle in the Ivie bush of a Taverne!

242 Forrainers: craftsmen not free of the local trade guild.

'The Forrainers were licensed for three daies, the freemen so long as they would.' (Stow, Survey, 2Z5^{v} marginal note.)

244 Smithfield: market for live-stock, especially poor-quality horses. See II Henry IV 325-27 (1.2.47-49):

> Fal. I bought him in Paules, and hee'l buy mee a horse in Smithfield. If I could get mee a wife in the Stewes, I were Mann'd, Hors'd, and Wiu'd.

247 Chapman: customer.

247-48 I'd see...my love: cf. the proverb, 'See for your love, and buy for your money,' Ray, Proverbs, N4^{v}, 23.

249-50 I'l finde thee: cf. the situation at A Shoemaker, a Gentleman, E1^{v}:

> Leo. Dare you venture on a wife of my chusing?
> Cris. If both parties were agreed Lady.
> Leo. That's no venture, Ile promise she shall be yong, good Parentage, honest, let her beauty commend it selfe.

256-57 honest...healthes sake: avoid the risk of contracting a venereal disease through sleeping with other women.

260 feeder: a) one who eats; b) one who has sexual intercourse.

261 flesh: a) meat; b) women.

271 the: thee.

273 blinde Bargaine: agreement trusting to luck of which the outcome is uncertain; cf. 'buying a pig in a poke'.

274 in your bed: in the dark - at night or with the curtains drawn. Stephen is suggesting that he anticipate his marriage vows.

282 stout: obstinate.

288 I'l have thee with all faults: commercial phrase, meaning literally to accept responsibility in a contract for all defects; referring back to the bargaining imagery of 274ff. Stephen takes the phrase literally in his reply.

295 Beane...Cake: Twelfth Night custom. A batch of cakes was baked, with a bean in one of them.

296 fetch: decoy; something worthless.

302 Nap: Dilke's emendation to 'nit' is unnecessary; the Clown is contrasting the thick pile of the cloth (himself) with the parasite living in it (Stephen), and commenting obliquely on

Stephen's ragged clothing. Cf. also Daborn, The Poor Man's Comfort, G2:

> Leo. Me thought I heard thee name thy dependence on the banisht King.
> Osw. I did hang on him as others did, as long as he had nap, you ha my meaning.

Brewer, The Love-Sick King, B3:

> ...A most fine, dainty, nappy Lamb-skin, if a Lady would line her Petticoat, A sweeter Lamb-skin cannot kiss her Catastrophe.

303 cracke: boast; if the Clown points to Stephen and not himself at 'here', then used ironically.

306 no blacke stormes: a recurrent image; see Introduction, 'Style'.

310 blacke Munday: Easter Monday 1209. The Irish in Dublin rebelled against the English colonists, who were nearly wiped out.

312 opposite: Q's 'apposite' is the result of reading 'a' for 'o'.

314 weapon: with a double entendre.

320 Companion: an insult.

323 Tittere Tu Tattere: a) referring to Stephen's tattered clothes; b) member of the Tityre-tus, distinguished by wearing scarves. See Introduction, 'Date'.

329 the wrong way: to Hell, by contemplating suicide as a result of the mortal sin of despair. Heaven and Hell are traditionally approached by narrow and wide paths respectively. The Clown's suicidal intentions are not to be taken seriously.

3.1

5-6 If you...Cittizen: cf. The Shoemaker's Holiday, B1:

> Lincol. Why my lord Maior, think you it then a shame,
> To ioyne a Lacie with an Otleys name?
> L. Maior. Too meane is my poore girle for his high birth,
> Poore Cittizens must not with Courtiers wed. (1.1.9-12)

8 Traffique the mart: deal in the market. Bruine equates marriage with a business deal.

11 handled: a) in feeling for quality (while buying goods); b) fondled.

19-20 rifle...share: put them as prizes in a raffle with tickets

12d each.

20 good foode...plantation: either gullible, foolishly incompetent, or rogues. See John Smith, *New England's Trials*, B4:

> ...the former ships haue not made such good voyages as they expected, by sending opinionated vnskilfull men, that had not experienced diligence to saue that they tooke, nor take that there was.

C2^{v}:

> ...the honourable Company haue bin humble suiters to his Maiestie to get vagabonds and condemned men to go thither.

The colonists were unsuitable with little chance of survival; cf. the expression, 'cannon fodder'.

new plantation: New England or Newfoundland; possibly Virginia. (Herbert licensed *The Plantation of Virginia* for the Curtain in 1623; see n. 1.1.119.)

22-23 meddle...case: with a sexual innuendo. Cf. *Coriolanus* 2700-2702 (4.5.46-47):

> 3 How sir? Do you meddle with my Master?
> Corio. I, tis an honester seruice, then to meddle with thy Mistris.

23 case: here, woman.

26 deepe in this case: sexual innuendo; cf. n. 22-23 above.

28 Fill's: thill's - the place (understood) of the horse attached to the shaft drawing the cart (thill).

29 elder Tree: a) insulting reference to Speedwell's age; b) literally the elder, traditionally unlucky because Judas Iscariot hanged himself on one.

32 large deedes: sexual feats.

34 by my fathers Coppy: by inheritance; copy = manorial court-roll recording the tenure held by tenants who have 'copyhold'. Also a catch-phrase; cf., e.g., *The Puritan*, B1:

> ...he cozn'd the right heire beeing a foole, and bestow'd those Lands vpon me his eldest Son;...
> I know what I may do well inough by my Fathers Copy.

39 suit: Jane refers back to 36-38 and puns on 'actions' = 'legal cases'. 40-42 Lambskin takes 'suit' as 'articles of clothing'.

42 *defiles*: befouls with excrement.

44 *Tale*: a) story; b) buttocks.

45 *bounty*: valour.

46 *Bulloyne*: the last English expedition was in 1544.

Godfry: Godfrey of Boulogne, Duke of Lorraine, captured Jerusalem in 1098, was crowned King and ruled one year. (Stow, *Abridgement*, E1^{v}-2.)

47 *paraphrase*: comment, gloss.

48 *full longitude*: cf. *The Puritan*, F2^{v}:

> *Edm.* O no; I haue more names at home, Maister *Edmond Plus*, is my full name at length.

50 *every quality*: with the suggestion, 'sexual organs'.

56 *hot and harmelesse*: a) inoffensive thing to keep you warm; b) amorous but impotent.

64 *Tradesman*: one who has sexual dealings.

65 *set up*: with sexual innuendo.

67 *Laundresse*: prostitute (because a laundress 'takes up' linen). See Massinger, *The Picture*, B2^{v}:

> And were it not for my honesty I could wish now
> I were his leager landresse I would finde
> Sope of mine owne, enough to wash his linnen
> Or I would straine hard for't.

Dekker and Webster, *Westward Hoe!* 1607, A4^{v} (1.1.180-81):

> *Iust.* No Landresse deere wife, though your credit would goe farre with Gentlemen for taking vp of Linnen.

occupy: a) exercise a skill or trade; b) have sexual intercourse. Cf. Ben Jonson, epigram 117:

> Groin, come of age, his'state sold out of hand
> For his whore: Groin doth still occupy his land.

75 *Nick*: a) notch in tally stick; b) to nick = to cheat; c) sexual innuendo; cf. Brome, *The Damoiselle*, B7^{v}:

> *Val.* He found's abed last night i'th'nick, as we say.

77 *course*: coarse.

88 *Tooth drawer*: popularly known as 'kind heart'. Chettle's Kind-heart describes himself as 'famous for drawing teeth'. (*Kind Heart's Dream*, B1.)

105 *crosse it*: in the duelling posture.

106-7 *purse...felony*: sexual suggestion? (See Partridge, *Shakespeare's Bawdy*, pp. 170 and 196.) purse = male sexual parts; cf. Rowley, *A Shoemaker, a Gentleman*, K2-2^{v}:

> *Wife*. A boy I'me sure,
> Has a Purse and two pence in't.

felony = theft; implying that Speedwell might geld Lambskin?

109-10 *reputation...soyld*: explained more fully by Cavendish, *The Variety*, D5:

> (*Manly offers to draw*.)
> *Beau*: Sir, this is most uncivill, and your rashnesse, beside the forfeit of your own discretion, will lay an imputation to wound my fame; within my presence, and beneath my roofe, which should protect all strangers, to affront a Gentleman that visits me.

118-19 *please you...Garden*: device for getting one group of characters off stage and another on without a meeting; cf. *The Puritan*, G1^{v}-2:

> ...how shal I do to bee rid of these Knights, - please you Gentlemen to walke a while ith Garden, go gather a pinck, or a Iilly-flower.

122 *Gallyes*: as a slave; a form of punishment particularly associated with the Mediterranean countries especially France. After 1564, the minimum sentence in France was 10 years.

131-32 *this place promises/well*: because the first place was the most honourable. Cf. Dekker, *The Shoemaker's Holiday*, C4:

> *Fyrk*. Soft, yaw, yaw, good Hans, though my master haue no more wit, but to call you afore mee, I am not so foolish to go behind you, I being the elder iourneyman. (1.4.15-17)

135-36 Speedwell stands in front of Lambskin. If Speedwell looks over his shoulder he sees Lambskin's nose (a euphemism?); if Lambskin turns round, Speedwell's nose is at his back.

141 *Downes*: English Channel between the east coast of Kent and the Goodwin Sands.

159 (*Discover'd by my mother*): syntactically, would make more sense as the second half of the line. An afterthought, inserted into the text in the wrong place (by copyist or compositor)?

160 *Whose*: Mistress Foster's.

175 fame: Q's 'Same' is caused by confusing f and long s, then making s upper case for the first letter of the line.

181-82 keepe...Suitors: obscure. seeth = to boil or digest; the suitors are so contemptible they are only fit for a stew? So weak Jane could eat them? (Cf. 4.1.32-33.)

186 leagu'd: agreed, made a treaty.

193 sweet Beauty: Robert unwittingly echoes a mannerism of Lambskin and Speedwell.

194 handsell: omen, sign; an astrological image. Cf. 195 'fortunate season', 196 'happier time', 197 'Augurisme'.

198 houres: unpropitious times; continuing the imagery of 194 above.

209 field: a) garden; b) battle-ground.

211-12 walke into your/Garden: common source of sexual imagery. Cf., e.g., Middleton, *Your Five Gallants*, (ed. Bullen) 2.1 p. 157:

> Tai. Push! I did but walk
> A turn or two in the garden.
> First C. What made you there?
> Tai. Nothing but cropt a flower.
> First C. Some woman's honour, I believe
> Tai. Foh! is this a woman's honour?
> First C. Much about one,
> When both are pluck'd, their sweetness is soon gone.

212 Garden: with a play on garden = pubic hair.

sweetes: sexual pleasures.

213 Honesty: a) a plant; b) chastity, maidenhead.

215 Penny-royall: species of mint with small, round leaves, of great medicinal strength. Here, with sexual innuendo; cf. *A Shoemaker, a Gentleman*, quoted n. 106-7 above.

216 Sorrill: punning on 'sorrow'.

Sullenwood: southernwood; here, for the pun on 'sullen-'.

220 Hearts-ease: pansy; here, also taken literally: contentment. Cf. Greene, *A Quip for an Upstart Courtier*, B1:

> none can weare [hearts-ease] , be they kings, but such as desire no more then they are borne to, nor haue their wishes aboue their fortunes.

221 Roses: a) purity, natural beauty; b) chastity, maidenhead.

222 Gillyflowers: artifice, painted beauty, with the association of sexual immorality. Gill = woman or prostitute. Cf. *The*

Winter's Tale (New Arden, 4.4.82-83):

> ...streak'd gillyvors,
> Which some call nature's bastards:...

The contrast is between the (supposedly) natural beauty of the rose and the highly cultivated appearance of the gillyflower, sometimes streaked and achieved by cross-breeding. (Gillyflower: carnation and wallflower. See note to *The Winter's Tale* quoted above and Parkinson, *Parradisus Terrestris*, Y3 and engraving.)

223 Venus Violets: Venus' flowers are the rose and anemone. Water of distilled violets 'is commended in the French disease, to be profitable, being taken for nine dayes or more, and sweating vpon it'. (Parkinson 2A4.) Dog-tooth violets were believed to be an aphrodisiac by natives of Virginia. (*Ibid*, R1^v.) Venus: goddess of beauty and sexual lust.

224 Batchelors Buttons: see Greene, *A Quip for an Upstart Courtier*, B2^v:

> whose vertue is to make wanton maidens weepe when they haue worne it fortye weekes vnder their Aprons for a fauour.

230 bound: make boundaries for himself; recognize his own limits.

231 mount: raise or lift up.

244-45 poore;...such: 'For ye haue the poore alwayes with you.' *Matt.* 26.11, *Mark* 14.7, *John* 12.8, *Deut.* 15.11.

246 venter: dial. form of venture. at a venture = at random, without forethought.

256 contents be drawne: in a contract. contents: of the deal just made.

257 George must stay on stage here, to fetch Robert and Jane at 3.1.279.

296 in time: Q's 'and' does not make sense; Hazlitt's emendation 'in' is plausible and conveys the sense of the passage. 'By' is another possibility, paleographically less convincing.

318 happily: a) by chance; b) luckily, fortunately; c) falling aptly, at just the right moment.

321 Catherin Peare: 'bigge, and round at the one end, and long, and slender at the other'. (Markham, *The Pleasures of Princes*,

B2^{v}.)

322 Popperin: a) fruit from Poperinghe, Flanders; b) with a sexual innuendo. Cf. Heywood, *The Wise Woman of Hogsdon*, E2:

> ...What needed I to have grafted in the stocke of such a Choake Peare, and such a goodly Popering as this to escape me?

323-24 prick'd my/finger: with a sexual innuendo? Cf. Wilkins, *The Miseries of Enforced Marriage*, A4:

> Scar. [Women] are the stems on which do Angels grow,
> From whence Vertue is stild, and Arts do flow.
> Ilf. Let them be what Flowers they will, and they were Roses, I will plucke none of them for pricking my fingers.

All's Well that Ends Well, 2040-43 (4.1.17-20):

> Dia. I so you serue vs
> Till we serue you: But when you haue our Roses,
> You barely leaue our thornes to pricke our selues,
> And mocke vs with our barenesse.

3.2

3 afflict: cf. 1.2.96-97:

> DOCTOR 'Tis some affliction, that you are afflicted
> For want of affliction.

4 I must not distaste: I must not feel repugnance for.

7 Good man: a) male head of a household; b) host of an inn or prison keeper.

10-12 Crosses...crosse: a) misfortunes; b) coins (from the cross on the reverse with arms reaching the outer edge to stop clipping). Cf. Dekker, *Penny-Wise, Pound-Foolish*, ed. Pendry, p. 116:

> ...and when a man hath not a penny in his purse, then he swears he hath not one 'cross' about him - so that, as a penny is the least cross that a man can carry, there can be no greater cross than for a man to go without a penny.

18 kinde: a) good-natured; b) natural.

19 Counting-house: with a sexual pun on 'count-'; Stephen is metaphorically making love to his money-bags when he should be physically making love to his wife.

tumbling over: making love to.

33 *throwne it at a hazard*: lost it gambling.

made Ducks and Drakes: wasted. Proverbial; see Tilley D632, *ODEP* p. 207. Cf. Cooke, *Greene's Tu Quoque*, D4:

> *Purs*. A man may winne from him that cares not for't
> This royall *Caesar* doth regard no Cash,
> Has throwne away as much in Duckes and Drakes,
> As would have bought some 50000 Capons.

34 *silver flyes*: house flies, used as bait in summer for bleak, ruff and perch. (Markham, *The Pleasures of Princes*, E2.)

37 *to*: too.

50 *Sir reverence of*: with all due respect to.

Master in law: a) legal master; b) master by marriage.

54 *crost*: thwarted.

56 *Whores at liverie*: rented for personal, exclusive use.

57 *us'd you like a woman*: beaten you; cf. the proverb, 'A Spaniel, a woman, and a walnut-tree, the more they're beaten the better they be.' (Tilley W644, *ODEP* p. 758.)

64 *texted*: inscribed. (Text-hand: large, formal hand used to distinguish the text of a book from its gloss.)

75 *Is your...bookes*: image taken from accounting; but the idea of 'being in someone's good books' is also present.

bookes: account books.

76 *blotted*: erased.

79 *stampt*: image of the act of striking an impression, e.g., minting a coin, embossing, making a seal in wax.

82 *reade it*: continuing the image of 75-76.

almost: all most.

93 *Propinquitie*: blood relationship. Cf. *King Lear* 120-21 (1.1.112-13):

> Heere I disclaime all my Paternall care,
> Propinquity and property of blood.

117 *mistake*: a) misjudge; b) make an error in marrying him (miss-take). Cf. *The Winter's Tale* 681-86 (2.1.78-82):

> *Her*. Should a Villaine say so,
> (The most replenish'd Villaine in the World)
> He were as much more Villaine: you (my Lord)
> Doe but mistake.
> *Lea*. You haue mistooke (my Lady)
> *Polixenes* for *Leontes*.

121 prodigall's return'd: referring to the parable of the prodigal son, *Luke* 15.11-32.

3.3

2 Blazon: lit. shield or its armorial bearings; here, display.

8 throw Dice at all: the turning point in the plot; gambling imagery indicates that Old Foster's fortunes will follow Stephen's.

8-9 be/A compleate Merchant: a) take full advantage of the deal; b) gamble. to play the merchant = to cheat, get the better of someone, especially in gambling.

15 Karsies: lengths of kersey, a coarse, ribbed cloth.

19 Make so your rates: conditional; 'if you make your rates such'.

21 Peruse and deale: 'check over the contract and negotiate on our behalf'.

24 even gaine: 'if you find that I shall break even on the deal'.

30 Saint Catharins Poole: by the Tower of London.

32 the Gunner: at the Tower.

34 report: a) noise (of the gun); b) news.

44 criticall: especially dangerous. See *A Help to Discourse*, L3, for the critical days'of a mans life being collected throughout euery moneth':

> There are likewise in the yeare more especially to be obserued 3. dangerous Mundaies, to begin any businesse, fall sicke or vndertake any iourney. First Munday in Aprill, on which day *Caine* was borne, and his brother *Abel* slaine.
> Second Munday in August, which day Sodom and Gomorah was distroyed.
> 31. Of December, which day *Iudas* was borne that betrayed Christ.

49 Hye-gate: Highgate, now part of Greater London but originally a village outside the City to the north.

58 Cornehill: in the heart of the City, between Poultry and Leadenhall Street, and forming a triangle with Threadneedle Street and Bishopsgate.

62 take the wall: the cleanest part of the path, furthest from the gutter and sheltered from refuse thrown from windows; cf. *A Fair Quarrel* 4.1.147-50 where Chough argues his right to

take the wall.

63 eldership: a) rights of older brother; b) priority of man who has been wealthy longest.

83 Iockey's a Gentleman now: proverbial; see, e.g., The Owl's Almanac, H3^{v}: 'And Iockie that rodde on his Courser (haire to haire) shall suddenly leape into his tuftaffity' (marginal gloss) 'Iockie a Gentleman now'.

85 florish o're: prosper at the expense of.

90 cry there againe shortly: at a grate in the wall, for bread. There was no obligation on anyone to feed debtors; the practise of crying for alms continued until the 19th century. (See Pickwick Papers, p. 686.)

94 fish-wife: given to gossip and shouting with the implication of prostitution ('crying their wares').

112 Equipage: carriage and horses, but OED records no such usage before the 18th century (sb. III.12).

120 Straites: of Gibraltar.

124-27 This is...arise: parodying Deloney's A Most Sweet Song of an English Merchant Born in Chichester:

> A Rich Merchant man there was
>   that was both graue & wise,
> Did kill a man at Embden Town
>   through quarrels that did rise. 1-4

(Works, ed. F.O. Mann, p. 485.)

138-40 get thee...on thee: conflating two Gospel passages, Matt. 7.3 and 5, Matt. 5.29.

157-58 traytor/To confiscate my goods: i.e., that you should confiscate my goods (as a penalty for treason). Here, goods = the news Richard confiscates (holds back).

159 conceite: imagine.

164 fatall Raven: bringing bad news (ravens are traditionally unlucky). The Raven was white until it told Apollo that his innocent mistress was unfaithful, causing her death; Apollo turned it black for its ill news. Cf. Macbeth 389-91 (1.4. 35-37):

> The Rauen himselfe is hoarse,
> That croakes the fatall entrance of Duncan
> Vnder my Battlements.

172 Carybdas: Charybdis, a whirlpool in the Straits of Messina, opposite the sailor-devouring monster Scylla.

190 sak'd: sacked, i.e., plundered. Emendation is necessary to restore the rhyme. 'wrack'd' might be expected but would suppose greater clumsiness by compositor or scribe. The simplest explanation is foul-case error.

195 Ludgate: founded for freemen debtors, the least harsh of the London gaols.

Newgate: for felons; notoriously the most uncomfortable of prisons, from which convicts were taken to Tyburn. In 1419 debtors were moved from Ludgate to Newgate but returned in 1420 because 'by reason of the foetid and corrupt atmosphere that is in the hateful gaol of Newgate,' many freemen had died, 'who might have been living, it is said, if they had remained in Ludgate abiding in peace.' (Ordinance of the Court of Aldermen, quoted Babington, *The English Bastille*, p. 24.)

4.1

14 Bucklers: shields; by extension, skirts; female sexual parts. Cf. *Much Ado About Nothing*, 2439-42 (5.2.15-17):

> Bene. ...and so I pray thee call Beatrice, I giue thee the bucklers.
> Mar. Giue vs the swords, we haue bucklers of our owne.

take up the Bucklers: to show he has won. (To give the bucklers = to give the victory.)

16 stickler: see n. 2.1.30.

17 run at the Ring: a game in which a rider tries to take a ring suspended from a post with the point of his lance. Also with sexual innuendo; cf. *The Taming of the Shrew*, 442-43 (1.1.134-35):

> Sweet Bianca, happy man be his dole: hee that runnes fastest, gets the Ring.

20 stand: with sexual meaning; cut by the Lord Chamberlain from Planché's adaptation (fol. 464).

23 Elements: there were four: earth, water, air amd fire.

29 coppy: here, in the same sense as 'printer's copy' - a pattern, something to be followed.

32 *A man of Ginger-bread*: a coward. Cf. Ford, *The Queen*, D3:

> *Mop*. By these hilts, I had rather then a hundred ducates, I had but as much spirit: as to have drawn upon a couple of men in Ginger-bread, which a hucsters crook't legged whorson ape held up, and swore they were two taller fellows then you are.

35 *Ianuary and May*: old man and young woman. Cf. Heywood, *The English Traveller*, A4^{v}:

> ...you know cold Ianuary and lusty May seldome meet in coniunction.

38 *youth in a basket*: proverbial; see *ODEP* p. 929, Tilley Y51. With suggestions of a spoilt child; childish innocence; a simpleton. Cf. *Choice, Chance and Change*, E3:

> Yet to bleer the eies of fools he could plaie the knaue with setting on the face of an honest man: this youth in a basket, with a face of Brasse, vpon a little acquaintance...comes to me.

42 *Pinnace*: a) woman; b) prostitute. Cf. Jonson, *Bartholomew Fair*, 2.2.71-74:

> This Pig-woman doe I know, and I will put her in, for my second enormity, shee hath beene before mee, *Punke*, *Pinnace* and *Bawd*, any time these two and twenty yeeres.

51-53 *if now...height*: common image, from Plato's *Phaedo* 85E-86. See, e.g., Bacon, *Essays*, C4:

> The Answere of *Apolonius* to *Vespasian* is full of excellent instruction. *Vespasian* asked him, *What was Neroes ouerthrow?* hee answered; *Nero could touch and tune the Harpe well; But in gouernment, sometimes he vsed to winde the pinnes too hye and sometimes to let them downe too lowe*. ('Of Empire'.)

Massinger, *The Emperor of the East*, I3^{v}:

> *Theod*. You touch a string
> That sowndes but harshely to mee.

Massinger, *A Very Woman*, R5:

> *Mar*. A strange position which doth much perplex me:
> That every Soul's alike, a musical Instrument,
> The Faculties in all men equal Strings,
> Well, or ill handled; and those sweet, or harsh.
> How like a Fidler I have plaid on mine then!

Brewer, *The Country Girl*, D4:

> *Sir Oli.* Still that Note?
> Touch onely that dull string of death?
> *Lad.* When life
> Would willingly exchange it selfe with Death,
> What Musick sweeter?

71 *Lopt...branch*: cf. Dekker, *II The Honest Whore*, B2^{v} (1.2. 88-94):

> *Hip.* You had a Daughter too sir, had you not?
> *Orla.* Oh my Lord! this old Tree had one Branch, (and but one Branch growing out of it) It was young, it was faire, it was straight; I prumde [sic] it daily, drest it carefully, kept it from the winde, help'd it to the Sunne; yet for all my skill in planting, it grew crooked, it bore Crabs; I hewed it downe,
> What's become of it, I neither know, nor care.

79 *To thee*: Robert.

81-82 *we have stood...away*: proverbial; see Ray, *Proverbs*, I8^{v}.

82 *kist the Mistris*: hit the jack; see n. 2.1.19.

85 *new found land*: pun on 'Newfoundland'. Pamphlets such as Whitbourne's *A Discourse and Discovery of Newfoundland* (1622) described it and recommended colonisation. The image continues at 86-87.

86 *point*: a) headland; b) tie, lace; c) with *double entendre*.
put in: with sexual innuendo.

89 *forestall the market*: raise the price of goods (illegally) by intercepting and buying up stock before it can reach its market.

90 *firkers*: a) cheats; b) people of sexual prowess. Cf. Beaumont, *Philaster*, (2nd Folio), E4^{v}:

> *1 Wood.* That's a firker I'faith boy;...I have known her lose her self three times in one Afternoon...and it has been work enough for one man to find her, and he has sweat for it.

91 *play the merchant*: get the better of. See n. 3.3.8-9.

92 *suitors*: with a play on 'shooters'. Cf. Brewer, *The Country Girl*, E2:

> *Sir Rob.* A troublesome Captaine indeed sir;
> A suytor once, in her virgin dayes
> And Rivall to her husband, Sir *Iames Mosely*.
> But, mis'd the marke he aymed at - he shot faire;
> But *Mosely* fairer.

97 Gallymawfryes: contemptuous term; 'made up of bits and pieces'.

98 Cockney: a) effeminate man; b) derisive term for a city dweller as opposed to a country man; c) used insultingly of a Londoner.

Zenocrates: Tamberlaine's wife; see n. 2.1.54-55.

99 gon a fishing: with secondary meaning, 'to have intercourse'. Cf. The Winter's Tale, 274-77 (1.2.192-95):

> And many a man there is...
> ...holds his Wife by th'Arme,
> That little thinkes she ha's been sluyc'd in's absence,
> And his Pond fish'd by his next Neighbor.

102 Eles: with a play on 'heels'.

103 striker: a) one who strikes a blow; b) fornicator. Cf. Rowley, All's Lost by Lust, D1^{v}:

> Laz. Is she such a striker, my Lord?
> Dio. All at head,
> No where else, beleeve me Sir, we hold it base
> To strike below the wast.

Brome, The English Moor, C2^{v}:

> Ra: And I have read
> That your viragoes use to strike all those
> They mean to lie with: And from thence tis taken
> That your brave active women are call'd strikers.

See also the stage direction on F1 of A Warning for Fair Women: 'Browne steps out and strikes vp Johns heeles.'

105 He dares not doe't abroad: because a) Robert might fight back; b) he might be arrested under the 1613 proclamation against duelling.

109 Hee's no Rivall: because he is only a merchant and not a gentleman. Cf. the Clown to Autolycus, The Winter's Tale 3136-38 (5.2.123-25):

> you deny'd to fight with mee this other day, because
> I was no Gentleman borne.

117 lists: area used for tilts or tournaments.

128 in the Heralds bookes: as able to bear arms and thus gentlemen.

130 Simply though: catch-phrase. Cf. The Puritan, G2:

> ...simplie tho it lies here, tis the fayrest
> Roome in my Mothers house.

138 Sheepeskin: parchment; bond of debt. See note on Innocent

Lambskin, Dramatis Personae.

139 crackt: a) bankrupt; b) corrupt, worthless; possibly also physically weak.

Predecessor: the Wife's first husband (who has literally predeceased Stephen).

140 Serjeant: to arrest the debtors.

142 protection: issued by the Crown to its officers to prevent arrest for debt while on its business; a system open to abuse. See The Liberties...of London, Calthrop, B4-4^{v}, where a protection is given.

149 lime-bush: not the linden, but a bush smeared with bird-lime to make it sticky (as a trap).

151 hole in the Counter: a) the poorest, worst lodgings in the Counter (debtors' prison); b) with a sexual innuendo.

152 suitors: see above, n. 92.

175 Angels: see n. 1.1.247.

229 Norton Folgate: the liberty of Norton Folgate, an area immediately north of the City bounds, dividing Bishopsgate from Shoreditch.

236-37 For in...dwell: because good deeds are the visible signs of the man living in God's grace who, because he has already been saved, automatically lives a holy life and performs good works.

4.2

21 your name is registred: a normal formality; cf. Fennor, The Compter's Commonwealth, B2^{v}:

> I no sooner was entred...but a fellow...called mee to a booke...comming to it, hee demanded my name, I tolde him, and then hee set it downe as horses are in Smithfield at the Tole-booth.

35 pills with poyson to recure me: some venoms were thought to be medicinal; cf. Topsell, The History of Serpents, D5:

> It is manifest, that if any man be wounded of a Serpent, though the wound seeme incurable, that the bowels or inward parts of the same serpent, being applied to the wound, will cure the same;...in the Prouince of Caraiam, there be serpents...which beeing killed, the inhabitants of the Country doe pull out their gall...for it is very medicinall.

39 this old Wall-nut-tree: see n. 3.2.57.

41 these leaves: his clothes. Cf. Taylor, The Praise and Virtue of a Jail and Jailers, B7:

> Man is a tree, whose root doth grow aboue
> Within his brains, whose sprigs & branches round,
> From head to foot grow downward to the ground.

See also 4.2.71.

48 christian Galley: see n. 3.1.122.

49 youngest: newest.

50 beg at the iron grate above: for charity; see n. 3.3.90.

53 embleme: moral picture or allegory. Either there is a picture on the grate, or the grate itself is the emblem of cruelty.

59-60 picture...men: continuing the imagery of 53. Old Foster himself becomes part of the picture with his face at the grate. There is also the suggestion of a broad-sheet wood-cut on a stationer's stall, or a street sign hung out over a shop.

66 Basyliske: mythical reptile whose breath and glance are fatal. Cf. The Winter's Tale 496-98 (1.2.388-90):

> Make me not sighted like the Basilisque.
> I haue look'd on thousands, who haue sped the better
> By my regard, but kill'd none so.

67 thine eyes: Q's 'mine' is only possible if Old Foster sees his own eyes inherited by Robert, so that Robert is like a mirror to him. Confusion of 'mine' for 'thine' (perhaps caused by 'me' earlier in the same line) seems more likely.

79 And I doe thanke it: rhetorical flourish. Old Foster shows little gratitude for his losses.

103 Pellican: common emblem device.

> The Pellican, for to reuiue her younge,
> Doth peirce her brest, and geue them of her blood.
> (Whitney, A Choice of Emblems, L4.)

The parent is usually the pelican; family relationships are distorted among the Fosters.

104 SD OLD FOSTER: Old Foster's voice off-stage; see Introduction, 'Staging'.

105-6 Bread...mercy: the usual plea at London prisons was 'for the Lord's sake'; cf. Nashe, Works, I.300.13-15:

> ...at that time that thy ioyes were in the Fleeting,
> and thou crying for the Lords sake out at an iron windowe.

A Woman Killed with Kindness, (Revels), vii.76-78:

> ...Shall we hear
> The music of his voice cry from the grate
> 'Meat for the Lord's sake'?

See also Measure for Measure 2078-95 (4.2.5-18). Perhaps the cry was changed because of Sir Henry Herbert's dislike of stage profanity (cf. n. 1.1.119); but The Puritan gives the cry at Marshalsea as, 'Good Gentlemen ouer the way, send your reliefe'. (See Introduction, 'Staging'.)

134 your paines: Q's 'you' is clearly erroneous; probably 'your' twice in one line caused the mistake.

154 There let him howle: exact repetition of Old Foster, 1.1.45.

162 spred up a lofty sayle: cf. II The Honest Whore D1 (2.1.180-81):

> ...to stand with my cap in my hand, and vaile bonnet,
> when I ha spred as lofty sayles as himselfe.

Ibid, F1^{v}-2 (3.2.135-36):

> ...the sailes which thou doest spread,
> Would show well, if they were not borrowed.

183 Fosters: Q's 'Foster's' is misleading; the genitive plural is required, for which Q has no convention.

4.3

entrance her sister: i.e., sister-in-law.

18 coach-horse: cf. Shirley's description of two comic lovers:

> Bel. They will be well met.
> Is. But uery ill matcht to draw a Coach; yet at
> prouender there will be scarce an Oat betweene the
> leane iade, and the fat gelding. (The Wedding, B1^{v}.)

29 country Clyent: notoriously gullible; see Tailor, The Hog Hath Lost His Pearl, F3:

> Ca. ô that Conncellors
> Would thus re[s]olue mens doubts without a fee,
> How many country Clyents then might rest
> Free from vndooing, no plodding pleader then
> Would purchase great possessions with his tongue.

30 upon no great Tearmes: feels no great obligation. Also a play on terms = sessions of court of law.

34 *Mace*: a) Serjeant's symbol of office; see Calthorpe, *Liberties*, $C1^{v}$:

> it is granted that our Sergeants shall and may bear, and carry maces of gold...with the Kings Arms upon the same, within the city and *Middlesex*.

b) the fruit of the nutmeg, ground to spice; it is,

> good against freckles in the face, quickeneth the sight, strengtheneth the belly, and the feeble liuer. (Gerard, *Herball*, $4S3^{v}$.)

Cf. Fennor, *The Compter's Commonwealth*, $F4-4^{v}$:

> Yet this much I will say for them when a Gentlemans fortunes begin to be sicke and crasie, most commonly they will apply him with caudles and cordials which only haue but this fault they tast some thing too much of the Mace, a spice more familiar in *England* then in the *East-Indies*.

35 *binder*: a) causes debtors to be locked up; b) causes constipation.

37 *stoole*: motion of the bowels.

39 *loose liver*: referring to a) his way of life; b) his anatomy. Rowley makes the same pun when writing of the bawd Malena:

> ...there's sacke in this Tunne,
> That has eaten up a great deale of dead
> Flesh in her time, lights, longs and bad livers.
> (*All's Lost by Lust*, $B2^{v}$.)

43 *Shoulders love no such clappings*: Sergeants were known as 'shoulder clappers'. Cf. Fennor, *The Compter's Commonwealth*, F4:

> but the most rauening and cruell Monsters in our Land are the shoulder-clapping pursebiting mace-bearers.

44 *drinke*: take Tobacco.

Woodstreet: running north from West Cheap to Cripplegate. The Compter, at the southern end, was under the sheriffs' jurisdiction.

Pipes: a) for tobacco; b) for water piped into the prison? (Stow does not mention any; but the nearest outside supply would have been the pump at the corner of Lad Lane and Aldermanbury, about 200 yards away; see end-map in Kingsford's edition of *Survey*.)

56 *shoulder clappers*: see above, n. 43.

59 Poultry: at the east end of Cheapside; site of another Compter.

88 case: a) circumstances; b) clothes, covering; see n. 1.1.227.

90 sheare no sheepe: anticipating Lambskin's pun at 91; 'sheepe' and 'Skin' (89) suggest 'Lambskin' and the idea sheepskin = parchment or bond may also be present.

92 Calfe by your white face: proverbial; see Tilley C19, ODEP p. 98.

Calfe: an idiot.

white face: a) from fear; b) still playing on the image of sheep/lamb; the sheep's white face.

100 bumbast: a) to beat; b) drinking term; to finish off (a can of liquor) OED 2. Also playing on the opposition of 'bum-' and 'bellies'.

106 fram'd by one square: to frame = to prepare or shape timber (for building); square = carpenter's tool for determining angles and straight lines (as in modern tee-square and set-square).

107 great lights of heaven: sun and moon, which in classical mythology are siblings, making the image apt.

110 Would you kill: 'kill' must be at the end of the line for the rhyme with 'ill' (111); but this phrase is unsatisfactory either as the end of 110 (in which case the metre is awkward) or as a short line.

142 Sheriffe: sworn to office the day after Michaelmas and fetched in procession by all the Aldermen. (Stow, Survey, 1633, 2K3.)

144 in scarlet: colour of Sheriff's robes.

5.1

7 like yee: is pleasing to you.

23-24 if heaven...Cators: referring to the legend of St. Paul the Hermit.

> ...a strange miracle that Sainct Ierome reporteth of one Paule an heremit, who liued from sixteene to sixtie of Dates onely, and from sixtie to sixe score and fiue (at what time he died) he was fed by a little bread brought to him by a crowe.
> (Greene's Farewell to Folly, K4v.)

Cators: caterers.

35-37 Besides...rise: this passage could also be lined:

> Besides your debts being truly counted cannot be great.
> OLD FOSTER But all my wealth and state
> Lyes in the seas Bottome.
> MISTRIS FOSTER It againe may rise.

50 Not like a threatning storme: echoing his description of Stephen, 4.3.72.

79 I'm borne...aside: Old Foster is defined as a man by his reason (which sets him apart from animals); but being human, he is certain to err. Cf. Field and Massinger, The Fatal Dowry, K1:

> ...she was my ages comfort,
> Begot by a weake man, and borne a woman,
> And could not therefore, but partake of frailety?

82-83 not for joy...spurne: not entirely true. Old Foster has been swayed by the gold, and cannot be regarded as totally indifferent to it.

114 You are sav'd: taking 'believe' and 'sav'd' in the theological sense. Cf. Day, The Isle of Gulls, E3^v:

> Demet. Is that part of your beliefe?
> Boy. A principall poynt Sir.
> Demet. Renounce it then, for I beleeue you'le neuer be saud by't.

115 You cut...due: proverbial, 'to cut large thongs of another man's leather'. See Ray, Proverbs, M1^v, 15.

118 My wager: see 4.3.125. Stephen, not the Wife, offers to make the wager.

126-28 'Twill ne'r...crackt: see n. 4.1.51-53.

136 old Saint Marie's Spittle: a confusion; Bruine's hospital was St. Mary's Spittle near Shoreditch but Rowley has made it here a separate institution. See Introduction, 'Sources'. Elsewhere Rowley makes it evident that he is aware of the identification of the Domus Dei with the Spittle (see 4.1.231ff).

137-38 sit/'Bout what you will: cf. II The Honest Whore, C3 (2.1.50-51):

> Bel. But I must sit all stormes: when a full sayle his Fortunes spred, he loued me.

140 three: Q's 'thee' is clearly a mistake. Dilke's emendation corrects what is probably a simple spelling error.

142 Full and faire sayles: cf. n. 4.2.163.

147 Master Foster: probably Old Foster, but possibly Stephen; 'Master Foster, who is the new Sheriff, your brother...'

158 Ludgate unto Newgate: such a move took place in 1419 to deter debtors, Ludgate being too comfortable; see n. 3.3.195.

165 divell in red: Stephen is already in his Sheriff's robes.

167 conduit-pipe: recalling Mistress Foster, 1.1.128 and 3.1.289. Dekker uses a similar image:

> ...she shall drinke of my wealth, as beggers doe of running water, freely, yet neuer know from what Fountaines head it flowes. (II Honest Whore, B4, 1.2.171-73.)

176-78 to nature...duty: echoing the discussion of 1.1.41ff and 1.1.168ff, but reversing Old Foster's position.

179 Wouldst thou strike: i.e., would you damage my fortunes further. Stephen does not hit Robert as 181 makes clear; such an action would be out of character with his statement at 212ff.

180 Th'art no brother: cf. 1.1.180 and 1.1.185.

I'le be no man: 'I will cast off reason and the normal restraints of humanity'. Cf. above, n. 79.

183 Churle: Stephen's insult to Old Foster, 1.1.213.

186-87 salt teares...him: influenced by Richard III 344 (1.2.153)?

> Those eyes of thine, from mine haue drawne salt Teares.

The syntax is confused. Either 'than thy malice should draw salt tears from him', or 'make salt the tears which thy malice draws from him' (but why should Old Foster be making Robert's tears salt?). Neither interpretation is entirely satisfactory.

188 told: a) related; b) counted.

219 Leads to walke on: see Stow, Survey, F2^{v}, and Introduction, 'Sources'.

229 'Tis fairely given: Q indents but does not assign this speech. Since it is a new speech, it must be Stephen's.

230-33 The Plummers...convey: Dilke's emendation restores the metre plausibly, and it is possible that the compositor accidentally repeated 'from'. However, 'The ground from Paddington; from whence I'l have laid,' is possible, if irregular. Dilke further emends 233 to, 'Pipes all[a]long to London, to convey,' but this seems unnecessary; there are short lines elsewhere in the text.

246-47 I'l wracke...downe: cf. the Duke's attitude to Isabella in refusing to tell her that Claudio is alive, e.g.,

> But I will keepe her ignorant of her good,
> To make her heauenly comforts of dispaire,
> When it is least expected.
> (Measure for Measure 2194-96, 4.3.105-7.)

5.2

2 benvenues: bienvenues; welcomes.

10 faithfully: a) diligently, conscientiously; b) inspired by faith.

17ff Shall free souccour be: St Mary's Spittle was known for its charity; see Stow, Survey, X8^{v}-Y2^{v} and Armin, A Nest of Ninnies, p. 53:

> On Easter Sunday the ancient custome is that all the children of the hospitall goe before my Lord Maior to the Spittle, that the world may witnesse the works of God and man, in maintennance of so many poore people.

21 Testator: either one who makes a will, or the witness to it (OED 1 and 2); 'if you will testify to my gift, and these noble Gentlemen be my witnesses as well'. But 'witnesse with me' seems to suggest that Bruine and the nobles are witnesses together to the King. Perhaps Bruine means that he is giving the Domus Dei to Henry for him to leave to the poor; see line 40.

24 large: limitless, long, everlasting.

26 now...age: apparently self-contradictory; but briefly linking the play's time with the audience's.

27 two or three hundred yeere behinde us: the Domus Dei lasted almost exactly 300 years - granted a charter in 1235, surrendered during the Dissolution of the Monasteries (1536-40). Stow, Survey, E6, X8^{v}-Y1.

29ff Should bee vnhallowed: the Spittle and Shoreditch were a 'red-light' area; cf. Field and Massinger, The Fatal Dowry, F4:

> Romont. An heyre and rich,

> Young, beautifull, yet adde to this a wife,
> And I will rather choose a Spittle sinner
> Carted an age before, though three parts rotten.

Massinger, Middleton and Rowley, *The Old Law*, B4:

> ...the fewer Hospitalls will serve to,
> Many may be usd for stewes and brothells
> And those people will never trouble em to fourescore.

53 largely: widely.

57 originall: source.

78 froward: perverse, unreasonable.

98-100 What...abus'd: these lines could be arranged:

> What could I then but as his father erst
> so I agen might Throw him from my love? for worse
> is love abus'd -

where 'so I agen might' is a false start intended to be deleted but accidentally included. This still leaves 'erst' without a rhyme; the lines are corrupt or unfinished. (I am grateful to Mr. G.R. Proudfoot for this suggestion.)

106 & 107 deserve, swerve: cf. the rhyme at *II The Honest Whore* A4^{v} (1.1.155-57):

> Bel. when Children
> From duty start, Parents from loue may swarue.
> He nothing does: for nothing I deserue.

119 abridge: curtail, deprive, stint.

131 part was mine: because he would have inherited them.

132 me: Q's 'him' presents difficulties; it could be Stephen or Old Foster; but they are both trying to explain why they disinherited Robert and he is asking to be accepted back again so it does not make sense for Robert to plead for them. Certainly the King's reply is addressed to Robert.

134 impartiall eare: cf. 70.

142 eye watch: tautologous; perhaps one word should have been deleted as an alternative about which Rowley could not decide.

151 theater of Kings: either 'the world' or 'the kingdom'; cf. *Henry V* 3-4:

> A Kingdome for a Stage, Princes to Act,
> And Monarchs to behold the swelling Scene.

156 liberty with mine: 'I have paid off your debts and my own'. But Stephen's debts were paid off long before the beginning of

Act 4. The reference may be to the Keeper's fees, paid at leaving (some debtors were held for prison fees long after their creditors were satisfied).

159 say you Amen: spoken to the Wife.

162 Thou art onely wise: you alone are wise.

164 redownes: redounds; flows back.

178 free for all prisoners: cf. Stow, Survey, $F2^v$, and Heywood, II If You Know Not Me You Know Nobody, D1:

> For. M. Foster late Maior honestly pray,
> And Agnes his wife to God Consecrate.
> That of pitty this house made for Londoners in Lud-gate:
> So that for lodging and water here nothing they pay,
> As their Keepers shall answer at dreadfull Doomes day.

(But see Stow's chapter on 'Rivers and other Waters serving this City' which makes no mention of Foster in this context.)

183 not left unto succession: cf. Bacon, 'Of Riches':

> ...and deferre not charities till death: for certainely, if a man weigh it rightly, he that doth so, is rather liberall of another mans, then of his owne. (Essays, $F1^v$.)

190 Women are forgetfull: see Stow, Survey, O7; II If You Know Not Me You Know Nobody, $D1^v$; Introduction, 'Sources'.

204 I must goe before: Stephen's Wife survived him; see Introduction, 'The Foster Family'.

and 'tis said: not recorded as a proverb.

205 women goe first to bed: and are thus first asleep. Women were supposed to nag their husbands in bed; see, e.g., engraved title-page of Braithwait's Art Asleep Husband? and inscription:

> This wife a wondrous racket meanes to keepe,
> While th' Husband seemes to sleepe but do'es not sleepe:
> But she might full as well her Lecture smother,
> For ent'ring one Eare, it goes out at t'other.
> (Quoted Camden, The Elizabethan Woman, p. 240.)

220 this bonds: Jane's.

221 me: Mr. G.R. Proudfoot's suggestion. Q's 'those' disrupts the rhyme and does not make sense; 'as a third father' confirms that Bruine is referring to himself.

224 booty: a way of cheating at bowls. See The Bellman of London, G1:

> Many other practises there are in Bowling, tending to cozenage, but the greatest and grosest is *Booty*, in which the deceipt is so open and palpable, that I haue seene men stone blind offer to lay bets frankely, although they could see a bowle no more then a post, onely by hearing who plaid, and how the old *Gripes* had made their layes.

225 *except*; interchangeable with 'accept'.

228 *in Esse*: now, something definite, 'in hand'.

228-9 *in Posse*: some time in the future, something uncertain. Cf. *The Elder Brother*, B2^{v}:

> *Ang*:...If
> He Want a present fortune, at the best
> Those are but glorious dreames, and onely yield him
> A happinesse in *posse*, not in *esse*.

231 *The liveliest harmony*: returning to the musical imagery of 4.1 and 4.3.

238 *brazen Pen*: to last for ever. Cf. *Measure for Measure* 2357, 2359-61 (5.1.9, 11-13):

> *Duk*. Oh your desert speaks loud,...
> ...it deserues with characters of brasse
> A sorted residence 'gainst the tooth of time,
> And razure of obliuion.

Inspired by Stow's account of the copper plate at Ludgate? (*Survey*, F2^{v}; Introduction, 'Sources'.)

FINIS In most copies there is an end ornament below the FINIS, which is in the centre of the leaf. See Introduction, 'Printing'.

Bibliography

(Place of publication is London unless otherwise stated.)

Texts

Armin, Robert, A Nest of Ninnies, ed. J. Payne Collier for the Shakespeare Society, as Fools and Jesters, 1842.

B., W. and P., E., A Help to Discourse, 1621.

Bacon, Francis, The Essays of Sir Francis Bacon Knight, 1613.

Beaumont, Francis and Fletcher, John, Fifty Comedies and Tragedies, 1674.

————————————, The Honest Man's Fortune, ed. J. Gerritson, Groningen, Djakarta, 1952.

————————————, The Maid's Tragedy, 1619; anr. ed. 1622.

Brewer, Anthony, The Country Girl, 1647.

————, The Love-Sick King, 1655.

Brome, Richard, Five New Plays, viz. The English Moor, The Love-Sick Court, The Weeding of the Covent Garden or the Middlesex Justice of the Peace, The New Academy or the New Exchange, The Queen and Concubine, 1658, 1659.

————, Five New Plays, viz. A Mad Couple Well-Matched, The Novella, The Court Beggar, The City Wit, The Damoiselle, 1653.

————, The Queen's Exchange, 1657.

Brooke, C., The Ghost of Richard III, ed. J. Payne Collier for the Shakespeare Society, 1844.

Calthorp, Henry, The Liberties ... of the City of London, 1642.

Cavendish, William, The Variety, 1649.

Chamberlain, John, The Letters of John Chamberlain, ed. N.E. McClure, 2 vols., Memoirs of the American Philosophical Society vol. 12, Philadelphia, 1939.

Chapman, George, Jonson, Ben and Marston, John, Eastward Ho, 1605.

Chettle, Henry, Kind Heart's Dream, 1592.

Choice, Chance and Change, 1601.

Church of England, The Book of Common Prayer and Administration of the Sacraments, 1621.

————, Certain Sermons appointed by the Queen's Majesty to be declared and read, by all Parsons, Vicars and Curates, every Sunday and holy day, in their Churches, 1559.

————, The Second Tome of Homilies of such matters as were promised and entitled in the former part of Homilies, set out by the authority of the Queen's Majesty, 1563.

Cooke, John, Greene's Tu Quoque, 1614; anr. ed. 1622.

Cooper, Thomas, Thesaurus Linguae Romanae & Britannicae, 1565.

Cotton, Charles, The Complete Gamester, 1674.

Covent Garden Theatre, untitled scrapbook of cuttings, BL Th. Cts. 39.

Daborn, Robert, The Poor Man's Comfort, 1655.

Day, John, The Isle of Gulls, 1606.

Day, John, Rowley, William and Wilkins, George, The Travels of the Three English Brothers, 1607.

Dekker, Thomas, The Dramatic Works of Thomas Dekker, ed. F.T. Bowers, 4 vols., Cambridge, 1953-61.

__________, The Bellman of London, 1616.

__________, I The Honest Whore, 1604.

__________, II The Honest Whore, 1630.

__________, The Shoemaker's Holiday, or, The Gentle Craft, 1600.

__________, Thomas Dekker: The Wonderful Year, The Gull's Horn-Book, Penny-Wise, Pound-Foolish, English Villainies Discovered by Lantern and Candlelight and Selected Writings, ed. E.D. Pendry, The Stratford-upon-Avon Library IV, 1967.

Dekker, Thomas, Ford, John and Rowley, William, The Witch of Edmonton, 1621.

Deloney, Thomas, John Winchcomb, 1633.

__________, The Works of Thomas Deloney, ed. F.O. Mann, Oxford, 1912.

Dick of Devonshire, BL MS Egerton 1994.

Dickens, Charles, The Posthumous Papers of the Pickwick Club, ed. Robert L. Patten, Harmondsworth, 1972.

Dictionarium Historicum ac Poeticum, Geneva, 1579.

Donne, John, XXVI Sermons, 1661.

Every Woman in her Humour, 1609.

Fennor, William, The Compter's Commonwealth, 1617.

Field, Nathan, and Massinger, Philip, The Fatal Dowry, 1632.

Fletcher, John, Beggars' Bush, 1661.

__________, The Elder Brother, 1637.

Ford, John, The Queen, or, the Excellency of her Sex, 1653.

Gentleman's Magazine, vol. 94, 1824.

Greene, Robert, Greene's Farewell to Folly, 1591.

__________, A Notable Discovery of Cozenage, 1591.

__________, A Quip for an Upstart Courtier, 1620.

Greville, Fulke Lord Booke, Certain Learned and Elegant Works of the Right Honourable Fulke Lord Brooke, 1633.

Herbert, Sir Henry, The Dramatic Records of Sir Henry Herbert, ed. J.Q. Adams, Yale Studies in English, 1917.

Herodotus, Herodoti Halicarnassei Historiae Lib. IX, Frankfurt, 1594.

————, The Histories, trans. A. de Sélincourt, Harmondsworth, 1954.

Heywood, Thomas, The Brazen Age, 1613.

————, The Captives, BL MS Egerton 1994; Malone Society Reprint, 1953.

————, A Challenge for Beauty, 1636.

————, The English Traveller, 1633.

————, The Fair Maid of the Exchange, 1607.

————, II If You Know Not Me, You Know Nobody, 1632.

————, Love's Mistress, 1636.

————, A Maidenhead Well Lost, 1634.

————, The Royal King and the Loyal Subject, 1637.

————, The Wise-Woman of Hogsdon, 1638.

————, A Woman Killed with Kindness, 1607; ed. R.van Fossen, 1961.

Heywood, Thomas and Rowley, William, Fortune by Land and Sea, 1656.

Holy Bible, 1611 repr. 1623.

James I and VI, Edict and Severe Censure against Private Combats and Combatants, 1613.

Jonson, Ben, Ben Jonson, ed. C.H. Herford and P. Simpson, E. Simpson, 11 vols., Oxford, 1925-52.

————, Poems, ed. I. Donaldson, Oxford, 1975.

Killigrew, Thomas, Claracilla, 1641.

Markham, Gervase, The Pleasure of Princes, 1635.

Marlowe, Christopher, I Tamburlaine the Great, ed. C.F. Tucker-Brooke, Oxford, 1910.

Massinger, Philip, The Plays and Poems of Philip Massinger, ed. P. Edwards and C. Gibson, 5 vols., Oxford, 1976.

————, The Emperor of the East, 1632.

————, The Picture, 1630.

————, A Very Woman, 1655.

Massinger, Philip, Middleton, Thomas and Rowley, William, The Old Law, 1656.

Middleton, Thomas, The Works of Thomas Middleton, ed. A.H. Bullen, 8 vols., 1885, 1886.

————————, Anything for a Quiet Life, 1662.

————————, A Game at Chess, BL MS Lansdowne 690.

————————, The Inner Temple Mask, 1619.

————————, The Mayor of Quinborough, or, Hengist King of Kent, 1661; Hengist King of Kent, ed. R.C. Bald, Folger Shakespeare Library Publications, 1938.

Middleton, Thomas, The Phoenix, 1607.

Middleton, Thomas and Rowley, William, The Changeling, 1653; ed. N. Bawcutt, 1958.

————————————————, A Fair Quarrel, 1617; ed. R.V. Holdsworth, 1974.

Middleton, Thomas and Rowley, William, The Spanish Gipsy, 1653.

————————————————, The World Tossed at Tennis, 1620.

Munday, Anthony, Chruso-thriambos, ed. J.H.P. Pafford, 1962.

Mynshul, Geoffrey, Certain Characters and Essays of Prison and Prisoners, 1618.

Nashe, Thomas, The Works of Thomas Nashe, ed. R.B. McKerrow, rev. F.P. Wilson, Oxford, 1958.

Nixon, Anthony, A Strange Foot-Post, 1613.

The Owl's Almanac, 1618.

Parkinson, John, Parradisus Terrestris, 1629; repr. as A Garden of Pleasant Flowers, New York, 1976.

Planché, J.R., Fortune's Favourite; or; the Widow of Cornhill, BL MS Add. 42868.

————————, The Widow of Cornhill, Cumberland's British Theatre, vol. 8, 1829.

Plato, Phaedo, trans. R. Hackforth, Cambridge, 1972.

The Puritan, 1607.

R., J., A Collection of Proverbs, 1670.

R., W., A Match at Midnight, 1633.

Rowlands, Samuel, Diogenes' Lantern, 1628.

Rowley, Samuel, When You See Me You Know Me, 1613.

Rowley, William, MS letter to Philip Henslowe, BL MS Egerton 2623, fol. 25.

————————, All's Lost by Lust, 1633; William Rowley his All's

Lost by Lust and A Shoemaker a Gentleman, ed. C.W. Stork, Philadelphia, 1910.

———————, A New Wonder, A Woman Never Vext, 1632; ed. C.W. Dilke, Old English Plays being a selection from the early dramatic writers, vol. 5, 1814-15; ed. C.W. Hazlitt, A Collection of Old Plays ed. R. Dodsley, rev. C.W. Hazlitt, vol. 12, 1874-75.

———————, A Search for Money, or the lamentable complaint for the loss of the wandering Knight, Monsieur l'Argent, or come along with me, I know thou lovest money, 1609.

———————, A Shoemaker, A Gentleman, 1638.

Rowley, William and Shakespeare, William, The Birth of Merlin, 1662.

Rowley, William and Webster, John, The Thracian Wonder, 1661.

Shakespeare, William, Mr. William Shakespeare's Comedies, Histories and Tragedies, 1623; ed. C. Hinman, New York, 1968 ('The Norton Facsimile'); ed. P. Alexander, William Shakespeare the Complete Works, 1951.

Sharpham, Edward, The Fleir, 1607.

Shirley, James, Changes, or Love in a Maze, 1632.

———————, The Wedding, 1633.

Sidney, Philip, The Complete Works of Sidney, ed. A. Feuillerat, vol. 2, Cambridge, 1922.

Smith, John, New England's Trials, 1622.

The Soddered Citizen, BL MS Egerton 1994.

Stationers' Company, A Transcript of the Stationers' Registers 1554-1640, E. Arber, 5 vols., London, Birmingham, 1875-77, 1894.

———————, Records of the Court of the Stationers' Company 1576 to 1602 from Register B, ed. Greg and Boswell, 1930.

———————, Records of the Court of the Stationers' Company 1602-1640, ed. W.A. Jackson, 1957.

Stow, John, A Survey of London, 1618; anr. ed. 1633; cont. Strype, 2 vols., 1754; ed. C.W. Kingsford, 1908.

Strabo, De Situ Orbis, Basle, 1579.

Stubbs, Philip, The Anatomy of Abuses, 1583.

Tailor, Robert, The Hog hath Lost his Pearl, 1614.

Taylor, John, All the Works of John Taylor the Water-Poet, 1630.

———————, The Praise and Virtue of a Jail and Jailers, 1623.

The Times, November 10th, 1824.

Topsell, Edward, The History of Serpents, 1608.

Tusser, Thomas, Five Hundred Points of Good Husbandry, 1593.

Vox Piscis, 1627.

Whitney, Geoffrey, A Choice of Emblems, 1586.

Whitbourne, Richard, A Discourse and Discovery of Newfoundland, 1622.

Wilkins, George, The Miseries of Enforced Marriage, 1607.

Wily Beguiled, 1623.

Other Works

Allen, Shirley S., Samuel Phelps and Sadler's Wells Theatre, Middleton, Connecticut, 1971.

Babington, Anthony, The English Bastille, 1971.

Baker, D.E., Biographica Dramatica, or a Companion to the Playhouse, rev. I. Reed, S. Jones, 3 vols., 1812.

Beaven, Rev. A., The Aldermen of the City of London, 2 vols., 1908, 1913.

Bentley, G.E., The Jacobean and Caroline Stage, 7 vols., Oxford, 1941-68.

Bowers, F.T., 'Beggars Bush: A reconstructed prompt-book and its copy', SB XXVII, 1974, pp. 113-36.

Cambridge History of English Literature, 15 vols., Cambridge, 1907-16, 1927, repr. 1949.

Camden, Carroll, The Elizabethan Woman, London and New York, 1952.

Clark, A.M., Thomas Heywood, Playwright and Miscellanist, Oxford, 1931.

Cromwell, Otelia, Thomas Heywood: A Study in the Elizabethan Drama of Everyday Life, London and New Haven, 1928.

Doran, Madeleine, Endeavors of Art: A Study of Form in Elizabethan Drama, University of Wisconsin, 1954.

Fleay, F.G., A Biographical Chronicle of the English Drama, 2 vols., 1891.

————, A Chronicle History of the English Stage, 1890.

————, Shakespeare Manual, 1876.

Genest, Jean, Some Account of the English Stage, 10 vols., Bath, 1832.

Greg, Sir W.W., A Bibliography of the English Printed Drama to the Restoration, 4 vols., 1939-57.

————, Dramatic Documents from the Elizabethan Playhouses, 2 vols., Oxford, 1931.

Grivelet, M., Thomas Heywood et le drame domestique élizabéthain,

Études anglaises 4, Paris, 1957.

Halliwell, J.O., A Dictionary of Archaic and Provincial Words, 2 vols., 1847.

Harbage, A., Annals of English Drama 600-1700, rev. S. Schoenbaum, 1964.

——————, Shakespeare and the Rival Traditions, New York, 1952.

Hazlitt, W., Lectures on the Dramatic Literature of the Age of Elizabeth, 2nd ed., 1821, Tieck's copy BL 11826.n.2.

Hosley, R., 'The Gallery over the Stage in the Public Playhouse of Shakespeare's Time', SQ Winter 1957.

Howard-Hill, T.H., Compositors B and E in the Shakespeare First Folio, privately printed for limited distribution, Columbia S.C., 1976.

——————, A Reassessment of Compositors B and E in the First Folio Tragedies, privately printed for limited distribution, Columbia S.C., 1977.

Hoy, C., 'The Shares of Fletcher and his Collaborators in the Beaumont and Fletcher Canon', SB VIII 1956, IX 1957, XI 1958, XII 1959, XIII 1960, XIV 1961, XV 1962.

Jackson, MacD. P., Studies in Attribution: Middleton and Shakespeare, Salzburg Jacobean Studies 79, Salzburg Studies in English Literature, Salzburg, 1979.

Jones, E.L., Scenic Form in Shakespeare, Oxford, 1971.

Jordan, W.K., Philanthropy in England 1480-1660: A study of the changing pattern of English social aspirations, 1959.

Kendall, P.M., The Yorkist Age, 1962.

Lake, D., The Canon of Thomas Middleton's Plays, Cambridge, 1975.

Lamb, C., The Dramatic Essays of Charles Lamb, ed. B. Matthews, 1891.

——————, Specimens of the English Dramatic Poets, 1808, J.A. Symonds' copy BL C.28.b.17.

Lancashire, Anne, (ed.), Editing Renaissance Dramatic Texts, 1976.

Langbaine, G., An Account of the English Dramatic Poets, 1691, Oldys' copy BL C.28.g.1.

Lavin, J.A., 'John Danter's Ornament Stock', SB XXIII, 1970, pp. 37-42.

McKenzie, D.F., 'A List of Printers' Apprentices, 1605-40', SB XIII, 1960, pp. 109-42.

McKerrow, R.B., Printers' Ornaments and Devices in England and Scotland, 1485-1640, 1913.

Nicoll, A., History of the English Drama, 6 vols., Cambridge, 1952-58.

The Oxford Dictionary of English Proverbs, ed. F.P. Wilson, Oxford, 1970.

Partridge, E., Shakespeare's Bawdy, repr. 1968.

Plomer, H.R., 'The Eliot's Court Printing House, 1584-1676', The Library 4th ser. 11, 1922, pp. 175-84.

Pollard, A.W. and Redgrave, G.R., A Short-title Catalogue of Books printed in England, Scotland and Ireland and of English books printed abroad, 1475-1640, 1926.

Postan, M.M., and Powers, E., Studies in English Trade in the 15th Century, Studies in Economic and Social History vol. 5, 1933.

Robb, D.M., 'The Canon of William Rowley's Plays', MLR XLV, 1950, pp.129-41.

Rosenfeld, Sybil, Theatre of the London Fairs in the 18th Century, 1960.

Sandeman, Mrs. G.A., A critical study of the work of William Rowley, unpublished doctoral thesis for London University, 1974.

Schelling, F., Elizabethan Drama 1558-1642, Boston and New York, 1908.

Schoenbaum, S., Internal Evidence and Elizabethan Dramatic Authorship, 1966.

Shapiro, I.A., 'Tittere Tu and a date for Rowley's Woman Never Vext', RES 11, 1960, pp. 55-6.

Sisson, C.J., Lost Plays of Shakespeare's Age, Cambridge, 1936.

Southern, R., 'On Reconstructing a Practicable Elizabethan Playhouse', Shakespeare Survey 12, 1959, pp. 22-35.

Swinburne, A.C., The Age of Shakespeare, 1908.

Thrupp, Sylvia, The Merchant Class of Medieval London, Chicago, 1948.

Tilley, M.P., ed., A Dictionary of Proverbs in England in the Sixteenth and Seventeenth Centuries, Ann Arbor, 1950.

Ward, A.W., A History of English Dramatic Literature to the Death of Queen Anne, 3 vols., 1899.

Wiggin, Pauline G., An Inquiry into the Authorship of the Middleton-Rowley Plays, Radcliffe College Monograph 9, Boston, 1897.

Addendum

Gerard, John, The Herbal or General History of Plants, 1597.

Levin, R., New Readings vs. Old Plays, Chicago, 19

For Product Safety Concerns and Information please contact our EU representative GPSR@taylorandfrancis.com
Taylor & Francis Verlag GmbH, Kaufingerstraße 24, 80331 München, Germany

www.ingramcontent.com/pod-product-compliance
Lightning Source LLC
LaVergne TN
LVHW050625100826
845148LV00011B/1737

* 9 7 8 0 3 6 7 1 1 0 0 3 1 *